MW00576606

NATURAL MONOPOLIES IN DIGITAL PLATFORM MARKETS

Competition policy debates on digital platform markets are often premised on the idea that market fragmentation and the standard forces of competition and entry may provide a potential solution to excessive concentration and market power. In this work, Francesco Ducci provides readers with a different perspective based on the theoretical lens of natural monopoly. Ducci explores this framework through the development of three case studies on horizontal search, e-commerce marketplaces, and ride-hailing platforms, investigating the strength and limit of potential (and often heterogeneous) sources of natural monopoly at play in each industry. Building on these case studies, the book then derives from the application of the natural monopoly framework general policy implications for digital industries by identifying the respective institutional flaws and shortcomings of ex ante and ex post approaches to market power as one of the central challenges in digital platform markets.

Francesco Ducci is a Global Fellow at New York University, affiliated with the Centre for Law, Economics, and Organization. His research interests include competition policy, regulation, international trade, and law and economics.

GLOBAL COMPETITION LAW AND ECONOMICS POLICY

This series publishes monographs highlighting the interdisciplinary and multijurisdictional nature of competition law, economics, and policy. Global in coverage, the series should appeal to competition and antitrust specialists working as scholars, practitioners, and judges.

General Editors: Ioannis Lianos, *University College London*; Thomas Cheng, *University of Hong Kong*; Simon Roberts, *University of Johannesburg*; Maarten Pieter Schinkel, *University of Amsterdam*; Maurice Stucke, *University of Tennessee*

Natural Monopolies in Digital Platform Markets

FRANCESCO DUCCI

University of Toronto Faculty of Law

CAMBRIDGE
UNIVERSITY PRESS

CAMBRIDGE
UNIVERSITY PRESS

University Printing House, Cambridge CB2 8BS, United Kingdom

One Liberty Plaza, 20th Floor, New York, NY 10006, USA

477 Williamstown Road, Port Melbourne, VIC 3207, Australia

314–321, 3rd Floor, Plot 3, Splendor Forum, Jasola District Centre,
New Delhi – 110025, India

79 Anson Road, #06–04/06, Singapore 079906

Cambridge University Press is part of the University of Cambridge.

It furthers the University's mission by disseminating knowledge in the pursuit of
education, learning, and research at the highest international levels of excellence.

www.cambridge.org
Information on this title: www.cambridge.org/9781108491143
DOI: 10.1017/9781108867528

© Francesco Ducci 2020

This publication is in copyright. Subject to statutory exception
and to the provisions of relevant collective licensing agreements,
no reproduction of any part may take place without the written
permission of Cambridge University Press.

First published 2020

A catalogue record for this publication is available from the British Library.

Library of Congress Cataloging-in-Publication Data
NAMES: Ducci, Francesco, 1987– author
TITLE: Natural monopolies in digital platform markets / Francesco Ducci.
DESCRIPTION: Cambridge, United Kingdom ; New York, NY, USA : Cambridge
University Press, 2020. | Series: Global competition law and economics policy |
Based on author's thesis (doctoral – University of Toronto, 2019). | Includes
bibliographical references and index.
IDENTIFIERS: LCCN 2019050405 (print) | LCCN 2019050406 (ebook) | ISBN 9781108491143
(hardback) | ISBN 9781108867528 (ebook)
SUBJECTS: LCSH: Electronic commerce – Law and legislation. | Internet industry –
Law and legislation. | Antitrust law.
CLASSIFICATION: LCC K1005 .D83 2020 (print) | LCC K1005 (ebook) | DDC 343.07/21–dc23
LC record available at https://lccn.loc.gov/2019050405
LC ebook record available at https://lccn.loc.gov/2019050406

ISBN 978-1-108-49114-3 Hardback

Cambridge University Press has no responsibility for the persistence or accuracy of
URLs for external or third-party internet websites referred to in this publication
and does not guarantee that any content on such websites is, or will remain,
accurate or appropriate.

Contents

Figures

Tables

Acknowledgments

I owe a number of debts of gratitude, starting from the inception of this project in my doctoral dissertation at the University of Toronto in 2015 and throughout to the completion of this book. First and foremost, I would like to thank Michael Trebilcock, Edward Iacobucci, Anthony Niblett, and Roger Ware for their insightful comments and feedbacks through the various stages of this research. I am also indebted to Mariana Prado, Ariel Katz, Eden Sarid, Terry Skolnik, Haim Abraham, Claire Jensen, the Massey College community, and my family for their support during my graduate studies at the University of Toronto. Finally, I would like to thank the University of Toronto Faculty of Law and the Centre for International Governance Innovation (CIGI) for the financial assistance received during my doctoral research.

1

Introduction

Multisided platform markets characterized by network externalities have always existed as an economic paradigm, but in different technological forms.[1] The old village marketplace, physical shopping malls, or any traditional fair can be seen as multisided platform markets connecting buyers and sellers. They are all platform-meeting places where different agents that want to interact and transact with one another are brought together by an intermediary. The traditional printed ad-based newspaper is also a classic version of a platform connecting advertisers and eyeballs. More readers increase the value for advertisers that want to reach them, and readers generally are indifferent to or dislike ads. Due to these externalities across the different sides, newspapers can often be provided for free to create an audience for advertisers. Payment cards of various kinds, the first two-sided market closely studied in the industrial organization literature, are also a typical example of platforms that connect merchant and cardholders concluding transactions.

The current wave of technological change has created a new generation of multisided platforms that dominate the digital economy: online search engines connecting searchers with advertisers; social networks connecting users with other users and advertisers; e-commerce online marketplaces connecting buyers and sellers; sharing economy platforms connecting various kinds of service provider with consumers; price-comparison, reservation, and job search platforms, and match-makers for various professional services. Due to digitalization, the multisided business model has become one of the predominant forms of organizing economic activity in the age of big data, network effects, and algorithmic-based matching.

This new generation of digital multisided platforms and their widespread growth has generated lively and complex debates that touch on many important areas of public policy, ranging from concerns about privacy, misuse of personal data, consumer protection, spread of fake news, and excessive concentration of economic power. Even within the competition policy domain, the focus on multisided platform markets

---

[1] The term "multisided platform" is the most accurate way to refer to this economic paradigm. Equivalent terminology found in the literature, however, will at times be used interchangeably throughout this book, including "two-sided" or "multisided market."

has expanded as a result of the rise of large tech platforms, partially shifting away from the original question of whether new legal tools need to be developed in competition law cases to account for the economic interdependence of multiple sides.

The growth of digital platforms has, in particular, turned the attention of competition policy debates to the increasing levels of concentration characterizing various digital industries and the perceived weakness of competition and market forces to address market power in the digital economy, often emphasizing the inaptitude of established competition policy principles to deal with the economic and technological features of the digital platforms. For example, it has been argued that current antitrust laws are "unequipped to capture the architecture of market power in the modern economy"[2] and the digital economy will lead to "the end of competition as we know it."[3] Radical proposals to fragment excessively concentrated digital sectors have as a result gained prominence in the academic and policy debate, including calls to break up tech giants such as Facebook or Google,[4] or implement major reforms to the goals, doctrines, and fundamental principles pursued by antitrust policy to fight excessive accumulation of economic and political power[5] – for example, abandoning the consumer welfare standard in favor of more structural approaches that promote deconcentration of markets as an objective in and of itself.

In contrast, other commentators have instead emphasized a number of reasons against intervention in these digital markets, criticizing, among other things the use of labels such as "network effects" and "big data" as empty slogans that in reality do not determine inevitable market dominance, citing various counterexamples of platforms such as AOL, MSN Messenger, Friendster, Myspace, Orkut, that have declined despite network effects and collection of data;[6] emphasizing the detrimental risks of false positives[7] in highly innovative markets;[8] arguing that entry barriers

---

[2] Lina M. Khan, "Amazon's Antitrust Paradox" (2016) 126 Yale Law J 710.

[3] Ariel Ezrachi and Maurice E. Stucke, *Virtual Competition: The Promise and Perils of the Algorithm-Driven Economy* (Cambridge, MA: Harvard University Press, 2016).

[4] *Financial Times*, "Big Tech and Amazon: Too Powerful to Break Up?"; Jonathan Taplin, "Opinion: Is It Time to Break Up Google?," *New York Times* (January 20, 2018), online: www.nytimes.com/2017/04/22/opinion/sunday/is-it-time-to-break-up-google.html; *The Guardian*, "Elizabeth Warren Vows to Break Up Amazon, Facebook and Google if Elected President" (March 8, 2019), online: www.theguardian.com/us-news/2019/mar/08/elizabeth-warren-amazon-facebook-google-big-tech-break-up-blogpost; Jonathan Taplin, *Move Fast and Break Things: How Facebook, Google, and Amazon Cornered Culture and Undermined Democracy* (New York: Little, Brown, 2017); Scott Galloway, *The Four: The Hidden DNA of Amazon, Apple, Facebook, and Google* (Basingstoke: Penguin, 2017).

[5] Konstantin Medvedovsky, "Antitrust Chronicle – Hipster Antitrust" (April 18, 2018), available at www.competitionpolicyinternational.com/antitrust-chronicle-hipster-antitrust/.

[6] David S. Evans and Richard Schmalensee, "Network Effects: March to the Evidence, Not to the Slogans," SSRN Scholarly Paper ID 3027691 (Rochester, NY: Social Science Research Network, 2017).

[7] David S. Evans, "Multisided Platforms, Dynamic Competition, and the Assessment of Market Power for Internet-Based Firms," SSRN Scholarly Paper ID 2746095 (Rochester, NY: Social Science Research Network, 2016); David S. Evans and Richard Schmalensee, "Debunking the 'Network Effects' Bogeyman," SSRN Scholarly Paper ID 3148121 (Rochester, NY: Social Science Research Network, 2017).

[8] Hal R. Varian, "Economics of Information Technology" (2003) Univ Calif Berkeley, available at http://people.ischool.berkeley.edu/~hal/Papers/mattioli/mattioli.pdf.

are low, multihoming and low switching costs are negligible; and that competition is simply "one click away."[9]

In between, various intermediate positions support different degrees of stronger competition policy enforcements. Among others, Shapiro has suggested for example that strengthening of merger enforcement may be necessary, together with stronger enforcement against exclusionary conduct by dominant firms.[10] Tirole has endorsed a form of competition policy intervention oriented to competition for the market, one that fosters contestability of a potential monopoly position rather than competition within a market due to the winner-takes-all nature of digital industries.[11] Likewise, a number of official reports in various jurisdictions support variants of more interventionist approaches.[12] A disparate range of largely different policy proposals and approaches, as a consequence, animates policy debates on how to tame – borrowing from the words of the *Economist* – the new titans.[13]

The goal of this book is to provide a novel contribution and perspective to the challenges of competition and market power in digital platform markets through the theoretical lenses supplied by the natural monopoly framework. Traditionally, natural monopolies are associated with infrastructures such as electricity distribution, water supply, or railroads that entail large fixed costs and high barriers to entry. Due to large economies of scale relative to the size of demand, the cost structure of a natural monopoly is such that a single firm will serve a market more efficiently than competing firms. As a result, rather than promoting competition, entry, and fragmentation, the standard policy approach has been to welcome or encourage

[9] Federal Trade Commission, Regulation in High-Tech Markets: Public Choice, Regulatory Capture, and the FTC, Remarks of Joshua Wright, available at www.ftc.gov/system/files/documents/public_statements/634631/150402clemson.pdf; Joshua Wright, Koren Wong-Ervin, Douglas Ginsburg, Bruce Kobayashi, and James Cooper, Comment of the Global Antitrust Institute, George Mason University School of Law, on the European Commission's Public Consultation on the Regulatory Environment for Platforms (December 29, 2015), available at http://masonlec.org/site/rte_uploads/files/GAI_Comment%20on%20EC%20Platform%20Consultation_12-29-15_FINAL.pdf.

[10] Carl Shapiro, "Antitrust in a Time of Populism," SSRN Scholarly Paper ID 3058345 (Rochester, NY: Social Science Research Network, 2017). Carl Shapiro, "Protecting Competition in the American Economy: Merger, Control, Tech Titans, Labour Markets" (2019) 33 *Journal of Economic Perspectives*, 69.

[11] Jean Tirole, *Economics for the Common Good* (Cambridge, MA: Princeton University Press, 2017); Allison Schrager, "A Nobel-Winning Economist's Guide to Taming Tech Monopolies," *Quartz* (June 27, 2018), available at https://qz.com/1310266/nobel-winning-economist-jean-tirole-on-how-to-regulate-tech-monopolies/.

[12] See, for instance, George Stigler Center for the Study of the Economy and the State – University of Chicago Booth School of Business, *Report by the Committee for the Study of Digital Platforms Market Structure and Antitrust Subcommittee* (May 15, 2109); UK Report of the Digital Competition Expert Panel, *Unlocking Digital Competition* (March 2019); European Commission, *Competition Policy for the Digital Era*, Final Report (April 4, 2019); Australian Competition and Consumer Commission, *Digital Platform Inquiry*, Final Report (July 26, 2019).

[13] *The Economist*, "How to Tame the Tech Titans" (January 18, 2018), available at www.economist.com/leaders/2018/01/18/how-to-tame-the-tech-titans.

concentration toward a natural monopoly while at the same time regulating ex ante the natural monopolist's behavior and the resulting market power.

The natural monopoly paradigm becomes potentially pertinent in the context of digital platforms because, even though platform intermediation is in itself not a new economic model, technological change appears to enhance the tendencies toward concentration compared to older, traditional physical predecessors of platforms: the collection and analysis of data as the cornerstone of prediction technologies and algorithmic-matching services create important scale and scope economies that were not available to the same degree to the previous generation of platforms; the digital, as opposed to physical, dimension of intermediaries increases the potential for large supply-side scale economies with low or zero marginal costs, as well as expanding the scope of matching capabilities for users that benefit from network externalities. Due to these various forms of scale enhanced by technological change, the natural monopoly paradigm becomes as a result a more fruitful theoretical starting point to evaluate concerns about market power in current digital platform markets than one provided by competition, entry, and market fragmentation, as well as a useful benchmark to evaluate alternative policy approaches that are consistent with efficient concentration and winner-takes-all markets.

On this basis, the first objective of this book is to investigate whether and how technological change and digitalization have promoted the emergence of natural monopolies in digital platform markets, and, if so, what kind of natural monopolies. Through an in-depth analysis of three case studies – horizontal search engines, e-commerce marketplaces, and ride-hailing platforms – this book will particularly highlight the different ways in which digitalization and technological change augment the tendencies toward natural monopoly, but with different degrees of natural concentration and contestability across digital industries.

Building on the conclusions derived from the application of the natural monopoly framework, the second goal of this book is to then draw more general principles that may serve as guiding tenets for policy approaches to competition and market power in digital platform industries as a whole beyond the three analyzed sectors. Highlighting the specific institutional limitations of alternative forms of intervention, this book will contend that the economic and technological features of digital platform markets overall challenge the dichotomy between ex ante and ex post approaches to market power, and thus demand rethinking the interface between regulation and competition policy.

1.1 THREE CASE STUDIES: A SPECTRUM OF NATURAL CONCENTRATION

As the book attempts to illuminate through the concrete illustration of three case studies, there are various and heterogeneous economic factors potentially associated with natural monopolies in digital platform markets, which include in particular: supply-side economies of scale often with negligible marginal costs, demand-side network externalities (both direct and indirect), and economies of scale related to data collection and analysis. The presence of these various forms of scale does not mean that natural monopolies are inevitable or that the emergence of a natural monopoly is necessarily driven by the platform model alone. Rather, the complex interplay between various economies of scale and possible counterforces against natural concentration shows that the technological features characterizing the current wave of digital platforms overall increase the likelihood of natural monopolies compared to older, standard examples of platform markets, but also that natural monopoly features vary substantially across digital platforms with different degrees of natural concentration.

In the first case study, for example, the book suggests that horizontal search[14] has the features of a natural monopoly. First, a horizontal search engine such as Google Search has a cost structure with high fixed costs and very low, arguably zero, marginal costs on the supply side creating economies of scale akin to standard network industries. Second, access to data is another key driver of natural concentration. Data are essential because at the core a horizontal search engine is a general-purpose prediction technology rather than simply a matching technology. While the matchmaking function and indirect network externalities between advertisers and searchers arising from the multisided matching model are contributing factors to concentration, they play only a limited role and are, in fact, tangential to the inevitable tendency toward a single horizontal search monopoly. On the contrary, the value of data and the economies of scale and scope that arise from larger datasets are critical for the purpose of improving search algorithm *predictions* as opposed to matching, where more data increase the efficiency of search results in terms of quality-adjusted costs. Moreover, due to the *universal* reach of horizontal search, specific data can have a positive value not only for a given narrow search query but also for a larger subset of related queries for which the same data points can be valuable. The predictive and universal nature of horizontal search are such that data can give rise to a natural monopoly.

Different conclusions are, however, reached in the second case study of e-commerce marketplaces. While online shopping marketplaces benefit from positive network externalities between buyers and sellers, product differentiation represents an important counterforce against natural concentration. Likewise, economies of scale at play in the development of logistics do not appear strong enough to generate a natural monopoly. On the contrary, the competitive advantage of successful marketplaces comes from having combined a large online marketplace with efficient storage and delivery infrastructure better than competitors. Amazon, for example, faces competition from other online marketplaces, and it is not the only firm providing delivery, but it is the firm that combines

---

[14] The term "horizontal" or "general" refers to search engines that provide any type of results covering any search query as opposed to "vertical" or "specialized" search engines that focus only on specific topics.

these two aspects in the most efficient and successful way, which explains its dominance. The fact that the physical infrastructure developed for storage and logistics plays a major role in e-commerce also shows that dominance can only partially be explained by the fact that an online marketplace like Amazon (in itself a hybrid between marketplace and reseller) can be described as a multisided platform.

The third case study of on-demand transportation services provides more ambiguous result. On the one hand, ride-hailing platforms benefit from a technological upgrade of the traditional dispatch mechanism through algorithmic matching that relies on data about drivers and passengers, coupled with the ability to call a ride and pay through an app. Overall, this form of matching benefit from substantial demand-side economies of scale through the creation of large networks, suggesting the plausibility of some natural monopoly features – among other things, bigger and denser networks that reduce waiting times are critical for services offered on demand, and more users contribute to the development of rating and review mechanisms important for solving issues of asymmetric information. On the other hand, the value of network externalities and the ability to improve matching tapers off after a critical mass of users is reached and the supply-side costs of entry are not particularly high. These considerations suggest that competition may be possible depending on the specific conditions of demand in a given geographical market – including the size of demand, density of population, and availability of alternative methods of transportation. As a result, ride-hailing platforms are located somewhere in between the strong natural monopoly features of horizontal search and the e-commerce's lack thereof.

The concrete illustration of the heterogeneous economic features and context-specific regulatory issues at play in each analyzed sector illuminates broader principles that may be pertinent to digital platform industries as a whole. First, the evaluation of the natural monopoly framework shows that digitalization and technological change increases the likelihood of natural monopoly in digital platform markets, albeit with different degrees of efficient and natural concentration across industries. Second, the identification of various forms of scale at play in digital platform markets and their technological features suggest that, depending on the source of concentration, some of these industries may be characterized by different degrees of contestability compared to standard public utilities and network industries based on physical infrastructures. Where the latter are generally the result of subadditive cost structures on the supply side – for example developing an electricity grid – natural monopolies in digital industries may emerge due to different factors such as demand-side scale created by direct and indirect network externalities. These types of natural monopoly can in some instances potentially be made more contestable than standard network utilities through policy intervention that promotes switching across platforms and entry for displacement.

1.2 RETHINKING THE INTERFACE BETWEEN COMPETITION POLICY AND REGULATION

The identified structural features of digital industries resulting from different degrees of natural monopoly features and contestability, as well as market power concerns associated with concentrated market structures challenge in complex ways the dichotomy between regulation and competition policy intervention. This book in particular contends that digital platform industries test the institutional limitations of ex ante and ex post approaches, suggesting that solutions to their respective institutional shortcomings will inevitably entail the need to rethink competition and regulatory solutions as complementary rather than substitute approaches to market power.

In theory, ex ante approaches could be a first-best response to some of the problem associated with a natural monopoly platform. However, not only the relevance of the standard paradigm of price and entry regulation is limited to platforms that are naturally monopolistic, but even when pertinent the concrete institutional implementation of regulation is rather imperfect and replete with various institutional limitations, including the costs of regulation, asymmetric information, rapid technological change, and the risks of regulatory capture. Most importantly, regulation risks entrenching current established market positions and as a result can undermine or slow down the process of technological innovation and dynamic displacement generally characterizing digital industries. Hence, the various costs and institutional limitations associated with the concrete implementation of standard ex ante regulation implemented by an industry-specific regulator are likely in many cases to outweigh the magnitude of market imperfections that regulation attempts to address.

While in a limited set of instances alternative approaches such as franchise bidding may provide a substitute option to regulation, intervention against market power in digital industries will, in most cases, demand reliance on ex post competition policy intervention. The approach dictated by structural features of these industries will be one focused on facilitating a form of Schumpeterian competition and cycles of monopoly displacement rather than market fragmentation. In order to do so, competition policy must be able to achieve two necessary objectives: a) preserve a degree of contestability by encouraging the threat of entry and facilitating the process of displacement by targeting innovation-based harms; and b) address market power exercises such as monopoly leveraging and discriminatory access to bottleneck inputs in an effective and expeditious way, especially in sectors where contestability is expected to be lower.

On the one hand, this approach has many virtues. It avoids the institutional costs and complexities of ex ante regulation; it reduces the need to directly regulate certain forms of inefficient behavior; and unlike regulation, it fosters incentives to cyclical displacement and innovation. On the other hand, as in the case of standard price and entry regulation, this policy approach to digital platform competition is affected by its own specific institutional limitations and constraints, due to the quasi-regulatory approach imposed by the features of digital industries. For instance, achieving the goal of contestability may often require forms of regulatory intervention that enable portability across platforms to facilitate entry and switching for users. Similarly, addressing some of the central market power concerns such as discrimination and leveraging will be difficult to achieve through antitrust enforcement characterized by slow and complex procedures, case-by-case adjudication, and remedies such as the application of the essential facilities doctrine that ultimately require ongoing administration akin to regulatory oversight.

On the basis of these conclusions, this book contends that the features of digital platforms and the resulting market power issues at play in these industries overall challenge the standard dichotomy between ex ante and ex post forms of intervention and require rethinking the interplay between competition policy and forms of regulatory oversight as complementary forms of intervention. As highlighted throughout the book, such a complementarity is, in particular, dictated by critical institutional trade-offs and limitations of alternative policy approaches that are pertinent to digital platform industries in light of the identified spectrum of natural monopoly features and contestability.

The conclusions reached in this book depart from the prevailing positions in favor of or against intervention in digital markets. Laissez-faire arguments generally underplay the ability of dominant platforms to abuse market power to protect themselves from threats of disruption, to delay displacement, and to foreclose adjacent markets, placing excessive emphasis on the role of market forces alone to erode high profits and market power. For their part, many of the proposals in favor of stronger antitrust intervention place excessive emphasis on the ability of competition, entry (conceived in terms of static competition between platforms), and induced market fragmentation to solve market power concerns in digital markets: proposals that attempt to fix competition by way of substantive changes to competition laws, for example, abandoning the consumer welfare standard, or by way of horizontal break-up of tech giants to fragment markets, clash with the contention that technological change makes platform markets overall more prone to efficient and natural concentration. More refined and nuanced positions that build on and apply Schumpeterian arguments to the tech sector are closer to the position defended in this book, insofar as they focus on favoring entry that aims at monopoly displacement and dynamic competition rather than fragmentation and static competition. However, these positions often assume away critical differences within digital platform markets, as well as important institutional constraints of ex post enforcement that this book attempts to highlight, suggesting on the contrary the need for forms of regulatory intervention to complement competition policy enforcement.

1.3 OUTLINE

This book is structured as follows. Chapter 2 introduces the natural monopoly framework in the context of digital platform markets. First, it discusses the technological and economic features that differentiate the current wave of digital platforms from older traditional examples of platform markets and explains the general legal and policy challenges raised by the increasing centrality of platform markets as a whole. Then, the chapter identifies potential key drivers of natural monopoly in digital platform markets. This general framework is subsequently applied to the specificities of three digital industries: online horizontal search (Chapter 3); e-commerce marketplaces (Chapter 4); on-demand ride-hailing platforms (Chapter 5). Building on the conclusions reached in the case studies, Chapter 6 evaluates alternative policy tools and identifies general guiding principles to address competition and market power for digital platform markets, pointing to the institutional dimension of intervention and the way in which it requires rethinking the interplay between competition policy and forms of ex ante regulation. Chapter 7 concludes by highlighting the theoretical contributions of this book and some of the open policy questions.

2

Technological Change and Natural Monopolies in Digital Industries

This chapter evaluates the applicability of the natural monopoly framework to digital platform industries, using it as a basis for the subsequent development of three case studies. The chapter first explains *why* the natural monopoly framework becomes pertinent in digital markets, pointing to the ways in which technological change overall increases the tendencies toward concentration and to some of the key legal and policy issues raised by the increasing centrality of the platform model of market intermediation. Then, the chapter introduces the standard economic and regulatory paradigm of natural monopoly and evaluates *what* such a paradigm entails in the context of digital platform markets, assessing the complex interplay of various forms of scale possibly associated with natural concentration.

2.1 TECHNOLOGICAL AND ECONOMIC DRIVERS OF INCREASING CONCENTRATION

The role of technological change in shaping economic organizations has always been central to the development of competition policy and economic regulation. Early political economists coming from different ideological perspectives such as Marx and Schumpeter already saw in capitalism a system always in the process of revolutionizing itself and constantly shaken by technological progress. While Marx's view of capitalist economies necessarily tending toward monopoly contrasted with the conclusions drawn by Schumpeter based on his insight about market competition as being driven by a perennial gale of creative destruction, both converged in seeing the instability of market mechanisms as a force of economic change resulting from the continuous process of revolutionizing the instruments of productions.[15] As important as the process of selling the best product at the lowest price, the force of the competitive process driven by the creation of alternative, better, technologies that generate entirely new markets and destabilize the previous market equilibrium

---

[15]   Karl Marx, *A Contribution to the Critique of Political Economy* (1859); Joseph A. Schumpeter, *Capitalism, Socialism, and Democracy* (London: Harper & Brothers, 1942).

has shaped many industries and equally influenced the origin and development of competition policy.

In itself, the emergence of modern competition laws can, in fact, be read as a response to social and economic changes created by technological progress. The emergence of the railroad, steam engines, and changes in telecommunication technologies during the nineteenth century that created the conditions for large-scale production and growth in the scale of manufacturing enterprises gave rise to drastic economic dislocations.[16] Canada was the first country to enact competition laws in 1889 as a result of the increased concentration of economic power in the aftermath of the industrial revolution,[17] and one year later the Sherman Act was enacted in the United States, as a result of increasing concerns among small producers, farmers, and consumers who perceived themselves as negatively affected by the forces of such transformations.[18] While the history of various competition law regimes is often unclear and reflects the confluence of heterogeneous forces and interests affecting the determination of the ultimate goal pursued by antitrust legislation,[19] the opposition to the growth of trusts and the protection of small businesses succumbing to the emerging large manufacturing enterprises were central to the birth of competition laws,[20] at least partially a by-product of substantial technological changes.

In particular, the increase in economic activity that came with new technologies and expanding markets gave rise to massive economies of scale in production and to administrative coordination, which increased organizational efficiency in terms of greater productivity, lower costs, and higher profits. The emergence of managerial capitalism in large firms through a hierarchy of middle and top salaried managers did not exist in 1840, but less than a century later the modern multidivisional business enterprise replaced small traditional enterprises. At first, the large enterprise grew and dominated only a few sectors or industries where technological innovation and market growth were particularly significant. As technology became more sophisticated and markets expanded, administrative coordination replaced market coordination in an increasingly larger portion of the economy. By the middle of the twentieth century, mass production and retail, mass transportation, and distribution dominated major sectors of the American economy.

As noted by Chandler, who traced the birth of the modern enterprise, the organizational changes that helped create the managerial capitalism of the

---

[16]　See Bhu Srinivasan, *Americana: A 400-year History of American Capitalism* (New York: Penguin Press, 2017).

[17]　See Chapter 1 in Michael J. Trebilcock, Ralph A. Winter, and Edward M. Iacobucci, *The Law and Economics of Canadian Competition Policy* (Toronto: University of Toronto Press, 2002).

[18]　See Alfred D. Chandler Jr., *The Visible Hand* (Cambridge, MA: Harvard University Press, 1977); William Letwin, *Law and Economic Policy in America* (New York: Random House, 1956).

[19]　Henry Rogers Seager and Charles Adams Gulick, *Trust and Corporation Problems* (New York: Harper, 1929).

[20]　William Letwin, *supra*, note 18.

twentieth century were as significant and as revolutionary as those that accompanied the rise of commercial capitalism half a millennium earlier.[21] Where administrative coordination within the firm was the organizational response to the application of industrial technologies, the passing of antitrust laws was at least in part the legislative reaction to the same changes in transportation and communication and to the new processes of production and distribution that gave rise to the increasing number of combinations that occurred during the 1870s and 1880s.[22]

As competition law regimes matured and evolved, the impact of technological progress on market competition retained its centrality in various areas of competition policy. Among other things, it remained implicit in the longstanding debates on what market structure – monopoly or competition – better serves the process of innovation. Many theoretical and empirical studies have attempted to determine the linkages between technological change, firm size, and market structure. Notably, Schumpeter, among others, famously emphasized that market power and concentration are necessary as an incentive for firms to innovate due to economies of scale and the expense and risks involved in carrying out research and development.[23] In contrast, Arrow concluded that competition rather than monopoly creates better conditions for innovation,[24] and others have highlighted the various disadvantages that larger firms can incur in administering large administrative structures, which undermine rather than facilitative innovative R&D processes.[25]

Most recent empirical studies have concluded that innovation presents an inverted U-shaped relationship with firm size and market concentration,[26] where market concentration aids innovation up to a point, but then concentrated, oligopolistic industries with high barriers to entry may reduce incentives to innovate. Aghion, et al.[27] collected empirical evidence about the relationship between product market concentration and the intensity of innovative activity, showing that an inverted U-shaped pattern[28] results from the balance between what they call the "Schumpeterian" and the "escaping-competition" incentive:[29] on the one hand,

---

[21] Chandler Jr., *supra*, note 18.

[22] Massimo Motta, *Competition Policy: Theory and Practice* (Cambridge: Cambridge University Press, 2004); Trebilcock, Winter, and Iacobucci, *supra*, note 17.

[23] Schumpeter, *supra*, note 15.

[24] Kenneth Arrow, "Economic Welfare and the Allocation of Resources for Invention," in *The Rate and Direction of Inventive Activity: Economic and Social Factors* (Cambridge, MA: Princeton University Press, 1962).

[25] See, for instance, Oliver E. Williamson, "Economies as an Antitrust Defense: The Welfare Tradeoffs" (1968) 58, no. 1, Am Econ Rev, 18.

[26] F. M. Scherer and David Ross, *Industrial Market Structure and Economic Performance*, 3rd ed. (Boston, MA: Houghton Mifflin, 1990).

[27] Philippe Aghion, et al., "Competition and Innovation: An Inverted-U Relationship" (2005) 120, no. 2, Q J Econ, 701.

[28] This pattern was previously hinted at by Scherer. See Scherer and Ross, *supra*, note 26.

[29] Flavio Delbono and Luca Lambertini, "Innovation and Product Market Concentration: Schumpeter, Arrow and the Inverted-U Shape Curve," SSRN Scholarly Paper ID 2981677 (Rochester, NY: Social Science Research Network, 2017).

competition can increase the incremental profits obtained from innovation and therefore encourages R&D investments aimed at escaping competition in sectors where incumbent firms are operating at similar technological levels; on the other hand, in unlevelled sectors where product market competition may discourage innovation by laggard firms with already low initial profits, the Schumpeterian effect is at work (even if it does not always necessarily dominate). In sum, the desirability of competition versus concentration for innovation often depends on the technological state of the sector.[30]

The different forms and paces of technological change have also been critical in shaping enforcement policies and intervention in markets characterized by dynamic competition for the market as opposed to static competition within markets. Technological development is usually incremental, bringing into markets products or services that are marginally superior to current ones. At times, and perhaps most critically, it is instead based on more irregular and unpredictable breakthroughs that bring radical changes to markets and reduce or destroy the established position of incumbents or create entirely new markets. This radical form of innovation can either come from an existing firm or from a new market entrant and generally occurs in markets dominated and occupied by inefficient incumbents that suddenly face competitive threats from the rapid scaling up of disruptors in niche segments.[31] Bower and Christensen divide the forms of innovation into two types, sustaining and disruptive.[32] The former provides an improvement in something that consumers already value, the latter introduces a different and new set of features compared to the ones traditionally valued by consumers. In *The Innovator's Dilemma*, Christensen describes this latter form of disruptive innovation as not always necessarily associated with breakthrough innovation but with a phenomenon that transforms a product that was previously offered expensively at the high end of the market and that is made more affordable and accessible.[33] At the outset, the new features offered usually perform worse on many dimensions, but eventually manage to replace older goods or services due to novelty, lower costs, elimination of middlemen, or other inefficiencies. Where sustaining innovation is usually associated with competition within the market, disruptive innovation is associated with dynamic forms of winner-takes-all competition for the market. The two different competitive processes generally call for a different set of enforcement policies: the former generally based on neoclassical economic assumptions about competition, the latter based on the goal of encouraging ongoing cycles of monopoly displacement.

[30]　Philippe Aghion, et al., *supra*, note 27.
[31]　"Disruptive Innovations and Their Effect on Competition – OECD" (2015), OECD.org, available at www.oecd.org/daf/competition/disruptive-innovations-and-competition.htm.
[32]　Joseph Bower and Clayton Christensen, "Disruptive Technologies: Catching the Wave" (1995) 73, January–February, Harv Bus Rev, 43.
[33]　"The Innovator's Dilemma: When New Technologies Cause Great Firms to Fail," Clayton Christensen, available at www.claytonchristensen.com/books/the-innovators-dilemma/.

This longstanding relationship between technology and the origin of competition policy is resurrected today due to the current wave of technological change driven by developments in artificial intelligence, big data, and the growing importance of the digital economy, fuelling, as a by-product, discontent in many quarters with technology as a visible force of profound economic change.[34] Among other things, automation has significant effects on labor markets and trends in employment in many key sectors of the economy; digitalization is reshaping many traditional professions,[35] the future of education,[36] and the process of lawmaking;[37] artificial intelligence, and big data test the foundations of various areas of public policy and regulation.[38] With regard to competition, in particular, technological change has been associated with growing evidence of increasing levels of market concentration in industrialized economies,[39] particularly in the United States.

[34] Michael J. Trebilcock, "The Fracturing of the Post-War Free Trade Consensus: The Challenges of Reconstructing a New Consensus," a paper delivered at the University of Toronto Faculty of Law (2017).

[35] Richard Susskind and Daniel Susskind, *The Future of the Professions: How Technology Will Transform the Work of Human Experts* (Oxford: Oxford University Press, 2016).

[36] Claudia Goldin and Lawrence F. Katz, *The Race between Education and Technology* (Cambridge, MA: Harvard University Press, 2009).

[37] Richard Susskind, *The Future of Law: Facing the Challenges of Information Technology* (Oxford: Clarendon Press, 1998); Benjamin Alarie, Anthony Niblett, and Albert H. Yoon, "Law in the Future" (2016) 66, no. 4, *Univ Tor Law J*, 423; Anthony J. Casey and Anthony Niblett, "Self-Driving Laws" (2016) 66, no. 4, *Univ Tor Law J*, 429.

[38] For the impact of big data and algorithms on competition, see Ariel Ezrachi and Maurice E. Stucke, *Virtual Competition: The Promise and Perils of the Algorithm-Driven Economy* (Cambridge, MA: Harvard University Press, 2016); Ariel Ezrachi and Maurice E. Stucke, "Artificial Intelligence & Collusion: When Computers Inhibit Competition" (2017) Univ Ill Law Rev, 1775; Michal Gal and Daniel L. Rubinfeld, "The Hidden Costs of Free Goods: Implications for Antitrust Enforcement" (2016) 80, no. 401, *Antitrust Law J*, available at https://papers.ssrn.com/abstract=2529425; Maurice E. Stucke and Allen P. Grunes, *Debunking the Myths over Big Data and Antitrust*, Legal Studies Research Paper Series Research Paper #276 (Knoxville: University of Tennessee Press, 2015); Darren S. Tucker and Hill Wellford, "Big Mistakes Regarding Big Data," SSRN Scholarly Paper ID 2549044 (Rochester, NY: Social Science Research Network, 2014); Cecilia Munoz, Megan Smith, and D. J. Patil, *Big Data: A Report on Algorithmic Systems, Opportunity, and Civil Rights*, Obama Administration's Big Data Working Group (Washington, DC: Executive Office of the President, 2016).

[39] See, for instance, David Autor, D., et al., "Concentrating on the Fall of the Labor Share" (2017) 107, no. 5, Am Econ Rev, 180; Joseph Stiglitz, "Toward a Broader View of Competition Policy," in *Competitive Policy for the New Era: Insights from the BRICS Countries* (Oxford: Oxford University Press, 2017), p. 4; Jonathan B. Baker, "Market Power in the U.S. Economy Today" (March 20, 2017), Washington Center for Equitable Growth, available at https://equitablegrowth.org/market-power-in-the-u-s-economy-today/; Luigi Zingales, "Towards a Political Theory of the Firm" (2017) 31, no. 3, J Econ Perspect, 113; University of Chicago Booth School of Business, *Is There a Concentration Problem in America?* (Gleacher Center, 2017); Council of Economic Advisers, *Benefits of Competition and Indicators of Market Power*, Issues Brief (Washington, DC: Obama White House, 2016); "Too Much of a Good Thing – Business in America," *The Economist* (March 26, 2016), available at www .economist.com/briefing/2016/03/26/too-much-of-a-good-thing; Jonathan Tepper, *The Myth of Capitalism: Monopolies and the Death of Competition* (Hoboken, NJ: John Wiley & Sons, 2018).

For instance, the US Census Bureau data show increases in the revenue share enjoyed by the largest fifty firms in the timeframe between 1997 and 2012 in a large portion of US industries, with various industry-specific studies finding similar trends over longer periods of time.[40] According to other studies, more than 75 percent of US industries have experienced an increase in concentration levels over the last two decades,[41] with the HHI index increasing by more than 50 percent on average.[42] Other evidence points to declining levels of new firm creations each year across sectors,[43] the growing problem of horizontal shareholding in concentrated industries,[44] and increasing monopsony power due to excessive employer concentration in labor markets.[45]

Not all of these concerns are necessarily or solely linked to technology. Yet the rise of superstar digital platforms is seen as a particularly prominent manifestation of the role of technological change in fostering concentrated market structures. In this regard, Autor, et al., for example, suggest an interpretation for the fall in labor's share of the GDP in the United States based on the rise of superstar firms, particularly in high-tech industries.[46] High-tech sectors (but also parts of retail and transportation sectors) have increasingly "winner-takes-all" aspects, suggesting that firms may

---

[40] Council of Economic Advisers, *supra*, note 39. See also discussions in Carl Shapiro, *supra*, note 10; Jan De Loecker, Jan Eeckhout, and Gabriel Unger, "The Rise of Market Power and the Macroeconomic Implications," Draft, November 22, 2018.

[41] Gustavo Grullon, Yelena Larkin, and Roni Michaely, "Are U.S. Industries Becoming More Concentrated?," SSRN Scholarly Paper ID 2612047 (Rochester, NY: Social Science Research Network, 2018).

[42] This trend appears to parallel very high levels of merger activity, and a decline in the application of Section 2 of the Sherman Act. There is also evidence that the wave of mergers has improved productivity but has also raised mark-ups from 15 percent to 50 percent above the average mark-ups across U.S. manufacturing industries. See Bruce A. Blonigen and Justin R. Pierce, *Evidence for the Effects of Mergers on Market Power and Efficiency*, Finance and Economics Discussion Series 2016–2082 (Board of Governors of the Federal Reserve System (US), 2016).

[43] While decreasing rates of entry were identified only in specific sectors during the 1980s and 1990s, this decline affected all sectors in the 2000s. See Ryan Decker, John Haltiwanger, Ron Jarmin, and Javier Miranda, "The Role of Entrepreneurship in US Job Creation and Economic Dynamism" (2014) 28, no. 3, J Econ Perspect, 3; Ryan Decker, John Haltiwanger, Ron S. Jarmin, and Javier Miranda, *The Secular Decline in Business Dynamism in the U.S.*, Working Paper (College Park, MD: University of Maryland Press, 2014).

[44] José Azar, Martin C. Schmalz, and Isabel Tecu, "Anticompetitive Effects of Common Ownership," SSRN Scholarly Paper ID 2427345 (Rochester, NY: Social Science Research Network, 2018); José Azar, Sahil Raina, and Martin C Schmalz, "Ultimate Ownership and Bank Competition," SSRN Scholarly Paper ID 2710252 (Rochester, NY: Social Science Research Network, 2016); Einer Elhauge, "Horizontal Shareholding," SSRN Scholarly Paper ID 2632024 (Rochester, NY: Social Science Research Network, 2016); Eric A. Posner, Fiona M. Scott Morton, and E. Glen Weyl, "A Proposal to Limit the Anti-Competitive Power of Institutional Investors," SSRN Scholarly Paper ID 2872754 (Rochester, NY: Social Science Research Network, 2017).

[45] See, for example, Suresh Naidu, Eric A. Posner, and E. Glen Weyl, "Antitrust Remedies for Labor Market Power" (2018) 132, *Harvard Law Review*, 536.

[46] David Autor, et al., *The Fall of the Labor Share and the Rise of Superstar Firms*, Working Paper 23396 (National Bureau of Economic Research, 2017), at 23.

initially gain high market shares by legitimately competing on the merits of their innovations or superior efficiencies, but once they have gained a dominant position, they use increasing market power to erect various barriers to entry to protect their position.[47] Similarly, according to the *Economist*, the rise of tech titans, often accused in public debates of being too big, engaging in anticompetitive behavior, and threatening democracy,[48] poses a danger to competition and requires antitrust policy solutions in a world based on information and networks where digital companies may use network effects to exclude potential competitors, or implement new ways of exploiting their dominant position.[49]

Indeed, various proposals that have been proposed to address the dominance of tech platforms, driven by concerns over excessive concentration of both economic and political power, evoke an inevitable parallel between the current discontent with technological change and the growth of trusts and nineteen-century robber barons – including radical changes in antitrust law doctrines and goals with a return to the protection of small businesses and specific market structures, stronger enforcement against mergers and single firm conduct, or calls to break up digital platforms.[50]

There are, however, important considerations and distinctions to be considered when evaluating such parallels. First, the evidence of alleged decreases in the levels of market competition is not uncontested. In themselves, data on increases in the revenue share reveal little or nothing about trends in competition and market power in properly defined relevant markets[51] and do not provide informative evidence of concentration as reflecting changes in the levels of competition over time, or provide

---

[47]   See also Simcha Barkai, "Declining Labor and Capital Shares" (2017) Working Paper, available at www.london.edu/faculty-and-research/academic-research/d/declining-labor-and-capital-shares; Loukas Karabarbounis and Brent Neiman, "The Global Decline of the Labor Share" (2014) 129, no. 1, Q J Econ, 61.

[48]   "How to Tame the Tech Titans," *The Economist* (January 18, 2018), available at www.economist. com/leaders/2018/01/18/how-to-tame-the-tech-titans; Patrick Foulis, "Across the West Powerful Firms are Becoming Even More Powerful," *The Economist* (November 15, 2018), available at www.economist.com/special-report/2018/11/15/across-the-west-powerful-firms-are-becoming-even-more-powerful; "Competition, Not Break-Up, Is the Cure for Tech Giants' Dominance," *The Economist* (March 13, 2019), available at www.economist.com/business/2019/03/13/competition-not-break-up-is-the-cure-for-tech-giants-dominance?fsrc=scn%2Ftw%2Fte%2Fbl%2Fed%2Fauto.

[49]   Adrian Woolridge, "The Rise of the Superstars," *The Economist* (September 17, 2016), available at www.economist.com/special-report/2016/09/17/the-rise-of-the-superstars; "The Superstar Company: A Giant Problem," *The Economist* (September 17, 2016), available at www.economist.com/leaders/ 2016/09/17/a-giant-problem; Aindrajit Dube, et al., "Monopsony in On-line Labor Markets" (2018) Draft (Paper under Preparation).

[50]   See, for example, Tepper, *supra*, note 39. See, more generally, UK Report of the Digital Competition Expert Panel, *supra*, note 12; Australian Competition and Consumer Commission, *Digital Platform Inquiry* (July 26, 2019), *supra*, note 12; "Competition, Not Break-up, is the Cure for Tech Giants' Dominance," *The Economist* (March 2019), available at www.economist.com/business/2019/03/13/ competition-not-break-up-is-the-cure-for-tech-giants-dominance?fsrc=scn%2Ftw%2Fte%2Fbl% 2Fed %2Fauto.

[51]   Shapiro, *supra*, note 10.

an explanation as to whether economies of scale or network externalities,[52] increasing barriers to entry, exclusionary conduct, or lack of effective merger enforcement are driving these trends.

Second, the technological drivers of concentration are different. Where managerial capitalism was driven by the increasing sophistication of administrative coordination of large enterprises that exploited supply-side economies of scale, the contemporary form of organizing economic activity capitalizes on the use of big data and AI technologies to perform more and more efficient prediction and matching, which are often characterized by negligible marginal costs on the supply side and reliance on demand-side economies of scale due to network effects. Unlike traditional vertically integrated industrial enterprises based on a linear value chain, matchmaking platforms sit as intermediaries between users and create marketplaces for their interaction by reducing information and transaction costs, shifting the focus from internal production processes to the efficient management of network externalities and market access for various small service providers.[53] Moreover, many digital platforms have a global nature and offer services at a global scale, and are often characterized by a complex interplay between their international, digital reach and the importance of local, physical dimensions of their services.

As a result, while the similarities between nineteenth-century monopolies and digital platforms are evocative of recurrent parallels between waves of technological progress and cycles of increasing market concentration, proposed policy responses to alleged problem of increasing market power caused by the current wave of platform markets can therefore often be too vague and lack a rigorous evaluation of the following considerations: what is exactly new and specific about the current wave of platforms vis-à-vis older generations of platforms that may cause increasing concentration and display similitudes with the economics of superstars;[54] what types of market failure may be caused by increasing concentration in specific digital sectors in terms of market power abuses; and what are the most desirable policy approaches to address identified market power issues in digital platform industries.

In the next section, we go on to discuss some of the features of current technological developments associated with increasing levels of concentration that distinguish the current wave of digital platforms from older generations of platform markets. The chapter shows, in particular, that the increasing predominance of the platform model based on digital services and access to data as a central input for algorithmic-based matching and prediction technologies make current platforms potentially more prone to natural monopoly.

---

[52] Autor, et al., *supra*, note 39; James E. Bessen, "Information Technology and Industry Concentration," SSRN Scholarly Paper ID 3044730 (Rochester, NY: Social Science Research Network, 2017).

[53] As it is the case with platform intermediaries enabling individual drivers to provide taxi services, home owners to offer short-term rentals, or small business to better access consumers online.

[54] Sherwin Rosen, "The Economics of Superstars" (1981) 71, no. 5, *American Economic Review*, 845–858.

2.1.1 *Platform Intermediation and the Theory of the Firm*

Modern information and communication technologies have scaled up exponentially the viability and efficiency of the multisided platform business model that have existed for millennia.[55] Old village marketplaces, trade fairs, auction houses, yellow pages, bricks-and-mortar shopping malls, physical newspapers, and credit cards[56] are all older analogs to today's digital platforms and many of these markets have been under the spotlight of antitrust enforcement in the past. Where matching capabilities of traditional old physical platforms have been often limited by the boundary of physical spaces that imposed limits on the extent of markets and the offering of new goods and services, online platforms can expand due to digitalization the extent of the marketplace both geographically and in terms of increased matching potential between users, aided by the power of big data and algorithmic matching functions that were not available to the older physical predecessors of the platform.[57]

The increasing predominance of the platform model of intermediation can be explained through the lens provided by the theory of the firm. Coase's theory of the firm was based on the idea that the transaction costs of organizing economic activities determine the boundaries between markets and within the hierarchy of the firm.[58] Coase's insight was that using the market is costly: discovering market prices and negotiating contracts for each exchange can be avoided inside the firm because bargaining is replaced by authority. However, because authority has its own costs, as the firm gets bigger, the relative cost of authority and the price system is what determines the boundaries and sizes of firms. Since then, a voluminous strand of law and economics literature has advanced competing theories of the firm and why in market economies we have firms at all.[59]

---

[55]   See David Evans and Richard Schmalensee, *Matchmakers: The New Economics of Multisided Platforms* (Cambridge, MA: Harvard Business Review Press, 2016).

[56]   Paul Belleflamme and Martin Peitz, "Platforms and Network Effects," Working Papers 16–14 (University of Mannheim, Department of Economics, 2016).

[57]   Liran Einav, Chiara Farronato, and Jonathan Levin, "Peer-to-Peer Markets," NBER Working Paper 21496 (Cambridge, MA: National Bureau of Economic Research, Inc., 2015).

[58]   R. H. Coase, "The Nature of the Firm" (1937) 4, no. 16, *Economica*, 386.

[59]   See Robert Gibbons, "Four Formal(izable) Theories of the Firm?" (2005) 58, no. 2, J Econ Behav Organ, 200; Oliver E. Williamson, "Transaction-Cost Economics: The Governance of Contractual Relations" (1979) 22, no. 2, J Law Econ, 233; Benjamin Klein, Robert G. Crawford, and Armen A. Alchian, "Vertical Integration, Appropriable Rents, and the Competitive Contracting Process" (1978) 21, no. 2, J Law Econ, 297; Sanford J. Grossman and Oliver D. Hart, "The Costs and Benefits of Ownership: A Theory of Vertical and Lateral Integration" (1986) 94, no. 4, J Polit Econ, 691; Oliver Hart and John Moore, "Property Rights and the Nature of the Firm" (1990) 98, no. 6, J Polit Econ, 1119; Armen Alchian and Harold Demsetz, "Production, Information Costs, and Economic Organization" (1972) 62, no. 5, Am Econ Rev, 777. Oliver Williamson, "The Vertical Integration of Production: Market Failure Considerations" (1971) 61, no. 2, Am Econ Rev, 112; Oliver E. Williamson, *Markets and Hierarchies, Analysis and Antitrust Implications: a Study in the Economics of Internal Organization* (New York: Free Press, 1975); Oliver Hart and John Moore, "Contracts as Reference Points" (2008) 123, no. 1, Q J Econ, 1; Bengt Holmstrom and Paul Milgrom, "The Firm as an Incentive System" (1994) 84, no. 4, Am Econ Rev, 972.

The growth of platform intermediaries goes to the heart of the questions raised by the theory of the firm because platform intermediation is a solution to transaction costs that blurs the traditional boundaries between the two predominant forms of organizing economic activities: markets and hierarchies.[60] In particular, the centrality of intermediaries' choice to vertically integrate or allocate in different ways the residual control rights between independent service providers and the firm transforms the typical "make or buy" decision of vertical integration to an "enable or employ" trade-off in the context of two-sided intermediaries.[61] The latter dichotomy involves a preference for contractual relationships between buyers and sellers, to which the two-sided intermediary is not a party, but merely an enabler of such contractual relationships.[62] In this way, buyers and sellers connecting or trading through a platform keep the residual control rights regarding transactions and a platform acts as a catalyst by reducing the transaction costs and internalizing network externalities across the different user groups.

A plausible explanation for the growing predominance of the platform model through the lens provided by the theory of the firm, then, is that platforms are a response to the costs of the market, where the solution is neither administrative hierarchy, nor pure bilateral contracting, but the creation of marketplaces that intermediate across users. A platform can be seen, at a very basic level, as a firm that specializes in the production of coordination and matching services not available in the market to individual users. Such form of intermediation improves trade compared to purely decentralized matching where exchange is socially inefficient due to coordination, information, and search cost among users. Reintermediation through platforms[63] (as opposed to disintermediation) is a response to relative changes in internal versus external coordination costs and a solution to the costs of excessive information made available by technological developments.[64]

Technological change therefore contributes to increasing levels of concentration in two important ways. First, it favors a new wave of platform intermediation as the increasingly predominant model of the firm, where intermediaries rely on creating large networks of users that can match through the platform and where users generally benefit from larger networks due to network

---

[60] For example, through a reduction in asset specificity (when assets can be redeployed for alternative uses hierarchy is less necessary) and alteration of coordination costs enabled by digital technologies. See Arun Sundararajan, *The Sharing Economy: The End of Employment and the Rise of Crowd-Based Capitalism* (Cambridge, MA: MIT Press, 2016).

[61] Andrei Hagiu and Julian Wright, "Multi-Sided Platforms," Working Paper No. 15–037 (Cambridge, MA: Harvard Business School, 2014).

[62] Ibid, at 4.

[63] Geoffrey G. Parker, Marshall W. Van Alstyne and Sangeet Paul Choudary, *Platform Revolution: How Networked Markets Are Transforming the Economy and How to Make Them Work for You* (New York: W.W. Norton & Company, 2016) at 71.

[64] Tirole, *supra*, note 11 at 381. For a broader discussion on matchmaking and market design, see Alvin E. Roth, *Who Gets What and Why: The New Economics of Matchmaking and Market Design* (Boston, MA: Houghton Mifflin Harcourt, 2015).

externalities. Second, and in addition to this effect, the digital nature of the current wave of platforms further enhances the tendency toward concentrated market structures compared to older examples of platforms through extensive reliance on big data for algorithmic predictions and digital matching. As will be discussed, these factors enabled by digitalization and technological changes overall have the potential to enhance the likelihood of natural monopoly in current digital platform markets.

2.1.2 *Data, Algorithmic Predictions, and Digital Matching*

Standard multisided platforms are generally thought of as matchmakers, such as a shopping mall, a dating nightclub, physical newspapers, or credit cards, that rely on indirect network externalities across the groups of users that match through the intermediary. What is novel in the current wave of digital platforms is that digitalization, AI, and big data have expanded matching capabilities as well as enabled novel and sophisticated forms of prediction. Thus, current digital platforms provide a different mix of algorithmic predictions and matching for which data are a central input.[65]

A paradigmatic manifestation of the various changes dictated by technological change in platform markets is the growth of the sharing economy, a phenomenon that encompasses a variety of peer-to-peer exchanges (often described using terms like peer-to-peer, on-demand economy, and collaborative economy),[66] which has been particularly prominent in the transportation and hospitality

---

[65] See, for instance, OECD, "Big Data: Bringing Competition Policy to the Digital Era – OECD," (November 2016), OECD *Better Policies Better Lives*, available at www.oecd.org/competition/big-data -bringing-competition-policy-to-the-digital-era.htm; Competition Bureau of Canada, *Big Data and Innovation: Implications for Competition Policy in Canada*, Draft for Public Consultation (Gatineau: QC, 2017); Autorite de la concurrence and the Bundeskartellamt, *Competition Law and Data* (2016); Federal Trade Commission, *Big Data: A Tool for Inclusion or Exclusion? Understanding the Issues*, FTC Report (2016).

[66] See, generally, Rachel Botsman and Roo Rogers, *What's Mine Is Yours: The Rise of Collaborative Consumption* (New York: HarperCollins, 2010); Einav, Farronato & Levin, *supra*, note 57; Working Party on Measurement and Analysis of the Digital Economy, *New Forms of Work in the Digital Economy*, Background Report JT03398022 (Committee on Digital Economy Policies (CDEP), OECD, 2016); Chiara Farronato and Audrey Fradkin, "Market Structure with the Entry of Peer-to-Peer Platforms: The Case of Hotels and Airbnb" (2016) Unpublished Draft Prelim, available at https:// editorialexpress.com/cgi-bin/conference/download.cgi?db_name=   IIOC2016&paper_id=285; Jeremy Rifkin, *The Zero Marginal Cost Society: The Internet of Things, the Collaborative Commons, and the Eclipse of Capitalism* (New York: Macmillan, 2014); Daniel Rauch and David Schleicher, "Like Uber, But for Local Governmental Policy: The Future of Local Regulation of the "Sharing Economy," SSRN Scholarly Paper ID 2549919 (Rochester, NY: Social Science Research Network, 2015); Molly Cohen and Arun Sundararajan, "Self-Regulation and Innovation in the Peer-to-Peer Sharing Economy" (2015) 82 Univ Chic Law Rev Dialogue, 116; Edith Ramirez, Maureen K. Ohlhausen and Terrell P. McSweeny, *The "Sharing" Economy: Issues Facing Platforms, Participants & Regulators*, Federal Trade Commission Staff Report (Washington, DC: Federal Trade Commission, 2016); Cristiano Codagnone and Bertin Martens, "Scoping the Sharing Economy: Origins, Definitions, Impact and Regulatory Issues," SSRN Scholarly Paper ID 2783662

industries.[67] On the one hand, most sharing economy platforms match various services and service providers with consumers based on the standard multisided model, where the platform intermediates between different users' groups with interdependent demand. On the other hand, the technological features and pre-conditions for emergence of the sharing economy phenomenon are novel: thanks to digitalization and a significant reduction in search, information and transaction costs, unused or underutilized assets can be turned into productive resources – whether it is an underutilized vehicle, spare rooms, or specific skills to provide various on-demand services – where matching is done digitally through algorithmic technologies that rely on data as an important input. These technological developments have as a consequence raised a number of challenging policy questions,[68] including the application of traditional labor standards, issues of fair and transparent pricing, collusion between service providers and the platform facilitated by algorithms, and winner-takes-all tendencies enabled by network externalities and data.[69]

The rise of the sharing economy phenomenon is just an example of broader trends and technological innovations that distinguish current digital platforms more generally, where digitalization and technological developments have enabled various forms of scale through the use of data and AI technologies, both for the purpose of digital matching and for the development of prediction services, that were not available to older generations of platforms. Digitalization expands matching capabilities and can give rise to cost structures with low marginal costs, and data become a critical input to the development of successful algorithms, including matching, prediction, and pricing,[70] thanks to increases in computing power and growing

(Rochester, NY: Social Science Research Network, 2016); Working Party on Measurement and Analysis of the Digital Economy, *supra*, note 66; Benjamin G. Edelman and Damien Geradin, "Efficiencies and Regulatory Shortcuts: How Should We Regulate Companies Like Airbnb and Uber" (2015) 19 Stanf Technol Law Rev, 293; Derek McKee and Teresa Scassa (eds.), *Law and the "Sharing Economy": Regulating Online Market Platforms* (Ottawa: University of Ottawa Press, 2018).

[67] According to a 2015 report by PricewaterhouseCoopers, "five sharing sectors – travel, car sharing, finance, staffing and music and video streaming – have the potential to increase global revenues from roughly $15 billion today to around $335 billion by 2025. Airbnb for instance, has now more than 50,000 guests per night, having served over 50 million guests since it was founded in 2008, and a market capitalization of well over $20 billion." See PriceWaterhouseCooper, *The Sharing Economy*, Consumer Intelligence Series (2015); Georgios Zervas, Davide Proserpio, and John W. Byers, "The Rise of the Sharing Economy: Estimating the Impact of Airbnb on the Hotel Industry" (2017) 54, no. 5, J Mark Res, 687.

[68] Sundararajan, *supra*, note 60. See also Parker, Alstyne, and Choudary, *supra*, note 63; Yochai Benkler, "Sharing Nicely: On Shareable Goods and the Emergence of Sharing as a Modality of Economic Production" (2004) 114 Yale Law J, 273; Tom Slee, *What's Yours Is Mine: Against the Sharing Economy* (OR Books, LLC, 2016).

[69] See, for instance, Eric A. Posner, "Eric Posner on Why Uber Will – And Should – Be Regulated," *Slate* (5 January 2015), available at www.law.uchicago.edu/news/eric-posner-why-uber-will-and-should-be-regulated.

[70] Munoz, Smith, and Patil, *supra*, note 38.

sophistication in data analytics and AI.[71] According to the *Economist*, "data are to this century what oil was to the last one: a driver of growth and change. Flows of data have created new infrastructure, new businesses, new monopolies, new politics and – crucially – new economics."[72] Based on some estimates, the volume of data processed globally has experienced a compound annual growth rate of 25 percent from 2014 to 2019, and it is forecast to expand almost exponentially.[73] While the analogy with oil has limitations,[74] data are undeniably a central asset in the digital economy whose increasing centrality animates policy debates ranging from privacy protection, access, portability, and data ownership.[75]

Data are particularly associated with increasing levels of market concentration because the data value chain, from collection to storage to analysis, is characterized by important economies of scale and scope.[76] The larger the amount of data, the more refined the algorithm applying them can become, generating a positive feedback loop as more users generate more data, which, in turn, means higher service quality. When this takes place, the quality-adjusted cost of data collection and analysis can become smaller for larger platforms. The importance of data and access to larger datasets depends on the context-specific minimum point of efficient scale and the marginal value of adding additional data. For certain purposes, the point of minimum efficient scale may, for example, be easy to reach, as it is in the case of data on very popular queries for a general-purpose search engine;[77] in other cases, such as tail queries, platforms with smaller datasets may instead not be able to reach the point of optimality. In its merger with Yahoo, for instance, Microsoft argued that merging datasets and having access to a larger index would have positive effects on competition due to scale economies enabling stronger competition with Google.[78] Data collection and analysis can also benefit from economies of scope, whereby the aggregation of different types of data from a variety of different sources can make a significant difference in the improvement of algorithms more than the simple accumulation of general data alone.

---

[71]   H. Hu, et al., "Toward Scalable Systems for Big Data Analytics: A Technology Tutorial" (2014) 2 IEEE Access 652; Autorité de la concurrence and the Bundeskartellamt, *supra*, note 65.

[72]   "Data Is Giving Rise to a New Economy," *The Economist* (May 2017, 6), available at www .economist.com/briefing/2017/05/06/data-is-giving-rise-to-a-new-economy.

[73]   Cisco, *Cisco Global Cloud Index: Forecast and Methodology, 2014–2019*, White Paper (2015).

[74]   Data, unlike oil, are not finite and the cost of processing, storing, analyzing, and sharing data are likely to fall dramatically as technology advances.

[75]   Chris Jay Hoofnagle and Jan Whittington, "Free: Accounting for the Costs of the Internet's Most Popular Price" (2013) 61 UCLA Law Rev, 606; Jaron Lanier, *Who Owns The Future?* (London: Penguin, 2013).

[76]   Big data are often referred to as being characterized by the four Vs: volume, velocity, variety, and value.

[77]   Zhicheng Dou, Ruihua Song, and Ji-Rong Wen, A *Large-Scale Evaluation and Analysis of Personalized Search Strategies* (New York: ACM, 2007).

[78]   *COMP/M5727 – Microsoft / Yahoo! Search Business*, 2010 European Commission, available at https:// publications.europa.eu/en/publication-detail/-/publication/48450f81-c731-47ab-99f4-bfc9b4cc8d50 /language-en.

The relative importance of data also depends on whether a platform is at the core a matching or a prediction technology. For the purpose of algorithmic matching, reliance on data is likely to increase the tendency toward concentration compared to older, standard marketplaces and matchmakers; however, scale effects associated with larger datasets for the purpose of matching are likely to taper off after a sufficiently large and thick network is created, beyond which the quality of matching can only be marginally improved. In contrast, the more a platform is a prediction technology rather than a simple matchmaker (for example, search engines), the more the value and scale effects of access to data become pronounced. This is because the essence of prediction is ultimately about access to more information and data, where larger and complementary datasets dramatically improve the efficiency of predictions creating significantly larger economies of scale and scope compared to pure matching.

This effect becomes stronger as the range of covered predictions gets wider. For instance, in many contexts data may only be used for a circumscribed purpose, such as improving online shopping or a specific narrowly defined service. In such cases, once the marginal value of data starts decreasing, there may be little efficiency gain that can be obtained from adding additional data. When the domain of predictions expands, however, data can be used and reused for a larger set of purposes. As it will be discussed in the first case study, for a general-purpose search engine the domain of search results is universal and covers virtually any information available online; hence, specific data points not only improve the quality of specific queries, but may also be relevant for a broader set of related queries, which expands the desirability of developing larger datasets.

Hence, and in addition to the increasing prominence of the standard model of platform intermediation based on positive network externalities between different users (in themselves a potential source of concentration), technological change can foster market concentration even further by giving rise to various economies of scale associated with data, algorithmic matching, prediction technologies, and digital services. Overall, these additional forms of scale have the potential to increase the likelihood of natural concentration in digital platform industries.

2.2 THE ECONOMICS OF PLATFORMS: ARE NEW LEGAL AND POLICY TOOLS NEEDED?

A broader and distinct question from one of increasing concentration that is related to the growing centrality of multisided platforms is whether there is something intrinsically special about the economics of these markets that calls for the development of novel legal and policy tools. Addressing this issue entails an assessment of whether the presence of multiple interrelated sides alters in a significant way the economic analysis of specific issues related to competition and market power, and, if so, whether or not the prevailing legal framework is capable of accommodating identified economic differences. This question has been mostly pertinent to case law in the payment card sector, but it has pertinence for digital platform industries insofar as a proper identification of policy prescriptions relies on identifying economic features that may set some of these markets apart from standard ones.

This section argues that platform markets, digital or physical all together, should not be seen as altering by default the fundamental basis of established competition law principles, but rather calling for tailored and context-specific adjustments to fill the gaps of established legal principles that apply to all markets. Since multisided platforms represent a highly heterogeneous category, and because the analysis of specific economic issues based on multisided models can often find analogous treatment with standard single-sided industrial organization models, any desirable legal and policy change should avoid the fallacy of treating all multisided platform markets as an intrinsically different subset of markets. The same applies to digital platforms and the potential policy refinements that may be justified by the economic and technological features of some tech industries.

2.2.1 *Economic Literature on Multisided Platforms*

Markets with network externalities have been a subject of study in industrial organization from the 1980s, but the economic literature on network effects has largely focused on the size of and choice of standards[79] and has left unexplored many of the distinguishing features of multisided platform markets. Only a few studies in this older generation of literature on networks hinted at the two-sided nature of traditional business and products such as newspapers or credit cards.[80]

It is only in recent years that the theory of platform competition has become one of the most dynamic areas of research in industrial organization,[81] starting with seminal papers by Rochet and Tirole,[82] Caillaud and Jullien,[83] Parker and van

---

[79] For example, in the context of telephone networks and computer keyboards. See Jeffrey Rohlfs, "A Theory of Interdependent Demand for a Communications Service" (1974) 5, no. 1, Bell J Econ, 16; Michael L. Katz and Carl Shapiro, "Network Externalities, Competition, and Compatibility" (1985) 75, no. 3, Am Econ Rev, 424; Joseph Farrell and Garth Saloner, "Standardization, Compatibility, and Innovation" (1985) 16, no.1, RAND J Econ, 70.

[80] See, for instance, James N. Rosse, "Daily Newspapers, Monopolistic Competition, and Economies of Scale" (1967) 57, no. 2, Am Econ Rev, 522. See William F. Baxter, "Bank Interchange of Transactional Paper: Legal and Economic Perspectives" (1983) 26, no. 3, J Law Econ, 541 at 541–588, 545.

[81] See OECD, *Rethinking Antitrust Tools for Multi-Sided Platforms 2018* (Strasbourg: OECD, 2018); OECD Competition Committee, *Two Sided Markets*, Report and Supporting Documents (2009); Bernard Caillaud and Bruno Jullien, "Chicken & Egg: Competition among Intermediation Service Providers" (2003) 34, no. 2, RAND J Econ, 309; E. Glen Weyl, "A Price Theory of Multi-sided Platforms" (2010) 100, no. 4, Am Econ Rev, 1642.

[82] Jean-Charles Rochet and Jean Tirole, "Two-Sided Markets: A Progress Report" (2006) 37, no. 3, RAND J Econ, 645; Jean-Charles Rochet and Jean Tirole, "Platform Competition in Two-Sided Markets" (2003) 1, no. 4, J Eur Econ Assoc, 990.

[83] Caillaud and Jullien, *supra*, note 81.

Alstyne,[84] Evans and Schmalensee,[85] Armstrong,[86] and Rysman.[87] This new genera-tion of industrial organization scholarship has provided further advances in the formalization of decisions made by intermediary platforms and in the modelling of platform competition.[88] In advancing the understanding of these markets, the economics of two-sided markets owes a debt to older branches of industrial organi-zation on network externalities and multiproduct pricing, from which it also departs in important ways.[89] The literature on platforms also naturally intersects with the literature on the theory of the firm and vertical integration[90] in the study of inter-mediaries, contractual incompleteness and allocation or residual control rights – a perspective that sees platforms as a distinct form of economic intermediation.[91]

Despite the impressive growth of this branch of industrial organization, the literature does not provide a unanimous definition of what constitutes a multisided platform; rather, it highlights from different angles common dimen-sions of platform markets that are generally perceived as distinguishing them from standard markets, which are discussed in turn.

---

[84] Geoffrey G. Parker and Marshall W. Van Alstyne, "Two-Sided Network Effects: A Theory of Information Product Design" (2005) 51, no. 10, Manag Sci, 1494.

[85] David S. Evans and Richard Schmalensee, "The Industrial Organization of Markets with Two-Sided Platforms," NBER Working Paper No. 11603 (Cambridge, MA: National Bureau of Economic Research, 2005); David S. Evans, "The Antitrust Economics of Multi-Sided Platform Markets" (2003) 20 Yale J Regul, 325; David S. Evans and Richard Schmalensee, "The Antitrust Analysis of Multi-Sided Platform Businesses," in *Oxford Handbook of International Antitrust Economics* (Oxford: Oxford University Press, 2015).

[86] Mark Armstrong, "Competition in Two-Sided Markets" (2006) 37, no. 3, RAND J Econ, 668.

[87] Marc Rysman, "The Economics of Two-Sided Markets" (2009) 23, no. 3, J Econ Perspect, 125.

[88] Recent economic research has focused on formalizing pricing decisions made by platforms as a result of cross-market network externalities, emphasizing the idea that platforms need to set not only a price level, but also a price structure through membership fees and usage fees, and that the choice of pricing has important implications for welfare.

[89] Rochet and Tirole, *supra*, note 82 at 646. It builds on the literature on network effects in the way it formalizes the idea that each consumer receives a non-internalized externality from the choice made by other consumers of the same good or service; however, because in platforms this occurs between different consumer groups of complementary goods or services, the literature on two-sided markets has focused on price structures, decisions on multihoming and single-homing, and related issues of control rights that were largely ignored in the literature on network industries. The emphasis on these features of market intermediaries with inter-group network effects therefore distinguishes the litera-ture on two-sided markets from the literature on network effects, which has for the most part focused on optimal size of networks and adoption of standards. The economics of two-sided markets also overlaps with the study of multiproduct pricing and the study of price structures between comple-mentary goods, but it differs in the fact that in two-sided platforms consumers on each side do not internalize the externalities on the other side, while purchasers of complementary goods (the classic razor and the razorblade example) are assumed to internalize the net surplus obtained from the two products.

[90] Hagiu and Wright, *supra*, note 61.

[91] The spectrum of intermediation can range from a pure platform model, to input suppliers, resellers and vertically integrated organizations, and other hybrid forms, where firms can choose to adopt one model through contractual design based on specific trade-offs.

i) Indirect Network Externalities. The first of these distinguishing features is the presence of *indirect* network externalities. A network externality is the effect that one user of a good or service creates for the value of that product or service to other users, which can be positive (an additional user in a telephone network, the development of industrial clusters, etc.) or negative (congestion, traffic jams, etc.). Positive network externalities are therefore present if users' utility increases with the participation and usage decision of other users.

Platforms are characterized by indirect forms of network externalities because they occur when the externality is felt by a different group of users as opposed to users of the same group as it is in the case of direct network externalities (although both direct and indirect network externalities are often coexisting in network industries).[92] This indirect form of network externalities is typical of platform intermediaries because they must bring together two or more distinct groups of users simultaneously, creating a chicken-and-egg problem[93] whereby consumers on one side will not participate without the other side. In order to do so, platforms must balance demand on each side, both in terms of the volume of users and the typology of users that join the platform. Since users on one side generally do not internalize the positive effects generated by the presence of users on the other side, they need to be internalized by the platform intermediary.

Indirect network externalities can arise from both membership and usage,[94] and can be either bilateral (namely both sides can generate positive externalities for each other such as drivers and passengers joining a ride-hailing platform) or unidirectional (in advertising-based media, for example, advertisers benefit from more users, but not necessarily vice versa). When indirect network externalities are strong, they can potentially make a single network more efficient than competing platforms through aggregation of demand[95] – therefore, they are in general the most salient

---

[92] Rochet and Tirole, *supra*, note 82.

[93] Caillaud and Jullien, *supra*, note 81 at 310.

[94] The former is the benefit a user on one side generates for users on the other side by joining the platform, thereby becoming available or accessible for transactions (for example, buying a newspaper). The latter is the benefit that a user on one side generates for a user on the other side by actually engaging in transactions on the platform (for example, paying with a credit card). The importance of externalities may also vary depending on the maturity of the market, which may attenuate their relevance compared to the initial phase of platform growth.

[95] Direct network externalities can also play an important role. For instance, although a search engine's business model generally relies on attracting as many eyeballs as possible by providing the service for free in order to create an audience for advertising and extracting revenue from advertisers, the role of direct network externalities is arguably more important: the more searchers mean more data and more refined algorithms. This has positive spillover effects both on users who benefit from a better search service and advertisers who benefit from having more users as a result of the improved service. Direct network effects are also particularly prominent in social networks, where the value of aggregation comes more from having users on a single platform than the externalities between users and advertisers. In themselves, however, direct network externalities are not a distinguishing feature of multisided platform markets.

feature of platform industries that is theoretically pertinent to the application of the natural monopoly framework as developed in this book.

ii) **Nonneutrality of the Price Structure.** Other definitions emphasize different aspects of multisided platforms. For example, Rochet and Tirole highlight the nonneutrality of the price structure, pointing to the importance of both a price *level*, namely the sum of prices on each side, and a price *structure*, how the total price is decomposed across sides matters. In particular, since two-sided platforms can effectively charge different prices to the different groups of users, the volume of transactions and profit depends not only on the total price charged to all users, but also on the structure of prices charged to different user groups (unlike the neutrality of a tax incidence).[96] Rochet and Tirole note that if the volume changes with the reallocation of the total price between the two sides, the market is two-sided.[97] If, on the contrary, the volume of transactions depends only on the aggregate price level the market is one-sided. This may happen, for instance, when users are able to bargain and pass a given distribution of charges to the other side.[98] In line with this perspective, Filistrucchi suggests[99] that multisidedness should be seen as a matter of degree based on the levels of pass-through,[100] distinguishing in particular between markets where bargaining among users is generally infeasible (nontransaction markets like advertising-based media), and markets where the level of pass-through may vary depending on the importance of transaction costs among end users and limits imposed by the platform itself (transaction markets like payment cards networks).

iii) **Models of Market Intermediation.** A further perspective on multisided platforms is based on the choice of business model across a spectrum of intermediation models, where the distinction between two-sided and one-sided markets depends on the decisions of the intermediary, and where multisidedness refers more to

---

[96] Rochet and Tirole, *supra*, note 82.

[97] Suppose, for instance, a platform charges usage fees p_1 and p_2 to the two distinct user groups. The market is not two-sided when the volume of transactions on the platform depends only on the total price level, $P \equiv p_1 + p_2$. If instead the volume of transactions varies with p_1 or p_2 while holding P constant, the market is two-sided. See Ibid, at 644–655.

[98] Nonneutrality can fail for a number of reasons: for example, because of transaction costs and other frictions that make it impossible to pass a redistribution of charges to the other side (small value transactions, lack of low cost billing systems, inability to monitor); when one side incurs costs that are influenced by the platform and are not proportional to the number of transactions (volume insensitive costs); or when there are platform-imposed constraints on the pass-through (for instance, credit card no-surcharge rules). See Rochet and Tirole, *supra*, note 82.

[99] Lapo Filistrucchi, Damien Geradin and Eric Van Damme, "Identifying Two-Sided Markets" (2013) 36 World Compet, 33; Lapo Filistrucchi, "How Many Markets Are Two-Sided?" (2010) 7 Antitrust Chron, available at https://econpapers.repec.org/article/cpiatchrn/7.2.2010_3ai=5616.htm.

[100] For instance, heterosexual dating clubs are often cited as examples of two-sided markets charging different prices to men and women, but for an already established couple entering the club what matters is their total maximum willingness to pay, not the allocation of prices. Since they can renegotiate the price structure charged by the club, it does not matter how much each member of the couple is charged. When that is the case, the market is in fact one-sided based on Rochet and Tirole's definition.

"strategies" than "markets." Unlike other intermediaries, a platform provides room for direct interaction between buyers and sellers or structures its intermediary role in a way where sellers care about the success with buyers.[101] This is often a conscious contractual choice made by the intermediary, and choice over a business model is not fixed.[102] Hagiu and Wright in particular lay out fundamental distinctions between platforms and other business models, while highlighting the fact that the choice between these models based on the allocation of control rights depends on specific trade-offs.[103]

While these different perspectives on platforms fail to provide a clear-cut definition, they illuminate the fact that multisidedness is not an intrinsic feature of a market, but a matter of degree. Many definitions converge on this point. The Rochet-Tirole definition depends on the conduct of a platform, which echoes the perspective highlighted by Filistrucchi based on an assessment of the levels of pass-through of fee/price allocation between sides, and is not inconsistent with Hagiu and Wright's approach that two-sidedness is a strategic choice across a spectrum of business models. Hence, no black-and-white distinction should be drawn between standard markets and markets with multiple sides.[104] This position is further corroborated by the fact that multisided platform markets often display a high degree of heterogeneity despite sharing some common features.[105]

---

[101] This is different from the case of a reseller that sets a retail price and the upstream seller obtains a wholesale price, without caring about the success of the intermediary with the buying side. A pure merchant or reseller model is a pure buy-out contract that makes relevant externalities disappear, where the reseller often takes ownership and control over products from suppliers and chooses how to sell them in outlets. Conversely, a platform marketplace leaves room for suppliers to control key aspects of the offer and transaction. It must be noted, however, that in reality resellers often have more complex relationships with suppliers, for example, suppliers may care about marketing activities that affect demand.

[102] See Andrei Hagiu and Julian Wright, "Marketplace or Reseller?" (2014) 61, no. 1, Manag Sci, 184. Firms may start as a single-sided intermediary preferring to be resellers in order to avoid the initial chicken-and-egg problem, and once successfully established, switch to a platform model in order to attract third parties to trade directly with buyers via the firm's marketplace. Amazon, for instance, started as a reseller of books and then introduced a platform marketplace for certain products, by enabling third-party sellers to trade directly with consumers on its website thereby having two coexisting business models. More generally, there are various hybrid intermediate forms that can emerge in between platform and alternative models.

[103] On this basis, Hagiu and Wright suggest that multisided platforms are not only characterized by indirect network effects and the nonneutrality of price structures (the way prices are allocated on each side matters for welfare outcomes), but also by direct interaction between two or more distinct sides, and affiliation with the platform. See Hagiu and Wright, ibid.

[104] In some cases, a degree of multisidedness may be present but so negligible that can be simply ignored. Rysman, for instance, offers the example of an automobile as a platform between consumers and mechanics, where even if there are some network effects, they are of little importance in determining market outcomes. In other cases, multisidedness may be important enough that competition policy enforcement and regulatory interventions typical one-sided markets will potentially be fallacious when applied in markets that are two-sided. See Rysman, *supra*, note 87.

[105] For example, some platforms perform symmetric matching where the role of the platform is to match users (dating platforms), buyers and sellers (e-commerce marketplaces), or service providers and consumers (on-demand ride sharing platforms). Network externalities are generally symmetrical,

As a consequence, labeling a market as multisided is at best a useful proxy for important economic issues that may be at play in a market due to the presence of multiple, interrelated sides. In and of itself, however, this says little as to whether multisidedness is actually relevant for a particular economic question related to competition in a specific antitrust case; importantly, it also does not offer sufficient guidance on the nature of legal changes and adjustments that may be desirable in order to incorporate identified economic departures from a standard market. The central policy question, therefore, is not whether a market should be classified as multisided, but how important multisidedness is in determining outcomes of interest,[106] and whether the established legal framework can accommodate potential differences based on standard approaches. Evaluating *whether* and *what kind* of legal and policy adjustments may be justified by the specific economic features of platforms, therefore, requires both an economic and a legal perspective.[107]

2.2.2 *Identifying the Boundaries of Desirable Policy Changes*

Some of the contributions offered by the economic literature on multisided platform markets are now considered uncontroversial. For example, the presence of multiple relevant prices means that the relation between price and marginal cost on each side does not hold for efficient pricing even in competitive multisided markets. While generally elasticity of demand and marginal costs are the crucial components in determining pricing, in two-sided platform markets prices on both sides depend on the set of demand elasticities and marginal costs on all sides[108] and the nature and strengths of network externalities. As a result, the profit-maximizing price for either side may create an asymmetric price structure where one side is charged below marginal cost or even a negative price, which makes consideration of pricing on either side of a platform in isolation incorrect.[109] Other ways in which the presence of multiple interrelated sides alters economic analysis include technical modifications

---

meaning that each side generates positive network externalities for the other side. Other platforms instead perform asymmetric matching, where platforms subsidize users to create audience (audience-building). Examples include ad-based TV, advertising-based newspapers, search engines and social networks, where only one side wants to reach the other (ads and eyeballs). Some platforms simply help conclude already occurring transactions, for example, credit or debit card networks; others help coordinate on a given standard (videogames and operating systems).

[106] In this regard, a fruitful perspective comes from case law rather than economic theory. Evidence from antitrust litigation in platform cases in fact scales back the importance of such definitional exercise, because almost no case hinges on whether a market is single-sided or multisided. Rather, the source of contention generally rests on the consequences and effects stemming from multisidedness.

[107] See, for example, the discussion in Dennis W. Carlton and Ralph A. Winter, "Vertical MFN's and the Credit Card No-Surcharge Rule," SSRN Scholarly Paper ID 2982115 (Rochester, NY: Social Science Research Network, 2018) at 25.

[108] Rysman, *supra*, note 87 at 129–130.

[109] The low-price side could mistakenly appear as an attempt of predation and the higher price on the other side as an exercise of market power.

to market definition and the assessment of market power[110] such as adjustments to the SSNIP (small but significant and nontransitory increase in price) test, the evaluation of mergers,[111] exclusivity,[112] tying,[113] collusion,[114] and so on. In these domains of competition policy, a sound economic analysis requires accounting for the

[110] See, for example, Kate Collyer, Hugh Mullan, and Natalie Timan, *Measuring Market Power in Multi-Sided Markets – Note by Kate Collyer, Hugh Mullan, and Natalie Timan*, Hearing on re-thinking the use of traditional antitrust enforcement tools in multi-sided markets DAF/COMP/WD (2017)35/FINAL (OECD, 2017); Kurt Brekke, *Measuring Market Power in Multi-Sided Markets – Note by Kurt Brekke*, Hearing on re-thinking the use of traditional antitrust enforcement tools in multi-sided markets DAF/COMP/WD(2017)31/FINAL (OECD, 2017); Elena Argentesi and Lapo Filistrucchi, "Estimating Market Power in a Two-Sided Market: The Case of Newspapers" (2007) 22, no. 7, J Appl Econom, 1247; Marc Rysman, "Competition Between Networks: A Study of the Market for Yellow Pages" (2004) 71, no. 2, Rev Econ Stud, 483; Elena Argentesi and Marc Ivaldi, "Market Definition in the Printed Media Industry: Theory and Practice," SSRN Scholarly Paper ID 779107 (Rochester, NY: Social Science Research Network, 2005); David S. Evans and Michael Noel, "Defining Antitrust Markets When Firms Operate Two-Sided Platforms" (2005) 2005, Columbia Bus Law Rev, 667; Sebastian Wismer and Arno Rasek, *Market Definition in Multi-Sided Markets – Note by Sebastian Wismer and Arno Rasek*, Hearing on re-thinking the use of traditional antitrust enforcement tools in multi-sided markets DAF/COMP/WD(2017)33/FINAL (2017); Lapo Filistrucchi, *Market Definition in Multi-Sided Markets – Note by Dr Lapo Filistrucchi*, Hearing on re-thinking the use of traditional antitrust enforcement tools in multi-sided markets DAF/COMP/WD(2017)27/FINAL (OECD, 2017) at 14.

[111] For instance, see Ambarish Chandra and Allan Collard-Wexler, "Mergers in Two-Sided Markets: An Application to the Canadian Newspaper Industry" (2009) 18, no. 4, J Econ Manag Strategy, 1045; Enrique Andreu and Jorge Padilla, *Quantifying Horizontal Merger Efficiencies in Multi-Sided Markets: An Application to Stock Exchange Mergers – Note by Enrique Andreu and Jorge Padilla*, Hearing on re-thinking the use of traditional antitrust enforcement tools in multi-sided markets DAF/COMP/WD(2017)37/FINAL (2017). Lapo Filistrucchi, Tobias J. Klein and Thomas O. Michielsen, "Assessing Unilateral Merger Effects in a Two-Sided Market: An Application to the Dutch Daily Newspaper Market" (2012) 8, no. 2, J Compet Law Econ, 297; David S. Evans and Michael D. Noel, "The Analysis of Mergers that Involve Multisided Platform Businesses" (2008) 4, no. 3, J Compet Law Econ, 663.

[112] OECD, Exclusionary Practices and Two-Sided Platforms, Note by Andrea Amelio, Liliane Karlinger, and Tommaso Valletti, *Exclusionary Practices and Two-Sided Platforms – Note by Andrea Amelio, Liliane Karlinger, and Tommaso Valletti*, Hearing on re-thinking the use of traditional antitrust enforcement tools in multi-sided markets DAF/COMP/WD(2017)34/FINAL (OECD, 2017). See also Michael Katz, *Exclusionary Conduct in Multi-Sided Markets – Note by Michael Katz*, Note (Strasbourg: OECD, 2017). Particularly prominent have been cases of MFN clauses included in contractual arrangements between price comparison websites. See Jonathan B. Baker and Fiona Scott Morton, "Antitrust Enforcement Against Platform MFNs" (2017) 127, Yale Law J, 2176.

[113] Jean-Charles Rochet and Jean Tirole, *Tying-in Two-Sided Markets and the Honour All Cards Rule*, CEPR Discussion Papers 6132 (CEPR Discussion Papers, 2007). Andrea Amelio and Bruno Jullien, "Tying and Freebies in Two-Sided Markets" (2012) 30, no. 5, Int J Ind Organ, 436; Jay Pil Choi and Doh-Shin Jeon, "A Leverage Theory of Tying in Two-Sided Markets," SSRN Scholarly Paper ID 2834821 (Rochester, NY: Social Science Research Network, 2016) at 1333–1347.

[114] Yassine Lefouili and Joana Pinho, "Collusion in Two-Sided Markets," SSRN Scholarly Paper ID 3049356 (Rochester, NY: Social Science Research Network, 2017); Isabel Ruhmer, *Platform Collusion in Two-Sided Markets* (Frankfurt am Main: Verein für Socialpolitik, 2010); Ralf Dewenter, Justus Haucap, and Tobias Wenzel, "Semi-Collusion in Media Markets" (2011) 31, no. 2, Int Rev Law Econ, 92; Federico Boffa and Lapo Filistrucchi, "Optimal Cartel Prices in Two-Sided Markets," SSRN Scholarly Paper ID 2506510 (Rochester, NY: Social Science Research Network, 2014) at 14–19.

interlinks between the different sides of a platform, but this generally does not imply the need to alter the fundamental logic of established legal principles.

In other areas of competition policy, in contrast, the legal and policy implications of multisidedness can become more controversial. As exemplified in particular by predation and the application of a rule of reason-type balancing framework, this section highlights more problematic aspects of multisidedness and the different ways in which it can affect legal and policy approaches. On this basis, it then discusses the pertinence of these legal and economic issues for application of the natural mono-poly framework and the development of policy approaches in digital platform industries.

i) **Predation**. One of the early recognitions offered by the economic literature on platforms concerns predation. Since the price charged by a platform to one side may be below marginal cost or average variable costs due to the need to balance both sides, a skewed pricing structure with price on one side below costs does not reflect an anticompetitive predatory strategy[115] but rather profitable and efficient pricing.[116] On the basis of this recognition, the literature has suggested the need to adjust standard predation tests in order to account for the presence of multiple sides and prices. In themselves, these changes do not alter the fundamental logic of predatory pricing, but rather fill the gap of standard tests to account for the presence of multiple sides.

This contrasts with approaches that instead use the economics of platforms to justify a different, generalized, and often more lenient enforcement policy to pre-dation, for example suggestions that predation becomes unlikely or less likely in multisided markets compared to one-sided markets. These suggestions go against the findings of recent literature showing that, on the contrary, predation may occur both at the level of the total price[117] and at the level of the price structure,[118] and that when network externalities are significant, the prospects of recoupment may be in some instances even stronger in two-sided markets.[119] Hence, multisidedness can be used in order to justify different forms of legal and policy changes – some of which focused on the need to fine-tune established tools and approaches, other proposing a different policy framework for platform markets as compared to standard markets.

---

[115] See *Bottin Cartographes v. Google France*, Cour D'Appel, Paris Pôle 5, Chamber 4, November 25, 2015. Google was allegedly to engage in predation by charging zero prices.

[116] Stefan Behringer and Lapo Filistrucchi, "Areeda–Turner in Two-Sided Markets" (2015) 46, no. 3, Rev Ind Organ, 287 at 287–306.

[117] Amelia Fletcher, "Predatory Pricing in Two-Sided Markets: A Brief Comment," SSRN Scholarly Paper ID 987875 (Rochester, NY: Social Science Research Network, 2007).

[118] In fact, in such settings the presence of indirect network externalities can make predation more plausible, if competitors have limited ability to transfer the gains from lower prices on one side to the other side in terms of extra revenues, or if the platform is competing with a single sided firm, where an asymmetric price structure may theoretically enable exclusion of a single-sided firm (for instance, a subscriber-based service provider) competing with a two-sided platform (an advertising-supported service provider). See Amelio, Karlinger, and Valletti, *supra*, note 112.

[119] Katz, *supra*, note 112.

ii) **Balancing Competitive Effects**. Another controversial issue is the application of a rule of reason-type balancing framework in platform cases. One of the early doctrinal implications arising from the case law on multisided markets has been a reduction in the scope of per se illegality: not dissimilar to the developments that previously occurred in the area of vertical restraints, courts have acknowledged that forms of conduct and agreements that may appear per se illegal may often reflect efficiencies or more ambiguous effects that need to be evaluated under a rule of reason or effect-based approach. In particular, seminal cases that have arisen in the payment network industry with regard to interchange fees in various jurisdictions have opened the door to such shifts. In the US case *NaBanco*, for instance, where the interchange fee set by Visa was alleged to be a horizontal price-fixing agreement that violated Section 1 of the Sherman Act, the US District Court for the Southern District of Florida concluded that interchange fees were instead required in order to maintain an appropriate balance between card-issuing and merchant-servicing, reflecting a doctrinal shift from per se rules toward a rule of reason analysis based on the two-sided nature of the market.[120] Other jurisdictions followed a similar path in shrinking the scope of per se illegality to various forms of conduct in multisided markets,[121] and expanding the importance of the legal framework dealing with the balancing of competitive effects in platform cases.

The legal structure of a balancing framework in the platform context, however, remains in flux in many jurisdictions, depending on the way in which the following three central questions are addressed: should the relevant market be defined as including the platform as a whole or just one side of the platform; how should the welfare effects across the different sides be balanced; and how should the respective burdens of proof be allocated. Since there are potentially different answers to each of these questions, developing an appropriate balancing framework in platform cases has been the subject of major controversies.

One option, for example, is to look only at one side in isolation throughout the entire legal analysis. This approach, which has been adopted under US antitrust law until very recently[122] tracing back to *Philadelphia National Bank*

---

[120] As then confirmed by the Eleventh Circuit, "the fundamental economic interdependence between the card-issuing and merchant-signing banks ... demonstrated that redistribution of revenues or costs is a must for the continued existence of the product." See *National Bancard Corp(NaBanco) v. Visa USA, Inc.* [1986] 779 F 2d 592 (Court of Appeals, 11th Circuit) at 57.

[121] For example, the Court of Justice of the European Union (CJEU) clarified the distinction between restrictions "by object" and "by effect" under Article 101(1) in the context of two-sided market cases in the payment card systems sector in *Groupement des cartes bancaires (CB) v. European Commission*, 2014 Court of Justice (Third Chamber). There, the CJEU made it clear that agreements in novel or complex economic settings, such as multisided markets, should not be subject to a "by object" analysis.

[122] *National Bancard Corp.(NaBanco) v. Visa USA, Inc.*, *supra*, note 120; *Times-Picayune Pub Co v. United States*, [1953] 345 US 594 (US Supreme Court). In *Visa*, a case involving exclusivity rules imposed by Visa and MasterCard prohibiting the issuance of Amex and Discover cards by member banks, two interrelated, but separate, product markets on each side of the platform were identified.

case,[123] treats each side as a separate relevant market,[124] and does not allow anticompetitive effects in one side to be justified by greater competition on another side.[125] An opposite approach is instead to look at the platform as a whole and all sides during each step of a rule of reason-type framework. In the *American Express* decision,[126] the US Supreme Court has for instance embraced this framework by defining the relevant market as the whole platform (all sides of the platform are included within the relevant market) and then imposing as a burden of proof for plaintiffs evidence of *net* anticompetitive effect on all sides.[127] Only then does the burden shift to defendants to provide procompetitive and efficiency arguments. A further, more nuanced approach

Even earlier in the *Times Picayune* decision concerning tying of morning and evening newspaper advertising space, the US Supreme Court stated that "every newspaper is a dual trader in separate though interdependent markets" and concluded that the case involved "solely one of these markets." See also Gregory J. Werden, "Cross-Market Balancing of Competitive Effects: What Is the Law, and What Should It Be" (2017) 43, J Corp Law, 119; Daniel A. Crane, "Balancing Effects Across Markets" (2015) 80, no. 2, Antitrust Law J, 397.

[123]   *United States v. Philadelphia Nat'l Bank*, [1963] 374 US 321 (US Supreme Court).

[124]   *National Bancard Corp. (NaBanco) v. Visa USA, Inc., supra*, note 120; *Times-Picayune Pub. Co. v. United States, supra*, note 122.

[125]   *United States v. American Express Company*, 2016 Court of Appeals, Second Circuit. *American Express Co.*, 2015, WL 728563.

[126]   *Ohio v. American Express Co. (AmEx)*, 138 S.Ct. 2274 (2018). For commentary on the case, see Joshua Wright, and John Yun, "Burdens and Balancing in Multisided Markets: The First Principles Approach of Ohio v. American Express" forthcoming, *Review of Industrial Organization* (2019); Dennis Carlton and Ralph Winter, "Vertical MFN's and Credit-Card No-Surcharge Restraints" (2018) SSRN available at https://papers.ssrn.com/sol3/papers.cfm?abstract_id=2982115; Michael Katz, and Jonathan Sallet, "Multisided Platforms and Antitrust Enforcement (2017) 127 *Yale Law Journal*, 2142; Patrick Ward, "Testing for Multisided Platform Effects in Antitrust Market Definition" (2017)84 *University of Chicago Law Review*, 2059; Tim Wu, "The American Express Opinion, Tech Platforms & the Rule of Reason" (2018), available at https://ssrn.com /abstract=3326667; David Evans and Richard Schmalensee, "Ignoring Two-Sided Business Reality Can Also Hurt Plaintiffs" (2018) *Competition Policy International*.

[127]   In the case, the district court first found that American Express's no-surcharge rules restricted price competition among alternative platforms on the merchant side, resulting in a price increase in the charges imposed by the network to merchants. American Express urged the district court to depart from the narrower market definition on the merchant side in favor of a broader market definition defined by transactions encompassing both the services provided to merchants as well to cardholders. The district court rejected this approach following the traditional procedural route based on a narrow market definition. The district court also concluded that, even if the market were viewed as broadly as American Express argued, there would be no legal ground to accept a restriction of competition on the merchant side as a result of increased inter-brand competition on the cardholders side; and that even if such cross-market balancing is appropriate under the rule of reason in a two-sided context, the defendant failed to establish that no-surcharge rules are necessary to robust competition on the cardholders side, or that any such gains offset the harm done in the network services market. The Second Circuit, however, took a different position from the district court and concluded that the Department of Justice placed excessive emphasis on the merchant side of the platform and paid inadequate attention to the role of cardholders. The Second Circuit found that the district court did not take the concept of two-sidedness far enough and that the market definition was a fatal error because it ignored cardholders. The US Supreme Court confirmed based on the broad market definition approach.

attempts to strike a balance between these two approaches, by starting from separate relevant markets on each side, but then allowing for the evaluation of so called out-of-market efficiencies on the other side of the platform outside the boundaries of the relevant market. EU competition law has endorsed this procedural option under Article 101 TFEU[128] in the *MasterCard* case.[129] This approach emphasizes at the stage of market definition the different competitive conditions at play on each side, but then accounts for multisidedness at the stage of evaluating procompetitive effects and efficiency arguments (although with important procedural constraints in the European context).[130]

Differences between these alternative procedures are problematic because, depending on the way market definition in carried out, they draw different legal implications from multisidedness.[131] Where the first approach risks ignoring the

[128]   In general terms, the Guidelines on Article 101 TFEU suggest that where two markets are related, efficiencies achieved in separate markets can be taken into account provided that the group of consumers affected by the restriction and benefiting from the efficiency gains are "substantially the same." See *Communication from the Commission – Notice – Guidelines on the application of Article 81(3) of the Treaty (Text with EEA relevance)*, Guidelines Document 52004XC0427(07) (Brussels: European Commission, 2004) at 43.

[129]   See Case C-382/12, *MasterCard Inc. v. Comm'n*, 2014 EU:C:2014:2201.

[130]   In the MasterCard case, a question emerged as to whether efficiencies and positive effects outside the boundaries of the relevant market benefiting cardholders should have been considered in the context of two-sided markets, particularly given that Article 101 TFEU requires explicitly that consumers be awarded a "fair share" of the possible efficiency gains that are claimed by producers that result from an anticompetitive agreement. The Court concluded that only if there are *"appreciable objective advantages"* for consumers in the relevant market defined narrowly on one side of the platform (in that case, merchants) the advantages for different consumers in the connected market that is not the relevant market at issue (in that case, cardholders) could justify the restriction if, taken together, they are sufficient to compensate for the restrictive effects. On the contrary, if there are no appreciable objective advantages for consumers in the relevant market, any advantages for the consumers in the connected market cannot in themselves sufficiently compensate for the restrictive effects, unless consumers in both markets are substantially the same.

[131]   With regard to market definition, Filistrucchi argues that in a nontransaction market a product does not necessarily need both sides, and therefore it is always necessary to define two, interrelated markets (for example, ad-based newspapers). In a transaction market where there is a direct and observable transaction that occurs on the platform, conversely, a product needs both sides, externalities are bilateral, and this necessary complementarity between the two sides allows one to define a single platform market. Under this approach, Uber's passengers and drivers would be conflated within a single relevant market for on-demand rides' matching, rather than in two separate, but interlinked markets for on-demand transportation services for passengers and drivers' support services. See Filistrucchi, et al., *supra*, note 110. Katz and Sallet argue, however, that there are compelling reasons why defining separate markets is a preferable option in all cases, as long as the interdependencies are accounted for. Even when users transact on a platform, the level of competition on each side, the kind of competitors available, product differentiation, vertical integration, and user sophistication may differ. Moreover, the boundary between transaction and nontransaction markets is not always clear: matching occurs also in the case of advertising, where transactions can take place after and can theoretically be observed when technology allows tracking purchases and charging advertisers based on sales. See Michael Katz, and Jonathan Sallet, "Multisided Platforms and Antitrust Enforcement" (2018) 127, Yale Law Journal, 2142. On the excessive importance of market definition in platform cases, see Francesco Ducci, "Procedural Implications of Market Definition in Platform Cases" (2019) jnzo17, *Journal of Antitrust Enforcement* 1.

importance of multisidedness and the possible implications stemming from the interlinks between sides, the second approach risks going too far in the opposite direction, applying the economics of multisided platforms in a way that places excessive emphasis on market definition and creates procedural routes that may ultimately not allow a proper evaluation of the economic effects of a particular conduct or restraint in light of multisidedness.[132] More desirable approaches would instead seek to incorporate relevant features of platform markets independently from market definition and within the established legal principles applicable to standard markets.

Like in the case of predation, defining a market as multisidedness can have problematic consequences, insofar that it can be used to justify different legal and policy changes. Some represent tailored adjustments that do not alter the fundamental logic of established principles; other entail a different framework that departs from the approach applied in standard markets.[133] Where the first kind of policy adjustments accounts for multisidedness but treats markets with one or multiple sides alike, the latter assumes an excessively formalistic distinction between markets.

2.2.3 *The Relevance of This Debate for Digital Platforms*

This general debate on the different set of implications that should be derived from the literature on multisided platform markets is to an extent pertinent to digital

---

[132]   Carlton and Winter show this discrepancy by suggesting two alternative analysis for the evaluation of vertical MFN clauses in credit card markets, one based on a vertical framework and the other on two-sided market theory. They show that a two-sided market as opposed to a vertical framework is more favorable to firms accused of anticompetitive behavior, although the two forms of analysis are equivalent from an economic perspective. See Dennis Carlton, and Ralph Winter, "Vertical MFN's and Credit-Card No-Surcharge Restraints" (2018) SSRN available at https://papers.ssrn.com/sol3/papers.cfm?abstract_id=2982115.

[133]   In many jurisdictions, the balancing framework is based on the following structure: enforcers face the burden of showing competitive harms, and defendants can respond by proposing efficiency and procompetitive explanations. In US antitrust law, for example, the rule of reason under Section 1 and monopolization claims 2 of the Sherman starts with the plaintiff's prima facie initial burden to show harm to competition, followed by the defendant's burden to show a legitimate objective is served by the restraint, and in response, the plaintiff has the opportunity to show that the objective can be achieved by a substantially less restrictive alternative. The court then balances whether the challenged behavior is unreasonable. See *Continental TV Inc. v. GTE Sylvania, Inc*, [1977] 433 US 36 (US Supreme Court). There are also important differences and peculiarities across legal regimes. In European competition law under Article 101 TFEU, for instance, the burden is on the party alleging an infringement of Article 101(1) to provide sufficient and coherent proof of infringement, and then the burden shifts to the firm in question claiming the benefits of Article 101(3) to establish that the required saving criteria are met. The firm must prove that a fair share of the alleged benefits is passed on to consumers. Canada competition policy contains an explicit efficiency defense for mergers, which adopts a modified version of the total welfare standard (a balancing weigh approach). See *Canada (Commissioner of Competition) v. Superior Propane Inc.* [2003] 53 FC 529 (Federal Court of Appeal). For a discussion, see Edward Iacobucci, "The Superior Propane Saga: The Efficiencies Defence in Canada," in *Competition Law World: Fourteen Stories* (Alphen aan den Rijn: Kluwer Law International, 2013).

platforms, insofar as various policy approaches and proposals tend to be based on the notion that multisidedness and the platform model changes the nature of these markets. To be sure, this can go in either direction: the platform model and multi-sidedness can be used both as an argument to dismiss the desirability of enforcement, as well as a basis for radical and invasive forms of intervention. In contrast, the application of the natural monopoly framework and the attempt in this book to draw general policy principles for digital markets starts from the premise that identifying the boundaries of desirable policy approaches is not simply a study of multisidedness; rather, it entails a broader, context-specific, and case-by-case analysis of market features beyond the formal classification and distinction between single-sided or multisided markets.

On the one hand, the economics of platforms provides a possible theory as to why indirect network externalities between the different sides of the platform may in certain extreme instances give rise to a natural monopoly through the efficient aggregation of demand. On the other hand, however, concentration is generally a product of a larger set of conditions and forms of scale enabled more broadly by technological change and digitalization, which go beyond the narrow focus on the strength of indirect network externalities. This reveals a high degree of heterogeneity within digital platform markets, and a rather blurred distinction between markets with one or multiple sides. Hence, the potential need for novel policy approaches for digital platforms results from a mix of context-specific economic and technological features, which can often be simply tangential to the presence of the multisided platform model alone.

Having identified the reasons why the natural monopoly framework becomes pertinent in digital industries, as well as the important policy questions raised by the economics of multisided platforms at large, we now turn to the application of the natural monopoly framework in digital platform markets.

2.3 APPLYING THE NATURAL MONOPOLY FRAMEWORK

The notion of natural monopoly is an assumption about the nature of technological change and a given type of production technology. Standard network industries and traditional public utilities such as electricity, gas, water, and telecommunications, generally involve large fixed sunk costs of developing infrastructure such as transmission and transportation networks and negligible operating costs associated with the production of each unit, which results in low variable or marginal costs. As production increases, the large high fixed costs can be spread across larger output units, decreasing long-run average total costs and making a natural monopoly more efficient than market fragmentation and competition. Where in standard networks the role of technological change has been to undermine supply-side scale in some market segments causing a shift from natural monopoly regulation toward competition (such as in segments of the telecommunication, airline, or electricity industries), technology overall appears to have the opposite effect on the current wave of digital platform markets, enabling economic conditions that increase rather than decrease the likelihood of natural monopolies. After describing the general economic preconditions for the emergence of natural monopolies, the chapter identifies the specific determinants of natural and efficient concentration that can arise in platform markets, and then discusses different forms of regulatory intervention potentially pertinent to markets with natural monopoly features.

2.3.1 *The Standard Natural Monopoly Paradigm*

The distinguishing feature of a natural monopoly is that the most efficient way to serve the market is to have a single firm serving the entire demand, as a single firm is able to operate in the market at a lower cost than several firms operating in the market. Competition and fragmentation, on the contrary, is not viable for natural monopolies.[134] More than one provider would create wasteful duplication of facilities increasing costs of producing total output, whereas a natural monopoly is the only structure that takes full advantage of internal scale economies relative to the size of demand as a result of decreasing long-run average unit costs over all or most of the extent of the market.

An economic definition of a natural monopoly is that the product and firm cost functions are said to be subadditive at the output level.[135] That is, a firm producing a single homogeneous product is a natural monopoly when the cost advantage in producing any level of output within a single firm (rather than with two or more firms) holds over the full range of market demand.[136] The presence of economies of scale and decreasing average costs over the relevant range of output is sufficient to satisfy the technological definition of a natural monopoly, but not necessary for subadditivity: even if output of a single firm has expanded beyond the point where there are economies of scale, it may still be less costly for output to be produced in a single firm rather than multiple firms if market demand is not large enough to support efficient production by two firms for some levels of industry output.[137] Thus, the set of firm cost functions that are subadditive is broader than the presence of economies of scale and decreasing average costs over the entire range of industry output. The natural monopoly must exhibit economies of scale over some range of output, but it will still be subadditive in many cases beyond the point where

---

[134] Richard Posner, "Natural Monopoly and Its Regulation" (1973) J Repr Antitrust Law Econ, 335.
[135] Alfred Kahn, *The Economics of Regulation: Principles and Institutions* (Cambridge, MA: MIT Press, 1988); Richard Schmalensee, *The Control of Natural Monopolies* (Lexington, MA: Lexington Books, 1979); Jean-Jacques Laffont and Jean Tirole, *A Theory of Incentives in Procurement and Regulation* (Cambridge, MA: MIT Press, 1993).
[136] William W. Sharkey, *The Theory of Natural Monopoly* (Cambridge: Cambridge University Press, 1982).
[137] Paul Joskow, "Regulation of Natural Monopoly" in *Handbook of Law and Economics* (Amsterdam: Elsevier, 2007).

economies of scale are exhausted and until industry output is large enough to make it economical to add a second firm.

A similar analysis can be undertaken for multiproduct subadditivity, which requires both multiproduct cost complementarity (economies of scope) and a form of multiproduct economies of scale over at least some range of the output of the products.[138] Another important cost attribute of natural monopolies is the existence and importance of sunk costs.[139] Sunk costs that have already been incurred and cannot be recovered at least in the short or medium run, even if production ceases altogether, are no longer a portion of the opportunity cost of production. The case for regulation based on a noncontestable natural monopoly generally requires both significant increasing returns to scale and substantial sunk costs that represent a significant fraction of total costs.[140]

These economic features of natural monopolies set them apart from standard monopolies. A standard monopolist faces a downward sloping demand curve, and standard marginal and average total cost curves, where the marginal cost curve slopes downward and then upward when the firm begins to face diminishing marginal returns, and where the average cost curve slopes downward and then upward once marginal costs are greater than average total costs. In contrast, a natural monopoly benefits from an average total cost curve that decreases over a much larger range of output, experiencing economies of scale and decreasing average costs over a large range of demand. Average total costs start increasing well beyond the demand curve, making a monopoly more efficient than competition, where competing firms may not be able to reach the economies of scale that allow average total costs to decrease. Since cost subadditivity is a necessary and sufficient condition for a natural monopoly, while decreasing average costs is a sufficient but not necessary condition, two kinds of natural monopoly can emerge depending on whether both conditions are met: a strong natural monopoly, which benefits from decreasing average costs *and* subadditivity; a weak natural monopoly, which instead benefits from cost subadditivity but faces increasing average costs.

Although in practice it is not easy to draw a bright line between industries that are natural monopolies and imperfectly competitive industries where there are economies of scale but little cost sacrifice in having multiple firms in the market, identification of natural monopolies has generally led policy to promote concentration toward a single provider but also to regulate the monopolist due to various potential market failures resulting from a natural monopoly, including distortions of allocative efficiency and productive efficiency, exercises of monopoly power, and

---

[138] Ibid.

[139] William J. Baumol, John C. Panzar, and Robert D. Willig, *Contestable Markets and the Theory of Industry Structure* (New York: Harcourt Brace Jovanovich, 1982).

[140] See Joskow, *supra*, note 137. Sunk costs distinguish between incumbents and potential entrants and introduce a time dimension into the cost commitment and recovery process of a natural monopolist. See also M. A. Weitzman, "Contestable Markets: An Uprising in the Theory of Industry Structure: Comment" (1983) 73, no. 3, *American Economic Review*, 486–487.

externalities. In most cases, regulation is implemented by independent or quasi-independent industry-specific regulatory authorities, although in some jurisdictions, competition authorities are in charge of both competition law enforcement and sectoral regulation.

A first economic rationale for regulating natural monopolies is to improve allocative efficiency through price regulation. As for standard monopolists facing a downward sloping linear demand curve, the profit maximization strategy is to produce where marginal revenue equals marginal cost, which entails a deadweight loss and a suboptimal outcome compared to a competitive market where prices are set at marginal cost and allocative efficiency is maximized. However, unlike standard markets where high prices will induce entry and therefore competitive market forces can be relied upon to erode high prices, in the natural monopoly framework market forces and competition will not solve this allocative efficiency problem, which instead requires some form of ex ante price regulation. A second efficiency-based argument for regulation of natural monopoly industries is restriction of entry. Since productive efficiency may require a single firm serving the entire market, regulation can limit inefficient entry to the market. Restrictions on entry have been based on the rationale of avoiding wasteful duplication of fixed costs, avoiding price skimming by firms that intend to serve only the most profitable segments of demand, or avoiding destructive competition that may cause instability or volatility in the industry.

The form of regulatory responses to these concerns has varied depending on whether a natural monopoly is strong or weak. With a strong natural monopoly, if the firm is forced to price at marginal cost a deficit occurs because average costs are higher than the point where demand meets marginal cost, due to the large fixed costs. Therefore, the first best response to the deadweight loss associated with monopoly is not available because price equal marginal cost will not be sustainable in the long term as the firm will not be able to recover its fixed costs of production. This problem may be tackled in various ways including, subsidies to the natural monopolist to cover fixed costs of product while pricing at marginal cost; different pricing policies such as average cost pricing that allow the firm to recover its fixed costs and obtain a fair rate of return on investments; or Ramsey pricing with different prices for different classes of consumers, depending on elasticity of demand (akin to price discrimination). With a weak natural monopoly, instead, the presence of increasing average costs implies that marginal costs are greater than average costs, suggesting that the firm can earn profits by pricing at marginal cost. The firm does not need a subsidy, but the regulator faces the problem of inefficient entry and price skimming. Weak natural monopolies may therefore justify entry restrictions.[141]

---

[141]   Various other efficiency rationales exist for entry restrictions, for example, in order to avoid wasteful duplication of fixed costs, destructive competition in cases of excess capacity that may lead to price volatility industry instability, selective entry through cream skimming, etc. See John Panzar and Robert Willig, "Economies of Scale in Multi-Output Production" (1977) 91 *Quarterly Journal of*

Another set of reasons for economic regulation is to address exercises of monopoly power and opportunistic behavior that may distort competition and harm consumers. Control of monopoly power, for example, may include not only monopoly prices, but also degradation of quality, lack of responsiveness to cost reductions and production efficiencies. When the natural monopoly is vertically integrated, market power can also be exercised by leveraging from the natural monopoly segment to adjacent upstream or downstream markets where competition is possible. Vertical integration in particular enables various forms of biases that favor the integrated natural monopoly and distort competition when the competitive segments rely on access to a bottleneck facility required by competitors to effectively operate in the market. The natural monopolist that controls such bottleneck can exploit the resulting market power and extend it over the competitive segments of the industry. Remedies to this problem of leveraging include both breaking up the vertically integrated monopoly by separating it from the competitive segment, and rules requiring nondiscriminatory access to the bottleneck facility.

2.3.2 *Determinants of Natural Monopoly in Digital Platform Markets*

Various factors driving concentrated market structures in digital platform markets may potentially be associated with a natural monopoly. As in standard public utility and network industries, economies of scale on the supply side may give rise to a natural monopoly platform. In digital industries, scale economies can be compounded by the fact that fixed costs for the development of a network or infrastructure (the degree of fixed costs of production is likely to vary substantially from one sector to another) are often coupled with negligible or zero marginal costs as a result of digitalization.

In addition to supply-side economies of scale, specific and unique to platforms is the presence of demand-side economies of scale in the form of indirect network externalities, which may represent a form of efficiency by aggregating demand and externalities across the different sides of the platform on a single network. For example, there are positive indirect network externalities between drivers and passengers joining the same ride-hailing network, home owners and renters joining the same short-term rental online portal, or buyer and sellers joining the same marketplace. Hence, a network becomes more valuable for users as the number of other users increases and externalities are aggregated on a larger network.[142] If network externalities are increasing over the relevant range of demand, they can be a source of natural monopoly conditions[143] where their positive strength makes aggregation over a single platform the most efficient market outcome. In order to do

---

Economics, 481; W. Viscusi, Joseph Harrington, and John Vernon, *Economics of Regulation and Antitrust* (Cambridge, MA: MIT Press, 2005).

[142]   Oz Shy, *The Economics of Network Industries* (Cambridge: Cambridge University Press, 2001).

[143]   Joskow, *supra*, note 137.

so, the benefit of aggregating users on a single platform and reducing inefficient fragmentation due to indirect network externalities must outweigh potential diseconomies of scale that may emerge on the supply side.[144] For example, when more users are connected to a network, it may still more efficient to have a single firm supplying the service even if the average supply-side cost per user rises, as long as the positive effect of aggregating network externalities outweigh diseconomies of scale on the supply side.

Adding to standard supply-side economies of scale and indirect network externalities typical of the platform model, other critical forms of scale may be associated with natural monopoly. First are direct network externalities. The distinction with indirect network externalities is important because direct externalities do not necessarily arise from or depend on the platform model. In the case of social networks, for instance, all users want to be on the same platform because of direct positive effects. Hence, in the case of social networks aggregating users on the same platform, direct network externalities are arguably more important than the indirect network externalities that may be present between users and advertisers.

Second, access to data can be a key factor driving concentration due to large economies of scale and scope enabled by technological change (see Table 2.1). Scale economies associated with data are likely to vary significantly depending on the context, the nature of the service, and type of data at stake. In many cases, after a certain point, data display decreasing marginal returns, which reduces the importance of additional data beyond a given threshold. In other instances, however, scale economies may be large enough that access to a larger dataset may be associated with the emergence of a natural monopoly. This is particularly plausible for the purpose of algorithmic predictions, for which the value of data is critical and arguably more important than the narrower function of algorithmic matching. When predictions are broad in scope, as it is the case for a general-purpose horizontal search engine, more data also give rise to economies of scope that further increase the importance of access to larger and more diverse data.

TABLE 2.1 *Drivers of natural concentration in digital platform markets*

Drivers of Natural Concentration
Supply-side economies of scale
Positive (platform-based) indirect network externalities
Positive direct network externalities
Scale in data collection and analysis
Low demand heterogeneity, product differentiation and multihoming

---

[144] For example, when the benefits of aggregating network externalities on a single network outweigh duplication costs.

At the same time, various opposing counterforces may reduce the likelihood of natural monopolies despite the presence of these various forms of scale. First, diseconomies of scale on the supply side may militate against efficient concentration. When diseconomies and positive network externalities are both present, the positive value of aggregating demand on a single platform needs to be strong enough to outweigh these diseconomies of scale for a natural monopoly to emerge. Second, another important factor against natural and efficient concentration is product differentiation and demand heterogeneity. Differentiated competition can give rise to coexisting platforms, both in the form of vertical differentiation (for example, same service with different levels of quality), and horizontal differentiation (platforms distinguishing themselves based on different features and services). This can result in users joining multiple platforms. Sellers, for example, may try to differentiate themselves either by providing products and services on multiple networks, especially when the fixed costs of producing a product compatible with multiple standards is low, or by selecting separate exclusive networks, in which case the choice of a different standard becomes a substitute for product differentiation.[145] Buyers may be willing to multihome when the costs are low and benefits substantial – another contributing factor to fragmentation and the existence of multiple platforms.[146] Hence, the less users' evaluation of the platform is homogeneous, the less likely it is that a natural monopoly will emerge due to the beneficial coexistence of multiple differentiated platforms. Finally, issues of congestion on either side may also result in users opting for multiple platforms.[147]

The interplay and combination of all these factors has the potential to increase the likelihood of natural monopoly in the current wave of digital platform markets enabled by technological change, especially compared to older and standard cases of platforms such as physical newspapers, shopping malls, or credit cards. Among other things, the critical role of data for algorithmic predictions and matching augments the efficiency of concentration. Digitalization creates large scale economies on the supply side with frequent zero marginal costs and reduces scarcity constraints providing higher latitude for the aggregation of network externalities. However, the emergence of a natural platform monopoly is neither circumscribed by the importance of indirect network externalities, nor an inevitable result of technological change and the platform model. It is, on the contrary, dependent on the more complex interplay of all the factors identified above that may favor or militate against natural monopoly conditions.

[145]   Rysman, *supra*, note 87, at 134.

[146]   In this regard, not all sides need to be single-homing for the market to tip. Single-homing by the more elastic side can lead to concentration even in presence of multihoming on the other side.

[147]   The results of congestion may not be entirely equivalent on physical and online platforms. For instance, congestion may result from the limits posed by increasing the physical size of platform, which will increase search costs; for online platforms these effects may be subtler: scarcity may be more easily alleviated, but congestion may still occur due to increasing information and transaction costs.

The presence of multiple, potential factors associated with technological change as possible drivers of natural concentration also suggests that natural monopolies in digital industries may often differ from standard network utilities, with important implications with regard to contestability. As was discussed above, the traditional definition of natural monopoly is generally based on subadditivity of the cost structure on the supply side. This feature of standard natural monopolies has generally emphasized the presence of a high degree of entry barriers, low and inefficient entry, and lack of contestability of a natural monopoly position. In digital industries, conclusions regarding contestability however may change, at least to an extent, for a number of reasons.

First, the rapid pace of technological change and the threat of potential disruption can represent, at least in some cases, a possible threat to an established monopoly position. These technological forces appear much stronger and faster in digital platform markets than in standard network industries. Second, and most importantly, drivers of concentration often tend to shift from the supply side to the demand side in the form of network externalities. Unlike the typical forms of scale and entry barrier of standard network industries, there appears to be as a result more room for policy intervention that promotes disruptive entry and reduces switching costs in the presence of network externalities – for example, targeted forms of portability across alternative providers. As a consequence, it is plausible to expect different degrees of contestability even within platform industries that display natural monopoly features. These identified potential differences compared to standard natural monopolies have important implications for policy approaches in digital platform industries. The more technological change gives rise to natural monopolies that can be made contestable, the more policy approaches that are more favorable to dynamic competition than standard price and entry regulation become relevant.

2.3.3 *Alternative Approaches for Naturally Monopolistic Markets*

While economic regulation has been the main response to natural monopolies, policy attitudes toward the natural monopoly problem have evolved over time responding to changes in technology, industrial structure, and dominant political ideologies.[148] First, the paradigm of economic regulation for network industries has lost some of its appeal in many industrialized countries, as a result of technology and shifts in ideological preferences toward privatization, deregulation, and competition.[149] In particular, technological and other changes have reduced or eliminated perceived natural monopoly features in some segments of network industries, undermining the significance of natural monopoly characteristics that

---

[148] Sanford V. Berg and John Tschirhart, *Natural Monopoly Regulation: Principles and Practice* (Cambridge: Cambridge University Press, 1988).
[149] Clifford Winston, "Economic Deregulation: Days of Reckoning for Microeconomists" (1993) 31, no. 3, J Econ Lit, 1263.

may once have been a legitimate concern in some sectors such as electricity or telecommunication. Moreover, the shortcomings and negative effects of regulation in practice led scholars and policy makers to question whether the costs of imperfect regulation were greater than the costs of imperfect markets.

As a result, the scope of price and entry regulation has been scaled back. First, some industries have been completely deregulated, others restructured to promote competition in potentially competitive segments and new performance-based regulatory mechanisms applied to core network segments of these industries that continue to have natural monopoly characteristics.[150] Industry-restructuring policies have in particular attempted to divide along the supply chain segments of the industry that are core natural monopolies from others that are potentially competitive activities. For example, in the electricity sector generation has shifted from perceived natural monopoly scale economies toward competition, while transmission and distribution remain natural monopolies. Similar shifts toward reliance on market forces have occurred in telecommunications, natural gas, and transportation industries.

Second, there are various alternative approaches to traditional economic regulation that, depending on the context, have been applied to network industries to mitigate the adverse economic consequences of unregulated natural monopoly. In some cases, this has included franchise bidding, which attempts to simulate competition for the market through auctions to a single firm on prespecified terms and conditions over a specified time period. The contenders bid on pricing and other aspects of service and this simulates a competition for the market that arguably does not require the same levels of ongoing regulatory oversight. In other instances, public ownership of network utilities has been favored in many countries, using governmental control as a way to direct the public firm toward the achievement of social welfare and public interest goals rather than narrow profit maximization. Competition policy, as well, can be used as a second-best alternative to natural monopoly regulation, for example where the costs of regulation are too high relative to the inefficiencies that regulation would address, or in cases where the natural monopoly is contestable, and enforcement can serve the goal of maintaining a high threat of entry.

All these factors become potentially critical in light of the identified economic and technological characteristics of digital platform industries, where the just described evolution of attitudes and approaches to natural monopolies will inevitably influence any attempt to trace the boundaries of a desirable policy framework

[150] Sam Peltzman and Clifford Winston, *Deregulation of Network Industries: What's Next?* (Washington, DC: AEI-Brookings Joint Center for Regulatory Studies, 2000); Paul Joskow, "Incentive Regulation in Theory and Practice: Electricity Distribution and Transmission Networks" in *Economic Regulation: Its Reform. What Have We Learned* (Chicago: University of Chicago Press, 2014), p. 291; Mark Armstrong and David E. M. Sappington, "Regulation, Competition and Liberalization" (2006) 44, no. 2, J Econ Lit, 325.

for digital platform markets. As the book will discuss more thoroughly in Chapter 6, the institutional dimension of each available policy instrument will in particular play a critical role in determining its desirability vis-à-vis available alternative forms of intervention.

2.4 CONCLUSION

Technological forces shape markets and firms, and today in particular the growing importance of big data, algorithmic predictions and matching, and platform intermediation are major drivers of concentration in the digital economy. As a result, natural monopolies in digital platform industries can be the product of various forms of scale, potentially giving rise to different degrees of natural concentration and contestability. On the basis of the general framework developed in this chapter, the book will now apply the natural monopoly framework to specificities of three selected digital platforms: horizontal search, e-commerce marketplaces, and ride-hailing platforms. The three selected platform markets share important commonalities that enable a useful comparison between them. They are all examples of global, digital platforms enabled by technological change that have been at the forefront of the academic and policy debates due to their winner-takes-all or winner-takes-most tendencies; they all use data as a critical input to perform algorithmic search, prediction, and matching; they all rely to some degree on network externalities across the sides of the platform, such as advertisers and eyeballs, riders and passengers, and buyers and sellers.

At the same time, the three evaluated platform markets and the identified common features display an important degree of heterogeneousness. Their global reach notwithstanding, for some platforms, the local nature of the service is of particular importance, such as ride-hailing. Despite their prevailing digital nature, some platforms benefit extensively from efficient physical infrastructure, which is at times arguably more important than the digital dimension of the service, as it is the case for e-commerce logistics. While all platforms perform a mix of prediction and matching, the importance of these two dimensions vary substantially across case studies, generating different degrees of scale associated with data and network externalities. Likewise, the role of scale economies on the supply side is also likely to differ across markets, some facing higher fixed costs than others, and different levels of variable and marginal costs.

Identifying the points of minimum efficient scale associated with data, network externalities, and supply-side scale economies is ultimately an empirical matter, but it is possible to identify the heterogeneous role of these factors in each platform market in a way that leads to different conclusions with regard to the possibility of a natural monopoly. This heterogeneity is exemplified and illuminated by the three case studies analyzed in this book, which appear to belong to a spectrum of natural concentration. Horizontal search for example shares features of a natural monopoly, due to high fixed costs and virtually zero marginal costs, and the scale and scope effects of data for general-purpose search engines. On the contrary, e-commerce marketplaces are not naturally monopolistic, despite benefiting to a degree from scale economies in logistics and network externalities between buyers and sellers. In between these two extremes, ride-hailing platforms represent a more ambiguous case, depending on the local conditions of demand in a given geographical context.

3

Horizontal Search

The first case study evaluates the characteristics of the horizontal (or general) online search market and concludes that a dominant search engine platform like Google fits within the natural monopoly framework. First, as in standard network industries, high fixed costs of developing a search algorithm and platform, and very low marginal costs of providing additional search services (marginal cost that are, in fact, close to zero on each side) create the conditions for a cost structure that make the market maximally efficient with a single provider. Second, the predictive and general-purpose nature of search makes access to data a central driver of natural monopoly. Access to data is critical for the purpose of search predictions because it generates extensive economies of scale and scope, which improve the efficiency and quality of the predictive algorithm when more searchers use the platform and generate more data. Moreover, due to the general, universal nature of horizontal search, the portion of positive marginal returns in the collection, aggregation, and analysis of additional data is further enhanced; the same data points may be valuable beyond a narrow query for a larger set of related queries where the same data may be relevant or complementary, improving the search algorithm overall. The combination of a cost structure with high fixed cost–zero marginal costs, and the importance of data and related direct network externalities among data-generating users set search apart from the other case studies and make natural monopoly tendencies analogous to, or perhaps stronger than standard network industries, such as electricity, telecommunications, or water supply.

The case study arrives at this conclusion by first looking at the evolution and market structure of online search, discussing available alternative business models, and highlighting the main competition policy issues that have emerged around Google. The case study then evaluates possible regulatory responses to the natural monopoly features of online search. In particular, it discusses some of the regulatory tools that can be used to deal with market power of a natural monopoly platform in horizontal search, highlighting how some of the often overlooked economic and technological features of search affect given assumptions about the applicability of traditional remedies. On this basis, it concludes that although under a natural monopoly framework structural remedies represent a clear-cut approach to over-come issues of market power leveraging from the natural monopoly to competitive segments, there is unexplored potential in rethinking access to general search as an essential facility, in light of reduced scarcity constraints offered by the technological characteristics of search.

3.1 THE EVOLUTION OF ONLINE SEARCH: FROM NEUTRAL TO UNIVERSAL RESULTS

Online search engines were originally designed following a ranking data model based on numeric metrics that counted the number of times a term appeared on a webpage.[151] Under this paradigm, the role of a search engine consists in crawling and indexing web content, and then ranking results based on selected criteria that attempt to determine the quality of results. Such a simple model based on the number of times a term appeared on a page, however, ignored valuable information about the interlinks between websites and lacked more sophisticated ways to deter-mine the relevance of results to the queries made by users. When Google started in 1997, it developed an alternative way of providing search results based on the so-called "PageRank" algorithm, which ranked results based not only on numerical scores, but on more sophisticated mechanisms to assess relevance of results. The PageRank algorithm achieved this by combining webpages' presence in links from other sites and the popularity with users searching similar queries, in order to better integrate relationships and interconnections among websites. As a result of this different and more efficient method of ranking search results, Google drastically increased the indexing of websites to over 1 billion pages by 2000.

Although developing an algorithm for online search can never be "neutral" in an absolute sense, as noted by the founders of Google in their original paper on developing their large-scale search engine, "with Google, we have a strong goal to push more development and understanding into the academic realm."[152] Noting that many early search engines migrated from the academic domain to the com-mercial and advertising-oriented business model, the founders of Google argued in the same paper that "while evaluation of a search engine is difficult, we have subjectively found that Google returns higher-quality search results than current commercial search engines."[153] In the Appendix of their paper, they warn against the dangers of turning an academically oriented search engine based on "neutral" ranking toward an advertised-based model:

---

[151] S. Brin and L. Page, "The Anatomy of a Large-Scale Hypertextual Web Search Engine" (1998) 30 *Computer Networks and ISDN Systems*, 107–117.
[152] Ibid, at 3.
[153] Ibid, at 15.

The goals of the advertising business model do not always correspond to providing quality search to users. For example, in our prototype search engine one of the top results for cellular phone is The Effect of Cellular Phone Use Upon Driver Attention, a study which explains in great detail the distractions and risk associated with conversing on a cell phone while driving. This search result came up first because of its high importance as judged by the PageRank algorithm, an approximation of citation importance on the web. It is clear that a search engine which was taking money for showing cellular phone ads would have difficulty justifying the page that our system returned to its paying advertisers. For this type of reason and historical experience with other media, we expect that advertising funded search engines will be inherently biased towards the advertisers and away from the needs of the consumers.[154]

The inherent conflict of interest between advertised and neutral search results is particularly insidious because it is very difficult to evaluate search engines and biases. Although market responses could discipline against blatantly evident search biases, the founders of Google acknowledge that less blatant bias are likely to be tolerated by the market:

For example, a search engine could add a small factor to search results from "friendly" companies, and subtract a factor from results from competitors. This type of bias is very difficult to detect but could still have a significant effect on the market. Furthermore, advertising income often provides an incentive to provide poor quality search results. For example, we noticed a major search engine would not return a large airline's homepage when the airline's name was given as a query. It so happened that the airline had placed an expensive ad, linked to the query that was its name. A better search engine would not have required this ad, and possibly resulted in the loss of the revenue from the airline to the search engine. In general, it could be argued from the consumer point of view that the better the search engine is, the fewer advertisements will be needed for the consumer to find what they want. This of course erodes the advertising supported business model of the existing search engines.[155]

The recognition that advertising can cause enough mixed incentives that contrast with the development of a neutrally competitive and transparent search engine was nonetheless not enough to stop the evolution of the original "neutral" ranking model toward the advertisement-based model as the predominant form of revenue for search engines, where ad-based results are added beside organic results. Meanwhile, this shift was also accompanied by the increasing growth of specialized search engines that provide answers only to specific topics and develop algorithms attuned to these narrowly defined results. As a result, two prominent forms of search engine emerged: the so-called "horizontal" or general search engines, which provide results for any type of query, and include general search engines including Google,

---

[154]   Ibid, at 18, Appendix A.
[155]   Ibid, at 19, Appendix A.

Bing, and Yahoo; and "vertical" or specialized search engines, which provide only results for specific types of query, such as local restaurants, online shopping, flights, and so on. Examples include Yelp, Zagat, Google Reviews, and TripAdvisor for restaurants reviews, Kayak, Google Flights, Expedia, Sky Scanner, and Trivago for online travel services such as flights and hotels, or Amazon for online shopping and e-commerce. Although the specialized nature of vertical search engines reduces their potential for growth compared to general search, at the same they can achieve product differentiation by specializing in a niche segment of the search market, and can in certain ways outperform general search due to the fact that users may reveal more accurate information and data, which, in turn, can allow for more targeted advertising.

While most search engines shifted to the advertising-based model, until about 2005 search engines did not directly provide content or immediate answers to queries, but simply generated a list of links combining a mix of organic and advertised results. Beginning in 2007, however, Google and other search engines introduced new interfaces often referred to as "universal" search, where the search engine merges within its general search page a variety of results from its own vertical search engines, which attempt to provide direct answers to queries rather than simply links to third-party websites. These results are given visual prominence at the top or in the center of the general search page, or are embedded in hardwired links.

As a result of these design developments, and despite the original philosophy advocated by its founders, Google led the development and evolution of the online search engine model by first switching from the original neutral "ten blue links" model to the advertising revenue model, and then by introducing hardwired links to proprietary services and the so-called "OneBox" interface that provided answers directly through Google's vertical search services. Before these changes, the end point of a search on Google was an external third-party webpage, and Google was at most a stopover point for users to access the relevant websites ranked by the search engine and to find the desired endpoint of a search. With the introduction of the "OneBox," Google started providing answers to users directly, becoming a direct content provider in competition with other specialized search engines (such as Google review in competition with Yelp, Google Shopping competing with Amazon, or Google flights with Expedia). As a result, three different types of result generally compose a horizontal search page:

a) Organic Results: A portion of the page remains based on "quality" competition among webpages determined by the relevance to the query as defined by the search algorithm, as previously occurred in the original neutral ranking data model.

b) Auction-Based Advertised Results: Areas of webpage space are only available to advertised results through auction mechanisms. In this space, competition among web content providers is simply driven by the number of bids to place an ad on a specific area of the webpage through the auction. For instance, in 2002 Google launched its AdWords service that allows firms to bid for higher ranking in the advertising listings found on search results pages, where advertisers can pay based on impressions/visualizations (as it is usually the case for media), or a pay-per-click basis (or a combination of bids and relevance).

c) Self-Preferential Search Results: Some results are provided directly by a search engine's specialized services (rather than third-party websites) and are often granted preferential treatment in terms of ranking, visual prominence, and dedicated space on the horizontal search page. For instance, in 2001 Google introduced Google News and in 2002 "Froogle," which then became Google Shopping, in addition to Google Finance, Google Maps, Google Flights, Google Places, Google Hotels, and so on. In addition to hardwired links in the hardwired bar at the top of the page (for example, links to Google Maps or YouTube), it introduced the "OneBox" interface, a portion of the webpage, usually as first results or in the center of the page, where Google provides visual prominence to its own vertical services (such as Google Shopping or Google Flights). For instance, in response to a search for "local restaurants," "flights," or "laundry machines," Google would not simply provide a list of links to external websites, but it would rank first, or give visual prominence to results provided directly by Google Reviews, Google Flights, or Google Shopping, irrespective of the relative quality of these services compared to vertical search competitors.

Figure 3.1 shows, for instance, a stylized graphic representation of a horizontal search page like the one provided by Google Search. The image shows proprietary links that are provided visual prominence (for example, Google Shopping); proprietary links that are not in competition with other providers (for example, Google Maps, Google Reviews, and hardwired links images, etc.); advertising results based on auctions; and some organic links to webpages.

3.2 ALTERNATIVE BUSINESS MODELS

As the developments of online search reveal, there are different business models that may theoretically be adopted to provide general search services: two-sided models based on advertising revenue; one-sided models with no advertising based on users' subscription (the neutral rankings provided for free was also based on a one-sided model); and hybrid models of partial vertical integration of content. The prevalence of a given business model has an impact on the nature of competition, the tendency toward market concentration, and the possible role of regulation (see Table 3.1).

A two-sided model matches searchers and advertisers, providing search results for free and relying on advertising revenue. Searchers provide indirect positive externalities for advertisers to whom a search engine sells advertising space. These positive indirect

TABLE 3.1 *Alternative structures for online search*

Pure Two-Sided Models	Hybrid Models	One-Sided Models
Example: Ad-based models without vertical integration	Example: Mix of partial vertical integration, ad-based results, and organic results	Example: Paid search subscription models

FIGURE 3.1 The structure of horizontal search results

network effects are, most of the time, not bidirectional.[156] Except for some rare cases where users are directly looking for ads, searchers are usually indifferent or most likely see negatively the presence of advertising when they do searches online. On the other side of the market, advertisers value the platform as the number of users increases, as this augments the audience pool and the amount of free data that can be extracted from users' queries, which, in turn, allows better targeting advertising. As a result of the nature of the network externalities at play in this market, providing the service for free to searchers increases the pool of users that can be reached by ads and maximizes the amount or type of data that can be collected and used to refine algorithms.[157]

The two-sided business model affects the nature of competition. Platforms will compete intensely for eyeballs (the source of data and positive externalities) and extract surplus from advertisers. Indirect network externalities from searchers can be a source of market power for the search engine.[158] In particular, the scale of data is a major source of competitive advantage, because smaller search engines need to reach sufficient scale in order to effectively compete, a problem that is particularly acute for tail queries where smaller search engines may not reach sufficient searches to refine quality results. The quality of data, which allows a search engine to amass targeted and personalized data concerning individual specific users by combining data from different services (which can include email, maps, and so on) can also increase the likelihood of a search engine becoming a bottleneck for advertisers over access to users. Through the aggregation of targeted data on specific users, a search engine can enable advertisers to reach specific "eyeballs" (not just general eyeballs), which makes access to that specific search engine even more valuable. This can give

---

[156] Some commentators have suggested that even an ad-based search engine like Google is not two sided, but rather a retailer of users' personal data, where two separate transactions take place. In the upstream market, Google buys users' personal information from large retailers and final consumers in exchange for search services, or payment. In the downstream market, it uses the personal information collected to resell targeted advertising to advertisers. Relying on this framework, Google is characterized more like a reseller than a two-sided platform. One reason why Google is not a two-sided market in this categorization is that the platform would still operate if the second side (advertising) ceased to exist under a different market configuration, and that network externalities run only from the number of users to advertisers and not vice-versa. See Giacomo Luchetta, "Is the Google Platform a Two-Sided Market?" (2014) 10, no. 1, J Compet Law Econ, 185. However, bilateral positive externalities are not necessary for a market to be characterized as two sided, and many two-sided markets, in fact, have two transactions taking place.

[157] Charging zero to users also avoids the high transaction costs involved in requiring users to pay even a very small amount for search services.

[158] There are alternative venues for advertising, ranging from "search" advertising in competing search engines, "nonsearch" advertising in online platforms such as Facebook, and the more traditional "offline" venues of advertising such as newspapers. With regard to substitutability among these different forms of advertising, it is necessary to determine whether online advertising can be a substitute to offline advertising; and within online ads, whether nonsearch advertising (such as Facebook) and search advertising (Google) can be considered as substitutes. The substitutability of these forms of advertising is important because it can significantly determine the assessment of market power. See Florence Thepot, "Market Power in Online Search and Social Networking: A Matter of Two-Sided Markets" (2013) 36, no. 2, World Compet, 195.

a search engine market power over advertisers, which can be exercised with price increases above competitive levels, reduction of quantity of the number of slots available for auction on a page in order to extract more value from bidding,[159] and exclusionary behavior or targeted discrimination or demotion against specific advertisers.[160]

On the users' side, the nature of competition among general search engines is based not on price but on quality metrics. Free search reduces the strength of competition insofar that it shifts from price to quality competition, which is arguably harder to evaluate given the credence nature of search. Market power can therefore be exercised as a reduction of the quality of search without losing a significant number of searchers,[161] while the credence good nature of search makes it less likely for users to effectively compare quality across available search engines and status quo biases identified by behavioral economists further exacerbate barriers to switching. This is confirmed by the enormous amounts of investments made by search engines to be the default option on Internet browsers and mobile software.[162] Despite the ability of users to switch among competing search engines that are just one-click-away, consumers may be less likely to multihome or switch to alternative platforms, because quality metrics such as the reliability of search results or levels of privacy protection are harder to assess than price differentials. As long as differences along these quality metrics are not substantial, they soften the incentives to switch and the intensity of competition on the searchers' side. Competition from smaller search engines does not necessarily prevent larger search engines from degrading the quality of search results, because it is hard for users to identify differences in quality and switch from familiar patterns from default options, absent blatant reductions in quality.

Compared to other models, the two-sided business model with free search and advertising can create some negative effects for competition. While a hypothetical paid search model would be less favorable to searchers in terms of price, the lack of pricing on that side could possibly make the market less competitive and potentially

---

[159]   Google has also expanded its reach as an advertisement network with its AdSense program, which provides a technical and commercial infrastructure for publishers that want to serve ads on their sites. The AdSense infrastructure allowed Google to serve both as a provider of technical infrastructure for content delivery and performance monitoring, and as a direct middleman between publishers and advertisers.

[160]   Some antitrust proceedings involved exclusivity, namely artificially restricting the possibility of third-party websites to display search advertisements from Google's competitors, in order to protect its dominant position in online search advertising. See European Commission, *Antitrust: Commission Takes Further Steps in Investigations Alleging Google's Comparison Shopping and Advertising-Related Practices Breach EU Rules*, Press Release (Brussels: European Commission, 2016).

[161]   See Maurice E. Stucke and Ariel Ezrachi, "When Competition Fails to Optimize Quality: A Look at Search Engines" (2016) 18 Yale J Law Technol, 70.

[162]   Apple has been paid $82 million in 2009, and $1 billion in 2013 for this partnership. See Rebecca Greenfield, "Why Google Pays Apple $1 Billion a Year", *The Atlantic* (February 12, 2013), available at www.theatlantic.com/technology/archive/2013/02/why-google-pays-apple-1-billion-year/318451/.

reduce the quality of the service, possibly undermining paid business models that could count on higher protection of privacy, less or no advertising, and higher quality of search. Positive prices also facilitate entry, while nonnegative price constraints at play with free search can reduce competitive forces.[163]

As an alternative to the two-sided model with free search and advertising, a search engine could hypothetically be based on a one-sided model with users' subscriptions and no advertised results. This would likely have some important effects. Pricing on the users' side could introduce more price competition on that side of the market, and the absence of advertising would increase the quality of organic search results, possibly increasing the willingness to pay of users. It is less clear whether the elimination of advertising would reduce or increase vertical integration. Without advertising revenue in general search, there would be even more incentives to vertically integrate and provide direct results through proprietary specialized search services where advertising revenue can be obtained. At the same time, a general search engine based on paid search without advertising-based results may compete on quality by providing specialized results from what it perceives to be better, specialized providers, possibly creating some degree of product differentiation and more degree of choice for users both in terms of specialized providers (for example, giving the choice to searchers to select default providers for maps or online shopping), and in terms of subscription options.

In hybrid models, instead, an online search platform may add to the mix of organic and advertised results its own proprietary results and content (which is the prevailing model that has been adopted by Google and other search engine providers). Most of the concerns raised by the hybridity of the business model are that partial vertical integration can allow a platform with market power to extend market power to adjacent markets, and these potentially problematic aspects of hybrid models find their root in the broader evolution of search toward universal results and increasing integration of general and vertical search. In a way, universal search represents a form of technological upgrade in the provision of search services, where integration leads to faster and more direct results. At the same time, the shift toward universal search also induces a form of scarcity compared to the original ten blue links model (from rankings to one result) that can be exploited by the horizontal search engine in the process of advancing direct provision of results.

3.3 HORIZONTAL SEARCH AS A NATURALLY MONOPOLISTIC MARKET

Horizontal search is highly concentrated. Figures 3.2 and 3.3 illustrate Google's market shares and revenue in the market for horizontal search. Google holds a 92 percent market share worldwide. In the US, its market share by share of search queries in 2019 is 88 percent (and 94 percent share in mobile search), while in Europe it is 97 percent and 92 percent in Canada.

---

[163] Jay Pil Choi and Jeon oh-Shin, "A Leverage Theory of Tying in Two-Sided Markets," SSRN Scholarly Paper ID 2834821 (Rochester, NY: Social Science Research Network, 2016).

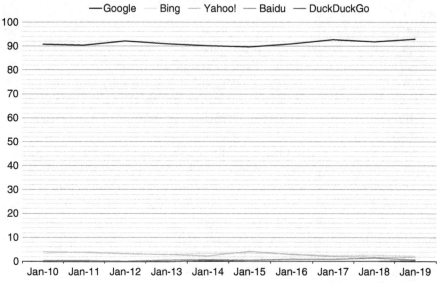

FIGURE 3.2 Worldwide search engine market share 2010–2019 (Source: Statcounter)

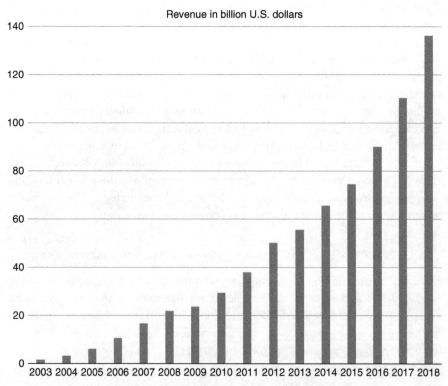

FIGURE 3.3 Google's global revenue 2003–2018 billion US$ (Source: Statista)

Google's revenue has also been increasing dramatically, from 1.5 to 136.3 billion US dollars between 2003 and 2016 worldwide.

There are a number of factors that may be used to explain why this market is highly concentrated. These include Google's superiority compared to existing competitors in investments and innovations, improvement of the search algorithm, and targeted advertising, all factors that certainly have played some role in allowing Google to outperform earlier search engines through technological improvements such as the introduction of the PageRank algorithm. Another common explanation is the multisided platform model based on free search and advertising that creates positive externalities between the two sides, which reinforces concentration tendencies. Indeed, the case study just highlighted how the model based on free search and advertising can in a way mute competitive forces compared to a hypothetical paid subscription-based model. However, the case study suggests that the major determinant of concentration is that horizontal search is a natural monopoly. The following factors in particular justify this conclusion, regardless of the impact of the platform model or Google's superior business strategy.

3.3.1 Cost Structure with High Fixed Costs and Marginal Costs Close to Zero

Developing a search engine involves high fixed costs and very low marginal costs. Developing an algorithm is R&D intensive, with high fixed costs in investments in physical plants, infrastructure for data centers and storage systems, hardware, support, and monitoring. These high fixed costs can be efficiently spread when search output increases. Marginal costs of providing an additional search service are instead very low. The marginal cost of providing an additional search service to searchers is, in fact, virtually zero, even accounting for refinements in algorithms; the marginal cost of advertising services is also very low or possibly zero, even considering the costs of an advertising sales force. With virtually zero marginal costs, average costs are likely decreasing over the total demand range. It is therefore plausible that cost subadditivity in delivering a general search service applies over the relevant demand output region and average cost may be decreasing over the same range, which makes the presence of a single dominant search engine the most cost-efficient way to serve the market. The cost structure is indeed similar to traditional natural monopolies.[164]

3.3.2 Network Externalities and the Value of Data for Horizontal Search Predictions

In addition to and related to the cost structure with skewed high fixed costs and low marginal costs, data are a central driver of efficient concentration in search. Access

---

[164] See Rufus Pollock, "Is Google the Next Microsoft: Competition, Welfare and Regulation in Online Search" (2010) 9, no. 4, Rev Netw Econ, available at www.degruyter.com/view/j/rne .2010.9.issue-4/rne.2010.9.4.1240/rne.2010.9.4.1240.xml.

to data is particularly important because the core function of search is prediction. In particular, for the purpose of algorithmic predictions, data can improve the efficiency in terms of quality-adjusted costs for a search engine with access to larger amounts of data and with the ability to complement different but related datasets. These scale effects that arise from access to data are much larger for the purpose of algorithmic prediction that they are for the purpose of matching. Hence, the importance of prediction over matching in horizontal search sets it apart from e-commerce marketplaces and ride-hailing platforms (for which, instead, matching is more important than predictions and thus access to data is not as critical). The importance of data is in this way linked with positive direct network externality among data-generating searchers. More users using the search engine means more searches are performed, which, in turn, means higher amounts of data can be analyzed, in terms of both scale and scope.

With regard to the number of searches performed on Google, for example, the number per day has been increasing from an average of 9,800 searches per day in 1998 to more than 5 billion searches per day in 2018, that is, over 60,000 search queries per second. Although some of Google's competitors have experienced a certain amount of growth in the number of queries, their share of and access to data remain marginal compared to Google. The increasing number of searches is critical because data from prior searches are the raw material from which search results are refined. The resulting economies of scale and scope in collection and analysis of data are such that the search engine that obtains access to bigger and more diverse data will have a marginal advantage over competing search engines that do not have access to the same amount of data. The ability to improve the efficiency of the algorithm as data increase in number is in a way a form of scale and decreasing quality-adjusted average costs over the demand range.

Moreover, the central role of data in fostering concentration is further augmented by the general-purpose nature of search predictions that are performed by a horizontal search engine. The reason why data are particularly significant for general purpose search engines and may display a large point of minimum efficient scale that make a single search algorithm more efficient than competition is that horizontal search encompasses the whole range of information on the web, covering virtually all aspects of knowledge, questions and answers that may be searched online (unlike vertical search platforms, including e-commerce and sharing-economy platforms, that only cover a limited subset of queries and topics). This universal scope of horizontal search may to a degree counteract the general pattern of nonlinear increasing returns to data. More specifically, it is usually found that for a given and narrowly defined query returns to scale become diminishing after a certain tipping point,[165] reducing the value of additional data. This explains for

---

[165]   Andres V. Lerner, "The Role of 'Big Data' in Online Platform Competition," SSRN Scholarly Paper ID 2482780 (Rochester, NY: Social Science Research Network, 2014).

instance why smaller competitors can compete even with fewer amounts of data on very popular queries (where it is easier to reach the minimum point of efficient scale), while, for tail queries,[166] scale in data may be harder to reach for smaller competitors.

While the principle of diminishing marginal returns to data pertains to narrow individual search queries, from the perspective of refining the general search algorithm as a whole, data have a much larger positive value (even when the same data points may display decreasing returns for the specific query). In horizontal search (unlike specialized search), the same data points can improve the efficiency of specific search queries but can then also be relevant to larger set of related queries for which those data can be relevant as well. As a result of the fact that more data can improve both specific queries and the overall efficiency of the search algorithm in other related areas of search, a horizontal search engine that can access and combine larger and diverse data can as a result outperform competitors that are not able to reach efficient scale for the general search algorithm as a whole.

As a result of these effects, an additional searcher (and perhaps also an additional advertiser) creates positive externalities for the search engine network as a whole, in that the overall quality of the general search algorithm increases with the quantity and quality of data collected from a larger pool of users and past searches, possibly *even* when the value of those data for a specific narrow query diminishes beyond a certain threshold. There may be limits on the amount of improvement to the overall algorithm that can be achieved from larger datasets, but the point of minimum efficient scale from this more holistic perspective is arguably much larger than from the perspective of a single query; future improvements in the models that are used for the development of search algorithms are likely to push these limits even further away, increasing the potential future advantage deriving from bigger pools of data and past searches.

3.3.3 *The Consequences of Natural Concentration*

The cost structure with high fixed costs–zero marginal costs and the role of data (and positive direct network externalities created by data-generating users) make general search a natural monopoly. Other factors further exacerbate this tendency toward concentration. First, the platform model relies on indirect network externalities that benefit advertisers. The more users use the search engine, the more valuable is created for advertisers, which, in turn, means more revenue extracted from advertisers by the search engine that can be invested in the refinement of the algorithm. Second, with the free price of search, the incumbent can exploit the degree of credence good of the service and use to some extent this information

---

[166] Publishing OECD, *Exploring the Economics of Personal Data: A Survey of Methodologies for Measuring Monetary Value*, OECD Digital Economy Papers No. 22 (Strasbourg: OECD, 2013).

asymmetry to reduce quality for users without facing aggressive price responses.[167] Moreover, the weakness of competition is also exacerbated by the importance of default options. As the behavioral economics literature explains, status quo bias seems to be a recurrent feature in online markets, where consumers' willingness to switch is reduced by the force of defaults. As confirmed in various antitrust cases in online markets (among others the investigations against Microsoft and Google), there are various ways through which the force of defaults can be enhanced, for example through preinstallation of specific software and services, or through search bias, which is a form of nudging toward the consumption of services by specific providers, which exploit the scarcity of web space and the transaction costs involved in choosing alternative providers. The force of default options appears particularly pronounced in online search.

In horizontal search, there is also little room for product differentiation. For instance, a general search engine could compete by ensuring better privacy terms, offering different ways of mixing organic/ad-based/proprietary results, or by stressing the pursuit of other ethical objectives, such as the search engine Ecosia, which links the promotion of the search engine to the support of environmental goals.[168] Choices of alternative business models, from ad-based, to subscription and the extent of vertical integration could also to some extent meet consumers' heterogeneous preferences. However, the room for product differentiation remains overall limited, partially as a result of various behavioral biases (consumers often lack objective quality metrics to judge small quality differentials, status quo bias may prevail due to branding and consumers' inertia, etc.). As a result, product differentiation remains a weak counter-force against natural concentration in horizontal search.

Framing a search engine as a natural monopoly has a number of implications when it comes to regulating its market power, which go beyond the standard intervention and remedies of antitrust enforcement. This can be seen by looking at the competition policy investigations against Google for market power leveraging.[169] The central case concerned search bias as a way to leverage market

---

[167] The free price has also other explanations. The behavioral economics literature, for example, has shown that a little price increase starting from zero can be perceived as a larger increase compared to a similar increase starting from above zero. Moreover, even assuming that users were willing to pay, a small price increase would increase substantially transaction costs.

[168] Ecosia's website, for instance, states: "A click on one of the search ads appearing above and next to Ecosia's search results generates revenue for Ecosia, which is paid by the advertiser. Ecosia then donates at least 80% of its monthly profits to plant trees in Burkina Faso, Madagascar and Peru." See "Ecosia – the Search Engine that Plants Trees", available at www.ecosia.org/.

[169] For a discussion, see Edward Iacobucci and Francesco Ducci, "The Google Search Case in Europe: Tying and the Single Monopoly Profit Theorem in Two-Sided Markets" (2019) 47, no. 1, Eur J Law Econ, 15. Luca, et al., also empirically investigate the impact of search bias and find a significant reduction in consumer welfare as a result of Google's favoring of its own products. See Michael Luca, et al., "Does Google Content Degrade Google Search? Experimental Evidence," Harvard Business School Working Paper 16–035 (Harvard Business School, 2016). See also Stucke and Ezrachi, *supra*, note 161; Alexandre de Cornière and Greg Taylor, "Integration and Search Engine Bias" (2014) 45,

power from horizontal search to other vertical search markets. By favoring and giving visual prominence to its proprietary results on Google search, Google induced the consumption of its specialized services, effectively tying them to general search through such bias.

The investigation was originally carried out by the US FTC[170] based on allegations of monopolization under section 2 of the Sherman Act. Vertical search websites alleged that Google unfairly promoted its own vertical properties through changes in its search results page, such as the introduction of the "Universal Search" box, which prominently displayed Google vertical search results in response to certain type of queries, including shopping or local restaurants. The FTC concluded that while Google's prominent display of its own vertical search results may have had the collateral effect of pushing other results below, the main goal was to allow quicker answers that would better satisfy users' search queries. No antitrust concerns were found in relation to the alleged tie between general search and vertical services[171] and the Federal Trade Commission closed its investigations in 2013. In a parallel investigation in Europe[172] originally focused on a number of different concerns,[173] the European Commission sent formal Statements of Objection to Google in 2016[174] for the preferential treatment granted by Google to vertical results

no. 3, RAND J Econ, 576; Benjamin G. Edelman, "Does Google Leverage Market Power Through Tying and Bundling?" (2015) 11, no. 2, J Compet Law Econ, available at www.researchgate.net /publication/277354792_Does_google_leverage_market_power_through_tying_and_bundling. Pinar Akman, "The Theory of Abuse in Google Search: A Positive and Normative Assessment Under EU Competition Law," SSRN Scholarly Paper ID 2811789 (Rochester, NY: Social Science Research Network, 2016).

[170] Federal Trade Commission, Statement of the Federal Trade Commission Regarding Google's Search Practices, In the Matter of Google Inc., FTC File Number 111-0163 January 3, 2013; Federal Trade Commission, *FTC Consumer Protection Staff Updates Agency's Guidance to Search Engine Industry on the Need to Distinguish Between Advertisements and Search Results*, Press Release (Washington, DC, 2013). The investigation included broader concerns of deception (where consumers could not identify which results were advertised results, and Google was required to provide information on the page about which results were determined by advertising auctions).

[171] Julie Brill, *Statement of the Commission Regarding Google's Search Practices*, Statement 111-0163 (Washington, DC: Federal Trade Commission, 2013).

[172] European Commission, *Antitrust: Commission Probes Allegations of Antitrust Violations by Google*, Press Release IP/10/1624 (Brussels: European Commission, 2010), Case AT. 39.740 Google Search (Shopping) (2018/C 9/08).

[173] These allegations include: i) unauthorized content scraping: Google was illegally scraping the content of reviews from competitors' websites without their permission and copying them in its own Google reviews. Such practice was found to be problematic, but Google voluntarily proposed a suitable remedy; ii) exclusivity agreements with advertisers: Google was forcing advertisers to enter into exclusivity agreements by preventing transfer of search advertising campaigns across AdWords and other platforms for search advertising. This was also found to be problematic and Google agreed to stop this practice; iii) limits to portability: Google put limits on the portability of advertising campaigns from its AdWords platform to the platforms of competitors, concerns that were also addressed by Google; iv) search ranking bias: Google was found to favor its specialized vertical search services on its general search ranking page.

[174] See European Commission, *Antitrust: Commission Sends Statement of Objections to Google on Comparison Shopping Service*.

from Google Shopping, as compared to those of its rivals. Although Google does not strictly require searchers to rely on its vertical search engine following the general search – links to services provided by rivals are still ranked – it nonetheless visually favors its own vertical search services providing them with prominent visual space at the center of the page in the OneBox, in particular Google Shopping. The investigation eventually led to the imposition of a $2.4 billion fine and a duty to provide equal treatment to competing specialized services.[175]

Under the lens of competition law enforcement, the concerns with search bias can be expressed as Google tying general search to its separate vertical search engines (by visually favoring its own specialized search services over those of the providers when providing general search results, ultimately excluding rival specialized search engines and reducing consumer's choice),[176] or, alternatively, as abuse of dominance through refusal to deal.

Framing horizontal search as a natural monopoly would, instead, suggest intervention based on attempts to leverage market power from the natural monopoly segment to potentially competitive segments and would possibly require a different set of remedies, including imposition of nondiscriminatory access to essential facilities, and evaluation of structural remedies to divide the identified natural monopoly from competitive segments. Indeed, the remedy imposed by the European Commission at the end of the antitrust investigation – a duty of nondiscrimination – already hints to this dimension of search.

3.4 REGULATING MARKET POWER OF A NATURAL MONOPOLIST IN SEARCH

Antitrust investigations and broader concerns over the negative consequences of a monopoly in search have led to various proposals to address Google's market power. One set of recommendations is designed to make search more competitive

[175] Google has also been facing separate allegations with regards to its mobile operating system Android that led to the imposition of a $4.3 billion fine by the European Commission. In particular, the European Commission found an antitrust violation in the tie between the app store Google Play and Google's search engine through preinstallation on Android mobile devices. Google used financial incentives to convince certain OEMs to adopt the tie and ensure preinstallation of Google's own applications or services, Google search in particular, required preinstallation of Google Search to certain manufacturers as a condition for licensing Google's app store, prevented manufacturers from selling single smart mobile devices running on alternative versions of Android not approved by Google (so-called "Android Forks"). The shift from desktop to mobile interned was possibly a threat to Google position in search, and preinstalment was a way to illegally tie Google Search app (and Google Chrome browser) on Android mobile devices. In the view of the Commission, preinstallation creates a status quo bias in favor of Google search compared to competing engines that need to be downloaded, ultimately resulting in foreclosure of rival search engines and innovation. See European Commission, *Antitrust: Commission Opens Formal Investigation Against Google in Relation to Android Mobile Operating System*, Fact Sheet Memo/15/4782 (Brussels: European Commission, 2015); Case AT.40099 – *Google Android*, July 18, 2018.
[176] Iacobucci and Ducci, *supra*, note 169.

through fragmentation and enhanced inter-platform competition. For example, some have suggested breaking up Google into smaller competing horizontal search engines. Other proposals to foster inter-platform competition suggest a generalized duty to give access to data, for example, under the essential facility doctrine,[177] to facilitate growth of smaller general search engines and entry by new ones. Both proposals aim at reinstalling competition among the newly created search engines, which would have the positive benefit of potentially reducing market power issues on both the users and the advertising side of the market, and it would also undermine the possibility of leveraging market power in vertical search markets. Alternative break-up proposals have included separating Google search from Gmail, YouTube, and other related services, or banning it altogether from entering certain vertical search markets by virtue of its dominance in general search.[178] A different set of policy recommendations instead gravitates toward distortions of intra-platform competition. Among others, the proposal to impose a form of search neutrality in result rankings as a way to avoid favoritism over specialized services, and mandate nondiscriminatory access to search results as an essential facility or the "gateway" to the Internet assume that competition among general search engines cannot be relied upon to discipline intra-platform competition and that intervention is needed to restore competition at play within a dominant search platform.

In this section, the case study rationalizes these proposals in light of the contention that horizontal search is a natural monopoly. If horizontal search is naturally monopolistic, it is generally most efficient to maintain the natural monopoly, because it can attain a lower production cost than could competitive firms in the same industry, Moreover, induced fragmentation will not stop the reemergence of a monopolist. Hence, proposals that focus on inter-platform competition and fragmentation have little scope for the treatment of a natural monopoly. At the same time, market power needs to be regulated in a number of ways. First, one may theoretically impose some form of price regulation (on the price of ad slots but possibly also on the price of searches if the regulator imposed a positive price) to avoid exercise of market power both on the search and on the advertising side of the market. Second, natural monopoly regulation would need to address issues of vertical integration between the natural monopoly segment (general search) and other potentially competitive segments (for example, certain specialized search services, or emails) to avoid attempts of anticompetitive leveraging that have already emerged in antitrust cases.

---

[177] Zachary Abrahamson, "Essential Data" (2014) 124, no. 3, Yale Law J, available at https://digitalcom mons.law.yale.edu/ylj/vol124/iss3/7. See also Cédric Argenton and Jens Prüfer, "Search Engine Competition with Network Externalities" (2012) 8, no. 1, J Compet Law Econ, 73.

[178] Tim Wu, *The Master Switch: The Rise and Fall of Information Empires*, 1st ed. (New York: Alfred A. Knopf, 2010).

When evaluating the boundaries of possible forms of intervention, it is important to stress the critical role played by the specific technological features of search, and the ways in which they alter important assumptions behind forms of market power abuse and the feasibility of remedies in ways that have been neglected in the literature. First, the technological evolution of search shows that the emerging concerns over market power – leveraging in particular – take place as part of a shift from ranked results toward universal search. On the one hand, more integration between horizontal and vertical services has some important efficiency benefits. Users may enjoy quicker answers, advertisers may have reduced transaction costs of dealing with multiple platforms, and the search algorithm can become even better as a result of a higher variety of data. On the other hand, this transition over universal search implies more artificial scarcity, which can be exploited through the process of merging horizontal and vertical into universal search. When search results are organic, rankings are not neutral in an absolute sense but follow specific parameters where winners are selected through a selected proxy for relevance. With advertised results, results are based on auctions and winners are determined by bids, which can be based on a per-click basis or based on the number of views. Differently from organic and advertised results, the introduction of universal search reduces the extent of available competition by imposing scarcity (one direct result instead of a ranking) in the transition toward more integration between horizontal and vertical search. In this light, a possible reading of leveraging cases is that they are attempts to ensure monopolization of specialized segments as the inevitable transition toward universal search occurs. The hard policy choice is determining and identifying the segments where such a shift is more problematic. For example, the integration on general search of direct answers to cinema running times or song lyrics does not seem so much of a concern, but what of direct answers to flight booking, job search, traffic and maps, or weather? In some cases, integration is not likely to pose competition issues of exclusion due to induced scarcity, while in others it may.

Second, the technological characteristics of search give an unconventional form to exercises of market power. For example, exercising market power over searchers takes the form of quality reduction rather than price increases but evaluating the quality of search results is inherently problematic and ambiguous, especially considering the continuous refinements of and changes to the search algorithm. Similarly, tying usually implies contractually conditioning the purchase of good A with good B or technological tying. In search, tying strategies are subtler. Search bias is a form of tie that induces the selection of specific tied goods through visual prominence and richer graphics, and preinstallation exploits status quo bias and end-user's inertia to achieve the same goal. Search bias and visual prominence induces more clicks, and status quo bias reduces incentives to switch and install alternative providers. Neither form implies a strict obligation to use two products together, as it is for conventional tie-ins. However, both are ways to induce the selection of tied goods exploiting some of the biases identified in the behavioral economics literature and confirmed by experimental evidence. Interventions need to wrestle with the idea that the technology of search makes market power abuses harder to detect.

Third and last, the technological characteristics of search determine the scope and feasibility of the principal remedies against market power. For instance, they complicate price regulation, because determining appropriate pricing for search queries or regulation of the quality of search is inherently problematic. In the same way, usual antitrust remedies against unconventional forms of tying are not straightforward because requiring the firm not to tie can have ambiguous meanings and these forms of subtle inducement make the notion of untying less straightforward (in the case of bias, this could mean banning visual prominence or hardwired links, or allowing visual prominence but giving searchers the option to choose which provider they would want in the OneBox, and in the case of preinstallation this could mean a screen choice among competitors or imposing preinstallation of the harmed competitor). Moreover, with regard to structural remedies the boundaries of separations in a technologically dynamic environment like search are more fluid and less clear-cut, unlike traditional public utilities, such as electricity or water.

At the same time, the technological dimensions of search also provide reasons why certain remedies may be more promising than is usually assumed. For example, while boundaries between different segments may be very hard to identify when implementing vertical break-ups and some important economies of scope from data may be lost after separation, the fact that discriminatory behavior is hard to detect may justify clean and clear-cut distance between the natural monopoly segment and adjacent markets offered by structural remedies. Similarly, mandated access to the essential facility has an untapped potential that stems from the fact that scarcity constraints are alleviated by the technological features of search engines, where access can be framed in statistical terms across equivalent searches and top results shared on a rotational basis. Hence, the problems of scarcity and shareability of essentials inputs generally confronted with physical facilities are overcome when the number of similar searches done on a search engine is statistically significant, which allows to reframe scarcity of rankings and top results in the web real estate from a probabilistic perspective and on a rotational basis. If the desired form of intervention were to impose equal access to a natural monopoly segment, this may benefit from the fact that it occurs in a world of lower scarcity constraints.

In light of the identified general technological features of search, the case study now evaluates the desirability of price regulation of searches and search ads, the role of competition law enforcement as a quasi-structural remedy, vertical separation remedies, and nondiscriminatory access to horizontal search as the essential facility.

3.4.1 *Regulating the Price of Searches and Search Ads*

The regulation of a natural monopolist's market power generally involves price regulation. For example, one may calculate the rate that would allow the search engine to cover its total cost plus a fair rate of return on investments, and impose price-cap regulation and ceilings on the increase in prices over search and advertising services.

Regulating prices of a general search engine presents an immediate hurdle created by the zero price for search. On the searchers' side, market power is exercised through reductions of quality and not by price increases and without positive prices, the regulator could only regulate quality of search rather than pricing. Alternatively, price regulation could be made possible by imposing a positive price to users, forcing the adoption of a different business model not based on free search, but on users' subscription. The regulator could then set subscription prices charged by the search engine. The advertising side of a search engine is where the natural monopolist may exercise market power through price increases (which is plausibly occurring given that marginal costs of providing advertising services are very low and advertisers are positively charged). In the advertising market, regulation would not only set the price that can be charged to advertisers for search ads placements, but possibly determine output and the number of ad slots that should be available on the general search page.

Beyond the problems raised by the current two-sided business model with zero price on one side, there are additional problems related to the determination of the regulated price. For searchers, there is no reference point of positive prices charged by other providers, and the quality of search has many dimensions, some of which are detectable (for example, the levels of privacy protection and the use of users' data), some harder to evaluate given that the nature of different search queries can vary (quality reduction can mean more advertising but ads can be valued differently by different customers). For advertisers, bids could be capped at a rate subject to cost recoupment for Google. However, determining the appropriate rate of return for a successful search engine that has obtained a natural monopoly position remains challenging, and regulating the amount of ad slots would also interfere substantially with web-page design. The issue of price regulation becomes even more complex when introducing the problem of vertical downstream integration and the different nature of search results. For example, should the price of all ads be regulated, or only certain segments on a case-by-case basis. As discussed below, caps on auctions may be introduced as part of a remedy that imposes equal access to specific competitive areas of search, but if the natural monopolist is also competing for bids on its own search engine price, regulation needs to account for the possibility that the pricing of auctions does not undermine the objective of the remedy.

All in all, monopoly pricing is not a concern for searchers given the zero price of search, although it must be noted that there are various forms of nonprice exploitation (reduction of quality, privacy, misuse of data) that may remain problematic on the searchers' side. Price regulation may instead be deemed necessary on the advertising side where market power can be exploited by the natural monopolist in search. It is not implausible that the market power obtained by Google's natural monopoly position in horizontal search is indeed exercised on advertisers, who pay well above the marginal cost of advertising services offered by Google.

The case for intervention against exploitative exercises of market power depends on the degree of allocative efficiency that this generates – for example, how large is the welfare loss for advertisers, how much is passed on to final consumers in terms of higher prices due to the higher costs of ad campaigns, and possible benefits that may arise for consumers due to less advertising output. In order to justify price regulation, one may have to identify the potential improvements to these market imperfections that price regulation promises to address and evaluate whether the expected benefits justify the costs associated with price regulation. It is plausible that the allocative problem associated with exploitative exercises of market power in horizontal search is not insignificant, given that the force of entry and market responses appear to be weak, but it remains unclear whether this market power concern may justify, on its own, direct intervention through price regulation.

An alternative to direct regulation is provided by market contestability. One of the real threats to the naturally monopolistic features of a market is technological changes that create enough shifts in market conditions that disrupt the natural monopolist. Because the very notion of natural monopoly depends on the state of technology in production, changes in demand, reduction of fixed costs, and rise in variable costs are all factors that may eliminate the preconditions for efficient concentration and change the desired policy approach, possibly leading to full or partial deregulation. A natural monopolist in search, analogously, is likely to face little effective head-to-head competition from existing competing general-purpose search engines; its major threat may instead come from niche markets that may eventually disrupt the technological foundations of its natural monopoly position. To the extent that this threat can provide a plausible constraint to market power exercises by a monopolist in horizontal search, competition policy may play a quasi-structural role to alleviate possible barriers against disruption created by the incumbent monopolist – for example, by blocking preemptive acquisition of potential competitors by a natural monopolist in search, or evaluating the possible role of defensive tying strategies in precluding the emergence of a potential disruptor. This enforcement approach that attempts to keeps at play a degree of contestability can at least mitigate market power exercises in the absence of price regulation.

3.4.2 *Structural Remedies to Separate the Natural Monopoly Segment*

Even if one were to reject the case for regulating price/quality of search and advertising services, there still remains, however, a compelling case for intervention

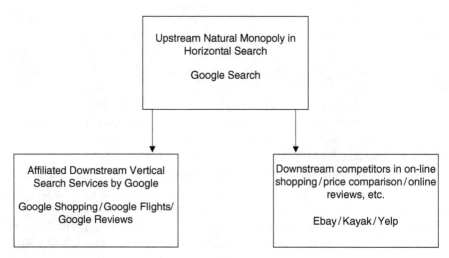

FIGURE 3.4 Upstream and downstream segments of search

to deal with discrimination and leveraging that can arise from vertical integration. In network industries, the natural monopoly in the distribution network can often support competitive upstream or downstream activities in which the natural monopolist itself participates and may have the incentives and ability to restrict access to an essential input by raising the price, lowering the quality, or reducing the timeliness of access relative to its own affiliates (see Figure 3.4). The standard concern with a vertically integrated natural monopolist is that it can leverage market power to monopolize competitive segments. For example, an electricity firm integrated in generation and transmission could limit competition from rival generators by raising the price that they pay for access to the transmission network, or a telecommunication operator can reduce competition from long-distance operators by raising price at which rivals access the local loop. Analogously, Google horizontal search is the "distribution network" for potentially competitive specialized segments where Google's downstream services (vertical search services such as Google Shopping or Google Flight) also operate. Foreclosing competition can occur by denying access to general search as the upstream input, but also through delays in providing access or lower quality, setting high prices for access to the input, which may give the search natural monopolist an advantage in downstream, specialized search markets.

As evidenced by antitrust case law, there is considerable evidence that Google is engaging in discriminatory behavior against rival vertical search firms and in favor of Google's downstream operations through search bias. Businesses compete for a place high up on Google's search rankings, and they also compete to buy well-placed positions in Google's paid advertisements. This leaves the natural monopolist in a position where it can ensure that rival services appear lower on the organic rankings, distort prices at which ad search is available to rival products, degrade their visibility, or enhance visual prominence of its own services. Discrimination and leveraging are particularly problematic because they distort both *intra*-platform competition in potentially competitive segments of specialized search, and *inter*-platform competition, insofar as this kind of behavior may be targeting nascent, potential competitors that may threaten an established dominant position in horizontal search.

A potential solution to these concerns is the imposition of structural remedies, either in the form of prophylactic bans or vertical separation between natural monopoly and competitive segments. Both remedies have the advantage of eliminating the problem of discriminatory behavior at the root, but have also specific limitations on their own, which are discussed below. Prophylactic bans preclude ex ante entry into specific markets. A version of this approach can be found for instance in Wu's separation principle,[179] who argues that Google should not be allowed to enter any vertical search markets based on the idea that "the people who move and carry information should stay at some distance from the creators of content, because they have a natural conflict of interest." The original proposal for a separation principle as applied to, among others, Google is not a regulatory approach but rather a constitutional principle of division of power applied to the information economy, but it is practically equivalent to the logic of prophylactic bans imposed on a natural monopolist, which attempt to prevent ex ante the incentive to leverage market power. One of the problems with this approach, at least from a competition perspective, is that it excludes by default a competitor from a competitive segment, ultimately making the market targeted by prophylactic bans less fragmented. Another issue is that in the abstract it is hard to find a grounded economic principle that can be used to distinguish downstream vertical search segments that require bans from those where entry by the natural monopolist should be allowed. In some markets, bans may be more desirable than others, and it remains unclear whether prophylactic bans should apply to all sectors or to specific segments.

Another form of structural remedy is vertical separation, which eliminates incentives to leverage market power by separating the natural monopoly segment from competitive adjacent markets. Rather than restricting entry, this remedy imposes various degrees of separation, from accounting to ownership, that eliminate the source of discriminatory behavior and anticompetitive cross-subsidization. In the same way as a standard network industry like electricity, where it might be desirable to separate the generation of the electricity from its transmission and possibly other competitive segments of the market, separation may be implemented between Google search and other Google's business, including specialized services like YouTube, Waze, DoubleClick, Google Shopping, or Gmail.

---

[179] Ibid.

One major problem in implementing this remedy is to identify clearly the point of separation from the natural monopoly asset, in this case, horizontal search from other specialized services. While the two may be distinct products for customers, they are, also in fact, interlinked as part of a process that tends toward more and more integration between the two. The introduction of universal search is in itself an example of how the boundary between the two forms of search can blur, possibly leading to a model where a general search engine platform becomes the direct provider of content merging together the two different products.[180] This can be seen even more dramatically in the change that may be created by digital personal assistants, which in many ways perform functions analogous to those of search and have the potential to further dictate direct responses and induce scarcity of results. Technological developments in search may potentially render separation problematic and if implemented would possibly require future amendments.

Once the point of separation is identified, there are still various synergies and efficiencies that remain to be considered before implementing the remedy. For example, vertical integration creates economies of scope in the analysis of data from specialized services that improve the quality of the predictive algorithm. Separation may reduce these synergies when the same data are used as inputs both for the natural monopoly and the competitive segment that is being divested. Moreover, separation can increase the cost for advertisers when the two services have some complementarity that is inevitably lost by separating the two entities.

Since vertical integration in the context of search can produce real efficiencies of various kinds that are lost with structural separation, it is important to evaluate how great are the costs and lost efficiencies arising from vertical integration vis-à-vis the benefits associated with the removal of the ability and incentive to discriminate, and then compare them with the costs and benefits of alternative forms of intervention, such as ongoing oversight implicit in an access remedy.[181] Overall, structural separation remains a remedy of last resort, and should be avoided when behavioral remedies are available and feasible.

3.4.3 *Access to Horizontal Search as an Essential Facility*

Behavioral remedies arguably provide a more promising approach to address vertical integration and discriminatory behavior by a natural monopolist in horizontal search. This is not only because access remedies avoid efficiency losses implicit is separation, but also because digital inputs encounter reduced scarcity and shareability constraints due to digitalization.

---

[180]   "Building the Search Engine of the Future, One Baby Step at a Time" (August 8, 2012), available at www.blog.google/products/search/building-search-engine-of-future-one/.
[181]   In this regard it must also be noted is that structural separation of search in distinct entities may still require a degree of ongoing monitoring.

As a starting point, it needs to be pointed out that concerns over discriminatory behavior at the root of recent antitrust investigations have led to broader proposals to introduce and enforce principles of "search neutrality." In general, search neutrality is the principle that search engines should return only the most relevant results without manipulation or biases. Yet the principle of neutrality in search is complicated by the fact that search engines, by design, cannot be completely impartial. Relevance is in itself a form of bias that ranks some results over others in the attempt to satisfy user's queries and preferences. Since relevance is subjective, search neutrality, in practice, has different meanings. It can imply a principle of transparency in a search engine's ranking algorithm, with obvious problems associated with auditing the algorithm; or it can imply a number of different more targeted constraints, such as intervention against active demotion of particular competitors, banning ad-based results altogether, or imposing limits to results provided by the search engine's specialized services. A narrow interpretation of search neutrality under a natural monopoly framework should be translated as a duty of equal treatment between verticals of Google and third-party downstream competitors, essentially a ban on self-preferential treatment in the general search segment as the essential facility. Such a remedy would attempt to ensure equal footing between downstream specialized search competitors and the vertically integrated natural monopolist in search.

Commentators have debated the possibility of applying the essential facility doctrine to online search engines,[182] and many have criticized the possibility of applying the doctrine to Google. Bork and Sidak, for instance, have argued that Google is not the "gateway" to the Internet, because users can switch to other search engines at zero cost, or navigate directly to websites,[183] elements that exclude the possibility of Google having a monopoly over search, while also proving the feasibility of duplicating the facility. They argue that a lower ranking cannot be considered a denial of access and that it is technologically infeasible to grant access to top results, because the facility cannot be provided simultaneously to all firms that require it, and that, in any case, it would be unpractical for a court to give access to top placements. Similarly, Lao criticizes the notion of neutral search that could lead to antitrust liability of Google,[184] because such exercise would be highly subjective, and no antitrust theory of harm would require search neutrality. Lao claims that Google does not possess monopoly power in an antitrust sense, no Google rival has been denied access, and the resource (first-ranked positions) is not shareable. In addition, Lao argues that the procompetitive effects of search bias outweigh any

---

[182] Marina Lao, "Search, Essential Facilities, and the Antitrust Duty to Deal" (2012) 11 *Northwestern Journal of Technology and Intellectual Property*, 275.

[183] Robert Bork and Gregory Sidak, "What Does the Chicago School Teach about Internet Search and the Antitrust Treatment of Google?" (2012) 4 *Journal of Competition Law and Economics*, 663, at 679.

[184] Marina Lao, "'Neutral' Search as a Basis for Antitrust Action?," SSRN Scholarly Paper ID 2245295 (Rochester, NY: Social Science Research Network, 2013).

incidental adverse effect on competition, and that imposing a duty to provide access would jeopardize the search engine evolution and distort competition in the broad online information market.[185]

Such conclusions are erroneous. In the light of the technological characteristics of search, there are, in particular, two major recurrent misrepresentations of how access to general search as the essential facility should be evaluated. The first error lies in the definition of what may represent a refusal to provide access to an essential input. Lao, for instance, argues that the facility could be the search engine itself, or the top-ranked results listings, and conclude that, in the former case, the facility can be shared but there is no denial, while in the latter case, the facility is not shareable, because there is only one first-ranked position, one-second ranked position, and so on. The critical input should, however, be evaluated pragmatically by looking at where the search engine imposes artificial scarcity and by taking into account the dynamic evolution of the general search page. Competitors, for instance, have required access to the area of the page with richer graphics (which appears to induce selection) where competition has been by default eliminated and substituted by Google's products, such as with the OneBox area or hardwired links. Discrimination can take various forms and includes subtle ways to restrict access to the essential input. Currently, the general search page is divided in three qualitatively different results, where competition is present for organic and advertised results but not for hardwired links and OneBox results. This part of the page is the central and qualitatively different section of the page where the natural monopolist discriminates in favor of its own services. The change in product design or technological upgrade of search through universal results has been accompanied by artificial scarcity to discriminate in favor of Google's downstream segments that provide vertical search services. The essential input is the horizontal search webpage "real estate," and refusal can be implemented in a variety of different ways that artificially restrict access to a critically important and available input.

A second related and critical mistake is that the input in horizontal search can in fact be shared more easily than standard physical facilities. Accepting for the sake of argument that access to top results is essential for competitive viability, Lao, for example, argues that Google's top results represent an intrinsically nonshareable property.[186] This, however, misinterprets the nature of search. It is true that a response to a specific query can provide only a limited number or results, or even one single result within the OneBox due to the limited web real estate space. This, however, is not necessarily true in a statistical sense when accounting for the number of identical or equivalent queries that are performed on the search engine. If, for instance, the same query is presented 1,000 times a day by different searchers, there is a possibility of sharing the facility within those 1,000 equivalent queries and

[185] Ibid, at 279.
[186] Lao, *supra*, note 182, at 304.

keywords. In the same way that Google already provides different responses to different users for the same query, and sometimes provides different results from the same query made by the same user, it would be plausible to suggest that the search engine could provide access by alternating in a probabilistic way top organic results or results inside the OneBox, possibly allocating a given default quota for Google's specialized results. This technological aspect of search makes the essential facility less constrained by scarcity and more prone to shareability.

A remedy of access to general search could therefore be implemented in the following way. The regulator would impose a duty on the natural monopolist to allocate web space through probabilistic ballots within the OneBox, and possibly other relevant areas of search. For example, Google could be required to statistically allocate in the OneBox a number of vertical competitors that are highly ranked based on organic results, leaving a quota of results as a default for Google's services. This option would retain the visual structure of the OneBox, and take seriously the qualitative difference created by visual prominence by forcing a form of competition within the OneBox. Alternatively, such spaces could be based on bids, but arguably the price should be capped, again leaving for Google a quota by default to avoid the problem of requiring Google to auction to itself. Finally, a complementary option could be to give consumers a choice to select their default option for particular vertical services, such as maps, shopping, or reviews. This remedy is similar to the one adopted in the Microsoft case on browsers, where Microsoft was required to give a choice of browser at the moment of installing the operating system. This option could be a viable complementary alternative to the expansion of access capabilities through statistically allocated results.

As a remedy, access to search as an essential facility has a number of limitations when taking the institutional dimension of intervention into account. First, regulating access would require ongoing oversight, either by an industry regulator or in its absence through competition policy intervention. The latter, however, must be able to administer and monitor access remedies through novel and faster procedures beyond standard antitrust ex post procedures, which generally entail complex legal and economic analysis and case-by-case remedies. Administering nondiscriminatory rules would, in any event, be complex, because the access remedy would have to account for the many ways in which the natural monopolist could succeed in monopolizing back the competitive segment by providing subtle undue benefits to its downstream entity, eventually asking the regulator to dictate many aspects of product design. Implementing the probabilistic ballot over areas of the search page would also be costly. It would be almost impossible to enforce this kind of remedy in the entire universe of search queries, and it could effectively work only for significantly popular queries and specific areas of search. Since the goal of the remedy is to provide nondiscriminatory access while the natural monopolist is operating in the same downstream market, imposing the rotation of ad-based results would necessitate dictating what kind of rotational results are allocated (should results only include organic results, or also include advertised results? In that case, should the price of bids be capped? What quota should be allocated by default to Google's specialized services?).

In spite of these considerations, the complexities associated with access remedies are not insurmountable, especially given the benefits that a properly enforced access remedy can bring in this context compared to structural approaches. Since the major challenges posed by nondiscrimination rules as a way to address leveraging by a natural monopolist in search are institutional rather than substantial, a focus of policy intervention may be to create the institutional preconditions for an effective application, enforcement, and administrability of behavioral remedies.

3.5 CONCLUSION

The first case study of this book advances the argument that horizontal search, which is a predictive technology that covers universally all general information and subjects on the web, is a natural monopoly. While the multisided platform model contributes to market concentration, because more searchers make it more valuable for advertisers, it is not the platform model alone that turns search into a natural monopoly. It is, instead, the combination of a cost structure typical of standard network industries and the central value of data in general search. On the supply side, high fixed costs and marginal costs of serving both users and advertisers close to zero resembles the price structure of standard natural monopolies, which is likely giving rise to subadditivity and decreasing average costs. On the demand side, an additional searcher not only provides a positive externality for advertisers but, most importantly, for other searchers because more users improve the quality and efficiency of search as a whole. The value of additional data for the efficiency of the search algorithm stems from two important characteristics of horizontal search: its core function as a prediction technology more than a matchmaking one; and the extensive domain of search predictions that need to be performed and covered by a general purpose search engine (as opposed to specialized or vertical search engines).

While the case for price regulation of advertising may not be immediately and necessarily compelling, regulating market power of a natural monopolist to address issues of leveraging and discrimination is necessary, given that the evolution of search and emerging antitrust case law show how the shift from neutral to universal search has been accompanied by attempts to extend market power to monopolize competitive segments. Access to general search as the essential input for downstream competition among specialized search providers can be restricted through various forms of discrimination by the natural monopolist that wants to favor its specialized services. The case study highlighted how the technological features of search make access remedies potentially appealing, insofar as they are less affected by scarcity and shareability constraints than it is often assumed.

The conclusions reached in the case study on horizontal search offer important lessons that may have some pertinence for policy approaches in digital industries at a more general level. On the one hand, traditional public utility-like regulation of price and access done by a hypothetical industry regulator may, in theory, address the identified market power problems associated with a natural monopoly search platform; however, a real-world regulator for horizontal search is likely to face a number of possibly insurmountable limitation and challenges, especially in technologically fast and fluid industries. These costs and uncertainties faced by a hypothetical stand-alone horizontal search regulator may outweigh the benefits of standard regulatory intervention. On the other hand, reliance on competition policy in the presence of a natural monopoly platform inevitably requires recourse to more structural and quasi-structural approaches, as well as remedies that are more regulatory in nature and demand a degree ongoing oversight and monitoring. This form of ex post intervention implies a set of institutional capabilities that often exceeds the current reach and comparative advantage of many institutions in charge of competition policy enforcement.

4

E-Commerce Marketplaces

The second case study looks at e-commerce platforms and, in particular, at the emergence of Amazon Marketplace as another possible candidate for natural monopoly regulation. Often accused of being the contemporary equivalent of nineteenth-century robber barons, and a major threat to jobs and wages, weakening communities, and squeezing smaller retailers.[187] Amazon's position in e-commerce has led to a number of proposals to tame its dominance.[188] For example, Nobel laureate Paul Krugman has accused Amazon of abusing monopsony power and called for stronger antitrust intervention, arguing that it has reached a position comparable to Standard Oil in the 1900s,[189] and the current US administration has also expressed willingness to evaluate possible antitrust options,[190] driven especially by concerns over jobs and smaller retailers. The neo-Brandesian or "hipster" antitrust movement has also advocated for radical reforms to current competition policy doctrines, on the grounds that consumer welfare and efficiency oriented policies have failed to address the types of anticompetitive conduct occurring in the digital economy, targeting in particular Amazon as owning the central infrastructure of online commerce that charges low prices to consumers while disrupting small retailers and increasing concerns over inequality.[191] These proposals seek to reorient competition law back to its older, polycentric orientation focused on the protection of the liberty of producers as well as the welfare of consumers, and on concentration of economic power as a threat to both the economy and democracy.[192] Public utility regulation has also been proposed on

---

[187] See, generally, Khan, *supra*, note 2.

[188] "Amazon, the World's Most Remarkable Firm, Is Just Getting Started," *The Economist* (March 25, 2017), available at www.economist.com/leaders/2017/03/25/amazon-the-worlds-most-remarkable-firm -is-just-getting-started.

[189] Paul Krugman, "Opinion | Amazon's Monopsony Is Not O.K.," *NY Times* (December 21, 2017), available at www.nytimes.com/2014/10/20/opinion/paul-krugman-amazons-monopsony-is-not-ok.html.

[190] CNBC, "Trump says Amazon has 'a Huge Antitrust Problem'," (May 13, 2016, available at www .cnbc.com/2016/05/13/trump-says-amazon-has-a-huge-antitrust-problem.html.

[191] Medvedovsky, *supra*, note 5.

[192] Alexei Alexis, "FTC Head Pushes Back on Calls to Expand Antitrust Law," (September 15, 2017), available at https%3A%2F%2Fwww.bna.com%2Fftc-head-pushes-n57982088021%2F; Virginia Postrel,

the ground that Amazon manages an essential infrastructure for Internet commerce,[193] and is de facto the gatekeeper of online retail and distribution.

This case study investigates whether Amazon's online marketplace should be characterized as a natural monopoly and regulated as such. Implicit in this hypothesis, as often framed in policy debates on excessive concentration in e-commerce, is the idea that a dominant online shopping platform benefits from positive network effects between buyers and sellers, which drive concentrated market structures. The case study reaches the opposite conclusion to the one presented in Chapter 3 on horizontal search. In particular, it provides an explanation as to why Amazon's e-commerce marketplace, unlike horizontal search, should not be described as a natural monopoly and why Amazon's competitive advantage instead lies in having efficiently invested in combining a large online market place with an infrastructure for delivery and logistics that is superior to the one offered by competitors. In concluding that Amazon Marketplace should not be described as a natural monopoly, the case study also points to the fallacy of ascribing to the platform nature alone (and indirect network externalities) the source of concentration and dominance. As the case study points out, Amazon online marketplace is not a pure platform but a hybrid between a reseller and a matchmaker, and the importance of its logistics and infrastructure, which is somewhat unrelated to the platform business model, is plausibly as important or possibly more important than the online marketplace itself.

The chapter first looks at the growth and evolution of Amazon and at some of the market power concerns that are linked to the winner-takes-all features of e-commerce. It then evaluates the possible sources driving concentration and shows that neither network effects nor scale economies are strong enough to make Amazon Marketplace a natural monopoly. Based on this conclusion, the case study points to some of the competition policy enforcement priorities that may be pertinent to e-commerce.

4.1 THE EVOLUTION OF AMAZON: FROM NICHE ENTRY TO THE EVERYTHING STORE

Founded in 1994 as an online book retailer, Amazon rapidly evolved into an online "everything store."[194] Guided by a vision to become the world's most customer centric company,[195] a few years after the creation of the original virtual bookshop, Amazon expanded into many sectors, including CDs and DVDs, toys, electronics, clothing, jewelry, cloud computing, data processing and networking services, consumer electronics, digital content, and food delivery. Today, it is the largest online

---

"U.S. Antitrust Law Is Not Broken," *Bloomberg* (September 29, 2017), available at www.bloomberg.com /opinion/articles/2017–09–29/u-s-antitrust-law-is-not-broken.

[193] Khan, *supra*, note 2.

[194] Brad Stone, *The Everything Store: Jeff Bezos and the Age of Amazon* (New York: Little, Brown, 2013).

[195] Ibid.

retailer in the United States.[196] In 2007, it also launched its popular e-book reader, Kindle, which allows customers to download e-books on the e-book platform rather than purchasing physical copies,[197] and now Amazon dominates the market for e-book devices, despite the entrance of multiple players such as Apple's iPad, Barnes & Noble's Nook, and Sony's Reader. Estimates suggest that Amazon might account for 70 percent of the online book market whereas Barnes & Nobles might have a market share of 15 percent and the remaining 15 percent is shared among more than 7,000 fringe e-retailers.[198] Similarly, its cloud-computing business, Amazon Web Services (AWS), is larger in terms of basic computing services than the three closest competing cloud offerings combined. Other services include original television content through Amazon Studio, and the voice-activated home digital assistants, Echo and Alexa. Most recently, Amazon also entered the grocery market with the acquisition of Whole Foods. Amazon's net sales have accelerated from $34billion in 2010, to $48 billion in 2014 and $107 billion in 2015, becoming the fastest company ever to reach more than $100 billion in annual sales.[199] It is the world's fifth most valuable listed company worth over $400bn, and as the biggest online retailer in America, it is still growing more quickly than the 17 percent pace of e-commerce as a whole.[200]

In its major business segment, e-commerce, Amazon's growth is the perfect example of niche entry that eventually disrupts an entire sector. After officially starting in a small market segment and branding itself as the "earth's biggest book-store," transforming book purchases from paper to digital, just a few years later its online marketplace became the virtual version of large retail stores and shopping malls with a vast selection of retail goods. Today, Amazon has expanded into almost every business line, with a full department directory that is promised to comprise "earth's biggest selection." On the demand side, Amazon achieved its success by pursuing a policy of low prices and convenience of delivery. Through Prime, Amazon has created a powerful instrument around consumer goods that depends not only on low prices, but also on reducing the frictions and transaction costs in buying and obtaining the goods. As stated by a former Amazon's representative, "it was never about [the fee]. It was really about changing people's mentality so they wouldn't shop anywhere else."[201] On the supply side, it developed and acquired a distribution network that allows it to manage logistics in a highly efficient way,

---

[196] See Statista, "Amazon – Statistics and Facts," available at www.statista.com/topics/846/amazon/; Financial Times, "The Whole Foods Fight is Amazon's Chance to Conquer Supermarkets," available at www.ft.com/content/71dfaf2e-52ae-11e7-bfb8-997009366969.
[197] Yabing Jiang, "E-Book Platform Competition in the Presence of Two-Sided Network Externalities," SSRN Scholarly Paper ID 2164395 (Rochester, NY: Social Science Research Network, 2012).
[198] Austan Goolsbee and Judith Chevalier, "Measuring Prices and Price Competition Online: Amazon and Barnes and Noble," NBER Working Papers 9085 (National Bureau of Economic Research, Inc., 2002).
[199] Jeff P. Bezos, *Letter from Jeff Bezos to Amazon.com Stakeholders (2015) in Amazon.com Annual Report (2015)* (2016); Amazon, *Form 10-Km for the Fiscal Year Ended December 31, 2015* (2016).
[200] *The Economist, supra,* note 188.
[201] Stone, *supra,* note 194 at 287.

benefiting from scale economies in storage and distribution. Since 2010, for example, Amazon has spent $13.9 billion building warehouses.[202]

Amazon's expansion in e-commerce has also comprised an evolution toward hybrid co-existing business models between marketplace and retailer, where the platform model has not always been as predominant as it is assumed. Beginning from e-books, Amazon started off not as a platform where the e-book provider acts as the middleman through whom readers consume content and publishers sell to readers,[203] but by buying books from publishers at wholesale acting more as a reseller than as a platform. In its Marketplace more generally, it also started by operating as a reseller, and only around 2000 did introduce a marketplace model allowing third-party sellers to sell their products directly to Amazon customers, while remaining also a direct reseller on its own platform. Eventually, the marketplace model became extensive. In 2013, for example, Amazon had more than 2 million third-party sellers that sold their products in the Marketplace, which accounted for about 40 percent of Amazon's sales,[204] and fees from sellers around the world who use Amazon reached $23bn in 2016, nearly twice what they were in 2014.[205] However, the marketplace model remains coexistent with the retail model and did not eliminate incentives to vertically integrate by entering various segments as a direct supplier of its own brand products. Due to this hybridity, Amazon can for example obtain transaction data on third-party selling on its platform to identify popular products and markets where it may be profitable to enter as a direct seller. An empirical assessment based on data on electronics, toys and games, home and garden tools, and sports and outdoors suggests that Amazon uses its Marketplace as a learning venue to decide whether or not it should enter certain product markets.[206] In particular, Amazon entry is more likely for products with higher prices, lower shipping costs, and greater demand, and likelihood of entry increases with a product's customer ratings.[207] The study also finds that Amazon is less likely to enter a product space of a third-party seller that uses Amazon's distribution system. Amazon's entry as a direct seller reduces shipping costs, but discourages third-party sellers from continuing to offer the products and discourages them from growing

---

[202] Daniella Kucera, "Why Amazon Is on a Warehouse Building Spree," (August 29, 2013), available at www.bloomberg.com/news/articles/2013-08-29/why-amazon-is-on-a-warehouse-building-spree.

[203] See, for instance, Jiang, *supra*, note 197.

[204] Mark Faggiano, "Fulfillment by Amazon: What Amazon Doesn't Tell Third-Party Sellers," (January 8, 2014), available at https://venturebeat.com/2014/01/08/fulfillment-by-amazon-what-amazon-doesnt-tell-third-party-sellers/.

[205] "Are Investors Too Optimistic About Amazon?," *The Economist* (March 25, 2017), available at www.economist.com/briefing/2017/03/25/are-investors-too-optimistic-about-amazon.

[206] Stone, *supra*, note 194 at 182. "If you don't know anything about the business, launch it through the Marketplace, bring retailers in, watch what they do and what they sell, understand it, and then get into it" (quote from Randy Miller, former Director of Merchandise Planning at Amazon).

[207] Feng Zhu and Liu Qihong, "Competing with Complementors: An Empirical Look at Amazon.com," (2015), available at https://mackinstitute.wharton.upenn.edu/wp-content/uploads/2015/04/Zhu-Feng-Liu-Qihong_Competing-with-Complementors.-An-Empirical-Look-at-Amazon.com.pdf.

TABLE 4.1 *Alternative structures for e-commerce marketplaces*

Pure Marketplace	Hybrid Platform	One-Sided Model
A marketplace with sellers setting prices and other selling conditions, etc. (eBay model)	Vertical integration in various segments in competition with independent third-party sellers	The firm buys products and resells them in the marketplace without giving access to independent third-party sellers

their businesses on the platform. Moreover, Amazon may present itself as the default seller even when third-party sellers' products are offered at lower cost with comparable shipping speeds and when these third-party sellers have high ratings (see Table 4.1).

Hybridity is not only at play in the choice of business model, but is also present in the relations between Amazon and third parties, which entail different forms of contractual arrangements that differ in the share of inventory risk and control Amazon takes on. For instance, some suppliers sell products through Amazon's website while still performing many of the related functions themselves, such as maintaining ownership, shipping, and setting prices on inventory. By contrast, under alternative arrangements, Amazon operates as a platform for third-party suppliers, but it takes inventory in its distribution centers and completes order fulfillment functions itself.

Amazon's philosophy based on growth rather than profitability has not only been sustained by this kind of aggressive market entry and vertical integration in various sectors, but also by a policy of low prices.[208] For instance, the price of e-books has often been set at $9.99 – in many cases, below the wholesale price – which has been labeled as predatory by publishers and other industry participants[209] and as the cause of extensive depression of physical bookstores, whose numbers in the US have dropped from 12,363 in 1997[210] to 8,407 in 2011.[211] Low prices have been adopted also in many other areas of Amazon Marketplace, including Amazon Prime, where observers have noted that Prime members cost Amazon more than annual revenue, losing on average $11 annually by collecting a $119 membership fee.[212] Due to large investments to enter new markets and low prices, Amazon remained unprofitable for

[208]   *US v. Apple Inc.* [2013] 952 F Supp 2d 638 (Dist Court, SDNY); *United States v. Apple, Inc.* 2015 2d Cir 28–29.

[209]   See Paul Aiken, *Guild's Tunney Act Filing to the DOJ*, Submission (New York: The Authors Guild, 2012).

[210]   US Census, Monthly and Annual Retail Trade Report, 1997, 2007.

[211]   See Richard Gilbert, "E-Books: A Tale of Digital Disruption" (2015) 29, *Journal of Economic Perspectives*, 165.

[212]   Brad Tuttle, "Amazon Prime: Bigger, More Powerful, More Profitable than Anyone Imagined," *Time* (March 18, 2013), available at http://business.time.com/2013/03/18/amazon-prime-bigger-more-powerful-more-profitable-than-anyone-imagined/.

years and even once it started generating profits in 2001, levels remained consistently low through the company's history and minimal in relation to its value on the stock market. Nonetheless, estimates suggest that Amazon will keep growing at a rate around 20 percent a year until 2025. While critics of Amazon see behind these strategies systemic forms of predation, supporters believe it is promoting the scale and growth that any platform would need in a market that is naturally prone to tip and accommodate only one or a few players.

4.2 CONCERNS ABOUT AMAZON'S MARKET POWER

In addition to Amazon's rapid growth path, some of the competition policy concerns about Amazon's strategies suggest a degree of winner-takes-all tendencies present in e-commerce. In order to put some of these issues in better perspective, this section reviews some of the competition policy concerns that have emerged around Amazon and evaluates the extent to which they reflect evidence of winner-takes-all market features typical of natural monopolies, looking in particular allegations of predation, structural dominance, discriminatory conduct, and vertical integration.

4.2.1 *Antitrust Investigations Regarding MFN Clauses*

The first major antitrust case that indirectly involved Amazon concerned a price-fixing strategy through the use of MFN clauses between Apple and several book publishers in an attempt to change the price of e-books charged by Amazon.[213] When Amazon launched its e-reader Kindle device and quickly became the leader in the e-book market, its business strategy was to sell certain new releases and bestsellers at a discount price of $9.99. E-books were distributed under a wholesale model, where publishers set a list price (retail price) and then sell e-books to a retailer for a wholesale price, typically a percentage of the list price. Since under the wholesale model the retailer is free to sell at whatever price it chooses, Amazon opted for selling at little or no profit often incurring a loss, arguably in order to encourage the adoption of Kindle. Publishers were concerned about Amazon's strategy and were reluctant to see the e-book market expand, because that would eat into profits from hardcover books and brick-and-mortar stores; consumers would also become accustomed to low prices, and the $9.99 price point would erode profits for all books. In addition, publishers also feared the disintermediation strategy that Amazon intended to pursue by directly negotiating with authors.

Publishers perceived that each of them, individually, would not be able to respond to these threats and force Amazon to change its pricing strategy. As a result, they saw a solution in Apple's desire to enter the e-book market. Apple

[213] *US v. Apple Inc., supra,* note 208; *United States v. Apple, Inc., supra,* note 208; *CASE COMP/ AT39847-E-BOOKS,* 2012 European Commission, available at http://ec.europa.eu/competition/anti trust/cases/dec_docs/39847/39847_26804_4.pdf.

intended to launch the iPad together with its own new iBookstore, but because it was not willing to match the below-cost prices charged by Amazon, it proposed to publishers certain contractual conditions as part of its strategy to enter the e-book market: i) establishment of an agency model, where publishers would have the freedom to set e-book prices in the iBookstore, and would keep 70 percent of each sale and the remaining 30 percent would go to Apple as a commission. This would solve Apple's issue of negotiating better wholesale prices with publishers and ensured Apple some profit on every sale; ii) price caps for certain books suggested by Apple slightly higher than Amazon's $9.99; iii) adoption of Most-Favored-Nation (MFN) clauses, which effectively forced the publishers to impose the agency model on Amazon and other retailers. If Amazon continued selling e-books for $9.99, publishers were in practice forced to set the same price for books sold on the iBookstore. However, the entrance of Apple in the e-book market increased the bargaining power of publishers vis-à-vis Amazon and allowed them to impose an agency model on Amazon.

While Apple characterized its contracts as a series of parallel but independent and lawful vertical agreements, the Court of Appeal for the Second Circuit dismissed Apple's arguments and affirmed the district court decision that the agreements constituted a per se violation of the Sherman Act, and that, in the alternative, they unreasonably restrained trade under the rule of reason. The Second Circuit found that the practice at issue consisted of a bundle of vertical and horizontal agreements that may be characterized as a "hub-and-spoke" conspiracy, where an entity on one level of the market structure (the hub) coordinates an agreement among competitors at a different level (the spokes). In particular, the court found that these vertical agreements were used to facilitate collusion among publishers, and that this con-stituted in a per se violation of Section 1 of the Sherman Act. The Second Circuit concluded that the relevant agreement was not Apple's vertical contract with the publishers, but the horizontal agreement that Apple organized among publishers to raise e-book prices.

Importantly, the court also rejected the alternative procompetitive explanation for the shift in business model aided by the MFN clause, namely that it was a necessary response to predation in order to enter the market. The court found that Amazon's low prices may have been the result of its superior efficiency and that Amazon was taking a risk in engaging in loss-leader pricing, losing money on some sales in order to encourage readers to adopt the Kindle. The European Commission, in parallel investigations, also concluded that similar practices between publishers and Apple had the object of restricting competition within the meaning of Article 101(1) TFEU.[214]

A separate group of MFN investigations, this time directly involving Amazon, was opened in various European countries with regard to the possible abuse of

---

[214]   *CASE COMP/AT.39847-E-BOOKS, supra,* note 213.

dominance resulting from the imposition of MFN clauses in the distribution agree-ments with publishers and sellers on Amazon's marketplace. MFN clauses required, for example, publishers to offer Amazon similar (or better) terms and conditions as those offered to its competitors and/or to inform Amazon about more favorable or alternative terms given to Amazon's competitors. The clauses covered not only price, but also many aspects that a competitor can use to differentiate itself from Amazon, such as alternative business (distribution) models.[215] The European Commission considered that such clauses could make it more difficult for other e-book platforms to compete with Amazon by reducing publishers' and competitors' ability and incentives to develop new and innovative e-books and alternative distribution services. The clauses may have led to less choice, less innovation, and higher prices for consumers due to less overall competition in e-book distribution.[216] Other competition authorities in Europe proceeded against Amazon for enforcing similar price parity clauses on the Amazon Marketplace platform.[217]

None of these investigations, while being the only major decided antitrust cases that directly or indirectly involve Amazon, pertains to the winner-takes-all or poten-tial natural monopoly features. The use of MFN clauses by Amazon is, in fact, not atypical and it has been a subject of investigation for abuse of dominance in various other platform markets, for example in the context of price-comparison platforms and hotel bookings.[218]

4.2.2 Predatory Pricing

Amazon has incurred significant losses supported by the willingness of investors to pursue long-term market leadership strategies in e-commerce. As already pointed out, below cost prices have occurred in the book sector, where Amazon allegedly sold at below cost physical books[219] and then extended its policy to the e-books, but also in other areas of its online shopping business, including Amazon Prime. Amazon's pricing has been framed in terms of loss-leader strategy, where low prices are justified on the ground that profit-maximizing prices for complementary goods can be below profit-maximization levels for one good because that expands demand for the complementary good. In fact, it appears that in aggregate Amazon's e-books business has been profitable and low prices not part of a predatory strategy intended

---

[215] European Commission, Antitrust: Commission Accepts Commitments from Amazon On E-Books, Press Release IP/17/1223 (2017).

[216] Ibid.

[217] Bundeskartellamt, *Amazon Removes Price Parity Obligation for Retailers on Its Marketplace Platform*, Case Report B6-46/12 (2013).

[218] See Baker and Scott Morton, *supra*, note 112; Jonathan B. Baker and Judith A. Chevalier, "The Competitive Consequences of Most-Favored-Nation Provisions" (2012) 27, *Antitrust*, 20; Andre Boik and Kenneth S. Corts, "The Effects of Platform Most-Favored-Nation Clauses on Competition and Entry" (2016) 59, no. 1, J Law Econ, 105.

[219] Authors United, *Letter from Authors United to William Baer, Assistant Attorney General for the Antitrust Division, US Department of Justice* (2015).

to generate monopoly power.[220] Low prices on both books and the reader may have also been a way to encourage early adoption and increase network benefits by coordinating consumers on its platform.[221] However, many commentators have claimed that Amazon is instead engaging in predatory strategy, selling many products below cost to drive competitors out of the market and subsequently recoup the losses. These allegations are of two forms: some based on specific products and areas of business that roughly correspond to potential antitrust markets; some based on a more general concern that investors may be funding a larger predatory strategy to win the book and other retail markets.[222] For neo-Brandeis, forms of predation go unchecked and are symptomatic of the inherent failure of the consumer welfare standard to address Amazon's predatory prices.[223] Proposals to address such gaps include presumption of predation for dominant platforms with a 40 percent market share in any given line of service, bans on personalized pricing and price discrimination,[224] or suggestions to expand the notions of predation beyond prices, in terms of quality and choice, lower wages, lower levels of business entry, and disruption of local ownership.[225]

Distinguishing competition from predation is generally harder than usual in markets with network effects and scale economies,[226] but it is plausible that low prices reflect competition for the market and a necessary strategy to gain dominance in a winner-takes-all market where growth is given priority over profits, regardless of whether such a market gives rise to a natural monopoly. Amazon's willingness to sustain losses indicates an expectation of dominance in e-commerce, where possibly winning the market may require large investments that include a phase of losses and low prices during the sorting out phase. While this confirms a form of winner-takes-most competition for the market that is at play in e-commerce, sustained low pricing in and of itself is not a sufficient proxy to distinguish a standard market with scale economies from a natural monopoly.

4.2.3 *Dominance in E-Commerce, Vertical Integration, and Discrimination*

Another set of antitrust issues that are more closely related to winner-takes-all features of Amazon's online marketplace encompass various allegations and concerns, including Amazon has excessive dominance in e-commerce, that its

---

[220] Oliver Budzinski and Karoline Henrike Köhler, "Is Amazon the Next Google?," Working Paper 97 (Ilmenau Economics Discussion Papers, 2015); John B. Kirkwood, "Collusion to Control a Powerful Customer: Amazon, E-Books, and Antitrust Policy" (2014) 69, Univ Miami Law Rev, 1.

[221] Joseph Farrell and Michael L Katz, "Competition or Predation? Consumer Coordination, Strategic Pricing and Price Floors in Network Markets" (2005) 53, no. 2, J Ind Econ, 203 at 205.

[222] Khan, *supra*, note 2.

[223] See Maureen K. Ohlhausen, *Antitrust Enforcement in the Digital Age, Remarks Before the Global Antitrust Enforcement Symposium*, Washington, DC, Georgetown University, 2017.

[224] Khan, *supra*, note 2.

[225] Ibid.

[226] Farrell and Katz, *supra*, note 221.

Marketplace is de facto the gateway to online commerce, providing essential infrastructure due to its role as a gatekeeper, and that it provides a marketplace for independent sellers while also selling its own products on its website.[227] A first concern is one of excessive power over sellers. Amazon is accused of abusing its power to control what products make it to the market, and pick winners and losers among vendors. Its dominance as the online retailer, for example, is often linked to the declining rate of new business formation over the past decade, a decline that results from excessive consolidation in the retail sector and increasing dominance of a few players. With regard to books, to take just one example, it has been accused of squeezing publishers by driving down the prices it pays for books, which resulted in a legal dispute with Hachette in which Amazon was accused of punishing Hachette in various ways when it pushed back on its pricing terms. According to a letter sent by Authors United to the DOJ, starting in March 2014, Amazon substantially interfered with the sale of millions of books published by Hachette Books Group.[228] Amazon stopped taking orders, started delaying shipping, eliminated discounts, and used rankings modifications and pop-up windows to redirect readers to non-Hachette books. These tactics allegedly reduced the sale of Hachette books by 50–90 percent. The letter also asserted that Amazon represented its rankings and recommendations as neutral while they were, in fact, biased by Amazon in various ways, such as prioritizing the books of authors and publishers that submit to Amazon's demands. Amazon's position and strategy over sellers is taken by some commentators as a sign of monopsony power.[229]

Another worry is vertical integration through mergers. Amazon's expansion and entry in multiple markets and lines of business is often cited as a central concern, on the grounds that cross-market presence allows Amazon to use monopoly power over the basic infrastructure of online shopping to monopolize various sectors.[230] Lack of effective merger enforcement has been pointed as one problem that allowed Amazon to obtain market power in part by acquisition.[231] The merger with Wholefoods is a recent prominent example of this concern. Merger policies have also been criticized for not making more effort to evaluate the role of data, in particular how ownership of big data could create concerns that may escape scrutiny in the analysis of vertical mergers. Arguments about merger policy also include the failure to address the predatory nature of certain acquisitions, as in the case of

[227] See Stacy Mitchell and Olivia La Vecchia, "Report: How Amazon's Tightening Grip on the Economy Is Stifling Competition, Eroding Jobs, and Threatening Communities" (November 29, 2016), available at https://ilsr.org/amazon-stranglehold/. See also the recent European investigation on Amazon's dual role as marketplace and direct retailer: European Commission, Antitrust: Commission Opens Investigation into Possible Anti-Competitive Conduct of Amazon (July 17, 2019), available at https://ec.europa.eu/commission/presscorner/detail/en/ip_19_4291.
[228] Roxana Robinson, "A Call to Investigate Amazon" (July 13, 2015), available at www.authorsguild.org/industry-advocacy/a-call-to-investigate-amazon/.
[229] Krugman, *supra*, note 189.
[230] Khan, *supra*, note 2.
[231] Ibid.

Amazon's acquisitions of potential competitors like Zappos and Diapers.com that were allegedly the result of previous predatory threats made by Amazon, which, after attempting to buy them, opened competing stores and sold items at a loss, forcing both firms to sell to it as a result. According to one narrative, Amazon was prepared to lose $100 million over three months in its attempt to force Quisdi to sell.[232] These concerns are coupled with the claim that once obtained through acquisition, dominance can be protected by exclusionary conduct through predatory pricing strategies that keep or drive out smaller competitors.

A further concern is related to discrimination. Biases in Amazon Marketplace between proprietary services and third-party sellers, analogously to the way Google search biases can discriminate in downstream specialized segments of search, can result from Amazon's hybrid business model as reseller on its own marketplace, which give incentives to prioritize its own products. These concerns have induced proposals to introduce some form of neutrality of results, nondiscrimination among third-party suppliers and Amazon's competing retail businesses, or prophylactic approaches to ban Amazon from being a retailer on its platform.

These concerns related to Amazon's market power in e-commerce and claims of structural dominance and control of essential infrastructures can be evaluated from different angles. A first possible interpretation is that Amazon Marketplace operates in a natural monopoly market, where concentration may be inevitable and efficient and may require ex ante regulation. A public utility framework would then include regulation of fees charged to buyers and sellers, and regulation of incentives to leverage monopoly power from the natural monopoly segment (its online market-place) to specific product segments that rely on its online infrastructure as an essential infrastructure for e-commerce.[233] This perspective would also negate the benefits of a horizontal break-up of Amazon Marketplace that would deny the benefits of concentration without preventing the reemergence of another dominant platform. Characterization as a natural monopoly requires more than winner-take-all tendencies, however. Scale economies on the supply-side and/or demand-side network effects need to be strong enough compared to total demand to make a single provider the most efficient market outcome and must counteract opposing forces such as demand heterogeneity and congestion that may make fragmentation desir-able. A second and common interpretation for Amazon's dominance is the result of the failure of current competition policy doctrines to deal with market power in the digital economy, as argued by the neo-Brandeis antitrust movement. This sort of proposals, concerned with both excessive concentration of economic and political power, ultimately aim at reforming antitrust to create more fragmented market structures, for example, among other things, by reforming the normative goals of antitrust intervention.

---

[232]   Stone, *supra*, note 194.
[233]   Mitchell and La Vecchia, *supra*, note 227.

The case study dismisses both the natural monopoly framework and the Hipster, neo-Brandeis explanation, and supports instead a perspective that sees e-commerce as characterized by large-scale economies and network effects, which create tendencies toward concentrated structures but without giving rise to a natural monopoly. This perspective does not advocate radical reforms but a more moderate evaluation of whether the strength of enforcement, or specific issues such as leveraging or vertical mergers need to be adjusted in light of increasing market power. Failing to identify a natural monopoly therefore expands the relevance of the debate about the reach of current competition laws in e-commerce without however entailing significant paradigmatic shifts in established goals and doctrines.

4.3 WHY AMAZON MARKETPLACE IS NOT A NATURAL MONOPOLY

Both the brief overview of Amazon's expansion and some of the competition policy concerns reviewed reflect a degree of winner-takes-all market tendencies in e-commerce. However, winner-takes-all tendencies are not necessarily synonymous with natural monopoly. There may be one firm in a market but no cost subadditivity, and there may be subadditivity in a market with a dominant firm and fringe competitors. A natural monopoly requires scale economies and/or network externalities that make a market more efficient when served by a single provider (a natural monopoly may exist even when the market is overly fragmented). In the context of e-commerce platforms and Amazon in particular, the possible sources of natural monopoly are that an online marketplace benefits from network effects between buyers and sellers, and that e-commerce relies on home delivery, which requires the operation of an infrastructure for storage and shipment whose development is characterized by economies of scale. This implies a degree of efficient concentration that inevitably will preclude the presence of a very fragmented market structure.

However, the case study argues that the forces that lead to concentration do not give rise to a natural monopoly in the case of Amazon. As the case study suggests, dominance in e-commerce is rather explained by the fact that Amazon online shopping marketplace, which competes with a number of other online large marketplaces and niche online sellers, is supported by the most sophisticated logistics infrastructure for storage, distribution, and delivery available in the market that is far superior to that offered by other competing providers. Neither the online platform nor the delivery infrastructure is naturally monopolistic, but their combination provides a competitive advantage over competitors. This section first shows that network externalities between buyers and sellers have limitations, and that there are important counterforces that limit efficient concentration. Then, it shows how the combination of an online store with an efficient physical infrastructure is in fact the key to Amazon's success in e-commerce.

4.3.1 *Network Effects Between Buyers and Sellers*

Online marketplaces for buyers and sellers benefit from bilateral network effects. More sellers benefit buyers by increasing the number offerings and available products, and more buyers shopping on a given platform increase the value of advertising on the same platform for buyers. These sorts of network externalities are such that creating a thick network on both sides of the market is a necessary precondition for any marketplace and can give rise to concentrated market structures.

However, network externalities in the context of online shopping have important limits when it comes to their potential role in creating a natural monopoly, in particular: limited strength of network externalities after a certain size is reached; ample room for product differentiation; possible issues of congestion; and extensive multihoming. First, it is plausible that the marginal utility of additional sellers or buyers will increase substantially during the initial stages of growth but that the value of network externalities may decrease after the platform has reached a sufficiently large size. This may limit the efficiency of concentration based on aggregation of network effects. This may explain for example why Amazon still faces important competition from various large e-marketplaces for many standard products. In fact, even though Amazon has a large market share of the e-commerce sector – in 2018, Amazon's market share in e-commerce was estimated at 49 percent in the United States and 22 percent in Europe[234] – it is not nearly as close to the share of Google in search. Moreover, while Amazon is relatively strong in the book market, if one considers markets product line by product line there are very few sectors where Amazon would appear to have no competition from large e-commerce stores. Alibaba, a top e-commerce platform founded in China in the 1990s, has an extensive global marketplace and it is one of the main Amazon's competitors. Walmart, which has introduced its own e-commerce, benefits substantially from its prior position as a major retail store and may possess an important competitive advantage compared to Amazon. Google Shopping, eBay, Kijiji, and Craigslist are other platform marketplaces offering an extensive range of products that compete with Amazon. Most of these platforms benefit from the same network effects between buyers and sellers, but these network effects have not tended toward dominance by a single platform.

Compared to horizontal search, the limits to the positive returns generated by network externalities is further limited by the lower positive returns to data collection that can be obtained when more users join an e-commerce platform, as opposed to the value of additional eyeballs and data for general-purpose search engines. As was suggested in the previous case study, data are central to online search because their core function is one of prediction more than matching. E-commerce

---

[234]   Ingrid Lunden, "Amazon's Share of the US E-Commerce Market is Now 49%, or 5% of All Retail Spend," *TechCrunch* (July 13, 2018), available at http://social.techcrunch.com/2018/07/13/amazons-share-of-the-us-e-commerce-market-is-now-49-or-5-of-all-retail-spend/.

platforms, on the contrary, while performing and relying to a degree on predictions and data (for pricing, ads, suggested products, etc.) have at their core a matchmaking role between sellers and buyers, for which data possess not nearly the same value. Thus, even though more buyers and sellers increase the volume of information and data on consumers' consumption patterns and on vendors (which, admittedly, gives Amazon some advantage especially compared to the ability of brick-and-mortar stores to obtain data on customer purchasing habits), there is not indefinite value to the accumulation of such data for the core function of matching buyers and sellers.

Second and related, there is an important degree of product differentiation at play in e-commerce, which includes myriad different product segments, and within the same segments different degrees of product quality, from cheap to luxury, from niche to mainstream. It is, therefore, likely that Amazon may face different sources of competition depending on the product market at issue, including competing major platform marketplaces and niche websites that provide online retailing. These considerations based on product differentiation and demand heterogeneity are further enhanced by the ease of multihoming and possible issues of congestion as forces limiting efficient concentration. Because alternative venues for buyers and sellers are available at a relatively low switching cost, multihoming can be expected to further limit the effects of network externalities toward a single monopoly platform. Likewise, congestion may not be as critical as physical stores, but it can reduce the optimality of a single virtual store: too many offerings can lead to excessive visual confusion or lack of proper separation between lower-end and luxury products, further leading buyers and sellers to multihome across online stores depending on the segment of the searched product. Without denying the presence of status quo bias and inertia, product differentiation promotes multihoming much more strongly than in horizontal search, thereby reducing the force of defaults in e-commerce.

There is an additional further reason why network externalities should not be expected to give rise to a natural monopoly in the case of Amazon Marketplace, which is that Amazon is not only a pure marketplace between third-party sellers and buyers but also a direct supplier. Because it does not simply act as a platform that relies on externalities between the two sides interacting through the intermediary, exploiting network externalities may conflict with incentives to reduce the number of sellers on the platform as a result of vertical integration in various downstream segments.

As a result, the various identified forces that reduce the efficiency of a single virtual marketplace, including the limits to the strength of these network externalities and the important role of product differentiation and consumers' heterogeneity, are significant enough to negate the power of network effects to give rise to natural monopolies in e-commerce.

4.3.2 *The Importance of Physical Infrastructure for Logistics, Storage, and Delivery*

The major technological upgrade offered by e-commerce compared to traditional shopping is arguably not the creation of virtual stores and inventories, but the physical infrastructure that enables rapid fulfillment and home delivery. Online marketplaces are analogous to large retail stores and shopping malls that have been present for a long time, except for the ability to obtain home delivery in a rapid and efficient way. What then creates an advantage in online shopping is not simply the importance of developing a sufficiently large virtual marketplace, but investing in a physical logistics infrastructure that allows offerings to be delivered in a short time and having a reliable and rapid customer service for completed transactions.

Amazon's business strategy of investing in a large infrastructure for logistics and delivery is its major competitive advantage over competitors. From fulfillment centers, sortation, and delivery centers, to Amazon Prime airplanes and air hubs, Amazon's physical network is the key enabler for the efficiency of online shopping. In practice, Amazon can outperform competitors not because the online market place is necessarily more extensive or superior to competitors, but because the service for home delivery is. In fact, in many cases, similar products may be available at a similar price on different online venues (or even at a lower price), but the convenience, reliability, and expedition offered by Amazon prevails over competitors. This is enabled by efficient investments in expanding the supply chain that starts from an online order and ends with door delivery, including inbound cross dock centers that receive products from vendors, multiple fulfillment centers for distributing and storing goods of different kinds, sortation centers, and delivery stations.

Developing such an infrastructure entails some fixed costs and benefits from a degree of economies of scale, but such scale economies are, however, not likely to be strong enough to create a natural monopoly. The capital costs involved in creating such an infrastructure are significant and some of the fixed costs can be diluted as output expands, but there may be some important diseconomies of scale in managing the infrastructure. Among other things, reducing fulfillment and transportation times requires adding more facilities that may entail a degree of wasteful inefficiencies in adding new facilities that requires costly duplication of inventory. Compared to standard utilities and natural monopolies such as an electricity network, the distribution and electricity grid is characterized by much larger scale economies, low variable costs, and much stronger scarcity constraints for the development of competing networks, which makes it a clear example of a natural monopoly. The physical infrastructure of e-commerce is instead not likely to entail a cost function that is subadditive, despite benefiting from scale economies. Fixed costs are lower, variable costs are higher, and issues of congestion and scarcity constraints for competing infrastructures are much smaller than a standard natural monopoly segment like an electricity grid.

Neither the logistics infrastructure nor a possible strategy to expand presence in from virtual physical stores in fact leaves Amazon immune from competition. For example, in the case of physical facilities, Amazon still has a much smaller footprint than Walmart. The latter benefits substantially, however, from having an established network of physical stores. The same infrastructure could in fact well serve both as store but also turned into storage and sorting facilities for online delivery. It is plausible that competing e-commerce network will be able to coexist in spite of the concentrated nature of the market.

Moreover, the segment of the supply chain that could possibly be closer to a natural monopoly is the last mile, from the last facility to the customer's doorstep, where Amazon is only marginally present and where there are a number of active competitors such as UPS and FedEx. The proximity of the last dispatching station to the served area is a large cost driver and according to some estimates, the last mile is for Amazon 28 percent of total transportation costs.[235] Because enough scale is needed to make direct delivery cheaper than outsourcing it, Amazon is building out a vast shipping and delivery operation with the aim of handling both its own packages and those of other companies. For e-commerce, scale to make last-mile parcel delivery to homes profitable is where the likelihood of natural monopoly is higher.

These arguments leading to the conclusions that regulating Amazon Marketplace does not find an adequate justification based on a natural monopoly framework also debunk the myth that network externalities are the major explanation for dominance or alleged natural monopolies in e-commerce. Not only are network effects associated with the platform model not strong enough to give rise to natural monopolies, but the segment of the supply chain that could theoretically resemble more closely a natural monopoly is the last-mile delivery from the last storage to the customer's home, where Amazon's position is less than established.

4.4 VENUES FOR STRONGER COMPETITION POLICY INTERVENTION

Rejecting the natural monopoly characterization for the Amazon Marketplace negates by default the desirability of regulation and increases the importance of competition policy enforcement to address possible abuses of market power, making a more compelling case for properly evaluating the potential need to reframe current antitrust approaches and enforcement policies.

Among the highlighted concerns, the most convincing case for stronger intervention is about leveraging, in particular, the problem of discrimination, demotion, or abuse of data by Amazon to enter certain retail segments by virtue of its position as a dominant marketplace. In this regard, Zhu and Liu provide an empirical study of

---

[235] Sunil Chopra and Peter Meindl, *Supply Chain Management: Strategy, Planning, and Operation* (London: Pearson, 2014).

the patterns of Amazon's entry into third-party sellers' product space. The likelihood of entry is positively correlated with the popularity and customer rating of third-party seller's products. The study suggests that small third-party sellers affected by Amazon's entry appear to be discouraged from growing their businesses on the platform subsequently, although the paper remains ambiguous on the overall social welfare effects of entry.[236] Khan also notes that certain acquisitions achieve similar goals but preemptively.[237] Most recently, the European Commission has initiated a preliminary investigation into Amazon's dual role as marketplace and rival to businesses that sell on its store. The critical concern is the use of data: Amazon is able to collect data on sales by third-party products, and can use these data to enter profitable segments with its proprietary brands and compete with third-party vendors, without even necessarily acquiring products as a traditional retailer or sharing data with other brands. Amazon Basics private label business, for example, started in 2009 and since then has opened around eighty private label brands, creating a frenemy scenario within its Marketplace.

Stronger investigations against this and similar types of potential abuse are a legitimate and desirable direction for enforcement. Depending on the magnitude of these concerns, this raises a complex and open institutional question already seen in the first case study: whether leveraging can be addressed through refusal to deal and abuse of dominance provisions and whether associated remedies can be effectively enforced through competition law intervention. As seen, the importance of this question stems from the fact that this kind of behavior can distort competition both at the intra-platform level and at the inter-platform level. The latter becomes particularly important in concentrated digital platform markets where small potential competitors may be targeted by a dominant platform in an attempt to stop their growth into substitutes.

The second venue for stronger intervention is vertical mergers. Critics argue that a new standard for merger review is needed, citing the role of data, but also the effects on workers, political power, and excessive concentration. Almost any of these concerns would require a different standard on its own and expanding the goals of merger review would transform it into a political assessment. At the same time, as has been recently pointed out by various commentators, there may be a stronger role in the evaluation of certain vertical mergers. Salop, for example, suggests invigorating vertical merger review, in particular in markets where economies of scale and network effects lead to barriers to entry and durable market power,[238] and Shapiro points to empirical evidence that supports moving in the direction of stronger

---

[236] Zhu and Quihong, *supra*, note 207.

[237] Khan, *supra*, note 2 at 770.

[238] Steven C. Salop, "Invigorating Vertical Merger Enforcement," SSRN Scholarly Paper ID 3052332 (Rochester, NY: Social Science Research Network, 2018); Jonathan Baker, Nancy Rose, Steven Salop, and Fiona Scott Morton, "Five Principles for Vertical Merger Enforcement Policy" (2019) Georgetown Law Faculty Publications and Other Works. 2148, available at https://ssrn.com /abstract=3351391.

merger enforcement, and calls in particular for a stricter approach to preemptive mergers of potential competitors.[239] These considerations may well be relevant in the context of e-commerce and Amazon. In markets with a dominant firm or tight oligopolies where entry is not easy, like e-commerce, vertical mergers challenge some of the traditional Chicago School assumptions and may lead to higher incentives to foreclose nonintegrated downstream rivals, increase entry deterrence, and eliminate the threat of potential competition, which may well exceed to possible efficiencies promised by vertical mergers.[240]

In sum, leveraging and discriminatory behavior against nascent firms as well as mergers of potential competitors appear to be important and legitimate venues for stronger antitrust enforcement. In this regard, however, a central policy question remains: can the objective of promoting contestability be vindicated by standard antitrust enforcement, or is it the case that this policy objective and the identified market power concerns may also require faster, simpler procedures and possibly remedies that imply ongoing monitoring, given the concentrated nature of this sector? These institutional questions represent one of the main challenges for an antitrust policy oriented at preserving contestability and potential competition that are pertinent to concentrated digital industries like e-commerce.

Other concerns are less straightforward. The first is predation. Khan argues that digital platforms like Amazon are positioned to recoup their losses in the future but bringing a predatory pricing case would be almost impossible to win, pointing to the inability of current laws to detect market reality in the digital economy.[241] The assertion that a predatory strategy is proved from estimates of future profits and stock prices alone is in itself too vague, however, because it is not clear whether the shift from low prices to future profits will be due to high volume sales and low prices, future high prices, efficiencies, or sustained predation.

The second dubious concern is about the failure of the consumer welfare standard. Some critiques propose alternatives that would include non-economic goals, the protection of competition as a process and the preservation of certain market structures to avoid market concentration per se.[242] The first objection to some of these proposals is that preserving the competitive process and market structures are, in fact, two different objectives. The latter resembles the ordoliberal ideals that have animated the origins of European competition law, while the former is something that in fact resonates in many ways with the Austrian and Chicago Schools' view of competition and does not clearly indicate the need for different normative goals in concentrated digital markets. The second straightforward objection is against pursuing simultaneously multiple conflicting objectives due to the associated issues of accountability, predictability, administrability, and enforceability. Third, the calls to

---

[239] Shapiro, *supra*, note 10.
[240] Salop, *supra*, note 238.
[241] Khan, *supra*, note 2 at 399.
[242] Khan, *supra*, note 2.

abandon the consumer welfare standard do not seem to be based on market power concerns in specific antitrust markets, but on excessive concentration across markets that results from presence across sectors as a whole, and the wealth inequality resulting from large corporate conglomeration. Amazon market shares in many markets, including retail and e-commerce are not nearly as large as other digital platforms like Google in search, but its presence is ubiquitous in a disparate area of retail and beyond e-commerce. Desires to change the forms of antitrust law seem to be driven less by market power considerations in an antitrust sense, and more by political choices about how corporate size expands across unrelated sectors.

Similarly uncompelling are the different critiques to the consumer welfare standard advanced by Tim Wu.[243] Responding critically to the Brandesian movement, Wu agrees that a postconsumer welfare antitrust may be in fact be desirable, but rejects the Hipster/Brandesian view that it should be substituted by the pursuit of multiple economic and noneconomic objectives. Wu instead would favor as standard based on "protection of competition" in lieu of consumer welfare. This objective would condemn a conduct that is meant to suppress or destroy the process of competition:[244]

> There is a fundamental and important difference between a law that seeks to maximize some value, and one that is designed to protect a process. The maximization of a value, particularly one as abstract as "welfare," necessarily puts enforcers and the judiciary in a challenging position, given that welfare is abstract and ultimately unmeasurable. In contrast, the protection of competition standard puts the antitrust law in the position of protecting the competitive process, as opposed to trying to achieve welfare outcomes that judges, and enforcers are ill-equipped to measure. In that sense, it makes the antitrust law akin to the "rules of the game," and makes enforcers and judges referees, calling out fouls and penalties, with the goal of ultimately improving the state of play, by protecting a competitive process that actually rewards firms with better products.

Thinking of enforcers and judges as referees with the goal of ultimately protecting the quality of play and rewarding firms with better products, or asking the referees to enforce the "rules of the game" in an effort to protect the process of competition from distortions instead of maximizing consumer welfare – on the grounds that the former objective better penalizes deviations and abuses that threaten to ruin competition – is, however, an empty statement insofar as it does explain what these "rules of the game" are. In other words, overseeing the process of competition still implies the need for an identifiable objective on the basis of which the process will be evaluated.

---

[243] See, generally, Tim Wu, *The Curse of Bigness: Antitrust in the New Gilded Age* (New York: Columbia Global Reports, 2018).

[244] Tim Wu, "After Consumer Welfare, Now What? The 'Protection of Competition' Standard in Practice" (2018) CPI Antitrust Chron, available at www.competitionpolicyinternational.com/wp-content/uploads/2018/04/CPI-Wu.pdf.

What then could be the guiding principles that determine the meaning of distortions to the process of competition? Two possible interpretation for intervention that promotes "competition as a process" appear plausible when evaluating Wu's argument: a first possible, literal interpretation is to envisage it as the promotion of market fragmentation and maximization of the number of players in a market – for example, blocking all mergers because, by eliminating a firm from a market, they reduce in a way the process of competition. This interpretation, however, overlaps substantially with the Hipster Antitrust approach and is unlikely to reflect a fair appraisal of Wu's position. A second potential interpretation, which brings the notion of competition as a process to its ultimate consequences and implications, is instead to see the competitive process, and hence its promotion and distortions, as the efficiency of the process of production and allocation of resources. In other words, competition as a process may simply be at the core another term for economic efficiency and the protection of efficient markets from distortions. Under this light, Wu's argument and its rejection of both the consumer welfare standard and Hipster Antitrust approaches conceptually overlaps, to a large degree, with economic efficiency as the guiding principle for protecting the "competitive process" benchmark that he suggests. This view fails to represent a complete departure from welfarist approaches. Yet Wu's critique remains valuable because it reveals the ambiguity of the term consumer welfare, which is ultimately a bundle of standards concerned with the efficiency of markets, both from a static and dynamic perspective, and not necessary just with consumer surplus.

In sum, while attacks to the consumer welfare standard attempt to develop alternative competition policy frameworks and novel policy approaches for competition in the digital economy, it appears necessary to distinguish, on the one hand, critiques concerned with non-economic factors, and on the other hand, critiques that instead focus on the meaning and outer boundaries of consumer welfare. The former entails a complex, open political question. The latter – more technical and economic in nature – does not seem to have a particularly meaningful role in dealing with possible market power concerns regarding Amazon and the e-commerce sector, once the consumer welfare standard is interpreted expansively as a concern about the efficiency of static and dynamic market forces.

4.5 CONCLUSION

Despite the fact that network externalities give rise to large e-commerce marketplaces and the physical infrastructure of online shopping for logistics and delivery is characterized by some scale economies, neither effect is strong enough to give rise to a natural monopoly. The positive effect of network externalities between buyers and sellers is not indefinite and not associated with the same scale in data that characterizes horizontal search; moreover, virtual stores are subject to issues of congestion and important product differentiation that cause multihoming and market fragmentation. Similarly, scale economies give a competitive advantage but are not sufficient to make a single provider the most efficient market outcome. The closest segment of the supply chain to a natural monopoly is the last-mile delivery, where Amazon's presence is not significant.

Instead of a natural monopoly explanation, the central reason for Amazon's dominance in online commerce is efficient investments in delivery, logistics, and storage infrastructure that make the service more convenient for consumers and better supports the virtual store compared to the service offered by competitors. These arguments exclude the desirability of natural monopoly regulation for Amazon's e-commerce marketplace, but increase the desirability of evaluating adequate forms of competition policy intervention. Among them, it appears necessary to take more seriously the kind of market power abuses that can emerge from Amazon's hybrid role as a marketplace and direct seller that can lead to anticompetitive leveraging and foreclosure within its Marketplace, and the review of vertical mergers.

5

Ride-Hailing Platforms

The third case study evaluates ride-hailing platforms and on-demand transportation services and shows that the natural monopoly tendencies in these markets are more ambiguous than horizontal search but stronger than for e-commerce platforms. Thinking of platforms like Uber or Lyft along a spectrum, they can be placed in between the strong natural monopoly features of Google and Amazon's lack thereof.

Forces that may theoretically drive concentration and that may possibly give rise to natural monopolies are network externalities between drivers and passengers, data, and economies of scale in developing and operating algorithmic-driven dispatch functions. Most critically, building a network relies on substantial network externalities between passengers and drivers. Especially when trying to reach a critical mass, an additional passenger joining the network adds value for drivers on the other side of the market, and vice versa. The development and operation of a centralized dispatch and matching system also benefits from data on passengers and drivers to operate instant matching and routing. Beyond subsidizing initial participation of drivers and passengers during the network's initiation phase, there may be also some degree of economies of scale in the development of software's research and engineering and the system of reviews and ratings between users that solves some of the market failures that may otherwise negatively impact on-demand ride services.

However, the relative role of network externalities, scale in data collection, and economies of scale on the supply side in generating a natural monopoly is limited by important constraints. While there may be some economies of scale in the operation of a dispatch system, fixed costs are not necessarily very high. Similarly, demand-side economies of scale associated with network externalities, while representing the central driver of concentration, are likely to taper off after a certain critical network mass is reached. Beyond a certain threshold, an additional passenger or driver may not add much to the efficiency of a given network, and more data may not be significant for the purpose of improving matching. These limits may leave room for competition between platforms and reduce natural monopoly tendencies. Data can nonetheless remain relevant for predictive purposes beyond the core matching function performed by ride-hailing platforms. For example, in a given geographical area, centralized algorithmic routing, planning, and traffic management may generate significant benefits in terms of congestion and efficiency of transportation, especially considering the advantages of carpooling and a plausible scenario based on automated vehicles. Data analysis and collection may therefore be characterized by a larger degree of scale for predictive purposes that may be at play independently from the platform-matching business model.

The chapter concludes that, overall, the technological features of sharing economy platforms are likely to shift the optimal scale toward larger networks compared to traditional taxi dispatch services. While it may still be the case that in dense urban areas duopolies or oligopolies between competing networks can be sustained,[245] ride-hailing markets can be characterized by a degree of efficient concentration at the *inter*-platform level that may generate a natural monopoly depending on the local conditions of a given market, including the strength of the identified forces related to efficient concentration, as well as the size of demand, the density of the urban area, number of trips per year, and available substitutes for transportation.

In addition, the chapter identifies a tension at the *intra*-platform level between efficient centralization versus decentralization within a platform that has important implications for regulatory intervention. At the level of individual drivers, ride-hailing platforms had a truly disruptive role and injected competition in the provision of taxi services by easing the entry restrictions for drivers that were imposed by a medallion system; at the same time, however, the way on-demand transportation platforms operate resembles the function of a centralized public regulator. For example, they regulate prices of rides, and attempt to solve negative externalities and asymmetric information with review systems. All these factors imply that even though the emergence of sharing economy platforms positively injected more competition in the provision of taxi services (by making entry easier for individual drivers), ride-hailing markets remain characterized by a degree of necessary centralized coordination at the *intra*-platform level, as well as a degree of efficient concentration at the *inter*-platform level.

On the basis of this framework, the chapter derives the following policy implications. Starting from the assumption that the elimination of entry barriers for individual taxi drivers is desirable, the tension between efficient concentration and competition presents a choice between different regulatory approaches to the structure of competition between networks (as distinguished from competition between individual drivers). In the first group are policy options that accept or

---

[245] Similar to Amazon, for which better investments in superior storage and delivery infrastructure provide a compelling explanation for its dominance, one of the main competitive advantages of ride-hailing platforms has been supplying a technological improvement and a more efficient and digital version of the outdated dispatch and payment system used by taxis. This technological improvement is the result of better strategic investments to innovate traditional services based on available technologies not exploited by taxi incumbents.

encourage the benefits of efficient concentration into a single regulated platform network provider, which are pertinent when natural monopoly conditions are present in a given local market. This would include, for example, regulating prices charged by the dominant network, or auctioning a temporal monopoly over the provision of the network service to a single platform through franchise bidding. More ambiguous cases can be presented by the prospect of weak natural monopolies, where entry is feasible but inefficient, and where the policy choice must balance the benefits offered by competition vis-à-vis costs of inefficient overfragmentation. In the second group belong, in contrast, policy responses that promote competition between platforms, for example, enforcement of competition laws with a particular emphasis on direct and indirect forms of exclusivity and tie-ins, coupled with the complementary role of regulatory tools like portability of users' profiles to promote switching across platforms. This approach may be pertinent both when natural monopoly conditions are absent, and in the presence of a natural monopoly where regulation is deemed to be too costly.

The structure of this third case study is as follows. It starts by introducing the central features and business models prevailing in the sharing economy phenomenon. Then, borrowing from the lessons that can be drawn from some of the competition policy concerns about Uber, it explains why natural monopoly features are ambiguous in the market for on-demand taxi and ride-sharing services and evaluates alternative regulatory options that may be justified depending on whether competition is feasible, whether the market is naturally monopolistic, or ambiguously situated between the two market structures.

5.1 THE STRUCTURE OF SHARING ECONOMY TRANSPORTATION PLATFORMS

The sharing economy model is based on turning unused or underutilized assets into productive resources, and using matching technologies to coordinate the providers of underused assets with consumers.[246] In the case of on-demand transportation services, the underutilized assets are privately owned cars that are used for on-demand taxi services. The matching technology is an app, which plays the function of a digital dispatch mechanism through which passengers can request a ride and complete a transaction directly on the platform without the need for cash. Sharing economy platforms have created all the necessary preconditions for a market for on-demand rides to emerge: the collection of data on both passengers and drivers and algorithmic matching that sets prices centrally reduce search and transaction costs and solve problems of market liquidity and temporal agglomeration. Mechanisms

---

[246] For a study on the effect of ride sharing on consumer welfare, see Peter Cohen, et al., "Using Big Data to Estimate Consumer Surplus: The Case of Uber" (2016), available at www.datascienceassn.org/sites/default/files/Using%20Big%20Data%20to%20Estimate%20Consumer%20Surplus%20at%20Uber.pdf.

such as ratings, reviews, and mandatory profiles on the app attempt to solve many of the information asymmetries and negative externalities.

On-demand transportation networks rely in part on the multisided platform business model: independent car owners can provide taxi services to passengers through an intermediary platform, which enables them to access the market without incurring high capital costs and provide services on a part-time or flexible basis. However, the actual structure of on-demand transportation platform is more complex and it is in fact based on a hybrid form of multisided platform. Such hybridity reflects some of the economic trade-offs that are central to the theory of the firm: should an on-demand ride services platform hire drivers, or restrict its role simply as an intermediary between independent contractors and passengers? Should the platform set prices or delegate the decisional authority on various aspects of the transaction to its users? Should a platform integrate the supply side, for example, with the introduction of its own autonomous vehicles, and should it integrate fully or partially allowing third-party service providers to compete on its network with its vertically integrated services?

Among possible structures and business models, there are in particular three major forms of intermediation that could apply to on-demand transportation services. Each has different consequences on concentration, competition, and market power, which are discussed in turn (see Table 5.1). First, there is a pure two-sided platform model, where the platform is simply providing a marketplace and has the minimal role of matching independent drivers and passengers. This model was not feasible for traditional taxis but it is made possible by the technology of sharing economy platforms (although as the case study argues, it remains undesirable). Second, there is a one-sided model, with a vertically integrated service provider that directly supplies transportation services with no significant two-sided network externalities at play. An

TABLE 5.1 *Alternative structures in the ride-hailing market*

Pure Two-Sided Market	Hybrid Models Between One and Two-Sided Markets	One-Sided Models
A competitive marketplace for independent drivers and passengers	Hybrid contractual arrangements on the supply side including centralized pricing with independent drivers; forms of employment based on commissions; partial vertical integration (competition between independent drivers and employed drivers or autonomous vehicles)	Vertical integration through employment of drivers or autonomous vehicles

example is a ride-sharing platform that substitutes independent drivers with employees or is based on autonomous vehicles. And third, there is a range of hybrid models along a spectrum of decentralization of economic decisions depending on the nature of contractual arrangements. As it is discussed more in detail in this case study, the present structure of on-demand transportation networks belongs to this category of hybrid platform model, with important implications for the role of regulation.

5.1.1 *The Pure Marketplace for Drivers and Passengers*

In a hypothetical pure two-sided platform model, independent drivers connect with passengers through an intermediary platform that provides a marketplace and simply enables matchmaking. Key control decisions are delegated to independent drivers. This means, for instance, that drivers are not employed or tied to a specific platform and can be affiliated with multiple platforms, and that they retain control over critical decisions regarding the provision of services through the platform. The platform's role is to enhance the network's value, by first solving the initial chicken-and-egg problem between different user groups and by developing a large network of users on both sides of the market that can transact through the platform. The thickness of the network is ensured through various mechanisms, especially at the early stages of platform adoption, such as divide-and-conquer strategies with cross-subsidies between sides to resolve issues of coordination failure,[247] or subsidizing the usage on both sides.[248]

The platform's role beyond developing a thick network and matching is dealing with market imperfections that may undermine transactions between independent users of the networks. Both the need to take advantage of indirect network externalities by efficiently balancing demand on each side, and the need to develop safety and trust mechanisms require the design of efficient platform rules for its members in order to increase the quantity and the quality of matches. For example, Uber's app reduces transaction costs for passengers by allowing the rider to view the estimated arrival time of their ride, car description, and the expected fare rate, which is then directly charged on the rider's account (although in some locations, cash payment is available). Moreover, platforms have developed rating mechanisms and require background and security checks for drivers and vehicles. Drivers must have some minimum years of driving experience, have car insurance, go through a background

---

[247] Bruno Jullien, "Competition in Multi-sided Markets: Divide and Conquer" (2011) 3, no. 4 Am Econ J Microecon, 186.

[248] These strategies have attracted antitrust scrutiny, as in the case of Uber facing a complaint for predatory pricing brought in the San Francisco Federal Court by a taxi company alleging that the platform is illegally subsidizing fares to drive competitors out of the market. See, for instance, *Desoto Cab Company, Inc. v. Uber Technologies, Inc. et al.*, California Northern District Court, available at https://www.pacermonitor.com/public/case/19745715/Desoto_Cab_Company,_Inc_v_Uber_Technologies,_Inc_et_al.

check, and own a vehicle that satisfies certain safety requirements. Failure to comply with platform's policies can lead to drivers being deactivated from the platform.

A two-sided platform can obtain revenue by imposing membership fees and/or transaction fees on its users. For instance, a platform may obtain revenue by imposing membership fees on drivers, and allow them to obtain the full amount of fares, or it can impose transaction fees on drivers without requiring access fees. In either case, the critical feature of a pure two-sided marketplace for on-demand rides between independent drivers and passengers is delegation of most other control rights to drivers, in particular the power to set prices. This could be facilitated by allowing individual drivers to preestablish their rates on the platform, so that drivers can compete among themselves on price while allowing passengers to know in advance the expected cost of alternative rides.

The pure marketplace model was not a feasible option for traditional taxi services. Excessively high negotiation and transaction costs conflict with the nature of a service that requires demand and supply to meet rapidly. Information asymmetries about prices for riders and cost for drivers preclude price comparison and increase the burden of search costs. These critical market imperfections made impossible the development of a pure platform marketplace for taxis. The technology of sharing economy platforms has changed many of these assumptions. In theory, a platform has the available technology to allow each driver to set the parameters used to calculate the final price of a ride, and then using a form of bidding auctions to allocate the cheapest rides to passengers (the price could also be set to be a function of waiting times), who would be able to evaluate in advance the expected rate of the ride. As discussed later, sharing economy platforms have not pursued this pure two-sided marketplace model and generally use a centralized pricing algorithm to determine the level of fares, which arguably is explained by the fact that centralized pricing remains more efficient than decentralization made possible by technology.

A pure two-sided platform model relies on positive and bidirectional network externalities between the two sides, and it can be expected to lead to high levels of market concentration. For example, on the demand side, users will likely want to join the platform with the largest network of drivers, creating a positive feedback loop effect between drivers and passengers that can grant the incumbent a competitive advantage. The incumbent can adopt insulating or divide-and-conquer strategies at the early stage of platform adoption to create a thick network that ignites after reaching a sufficient critical mass.[249] In addition to the relevance of the network's size, first mover advantage and the force of default options and status quo bias can create other significant advantages for the incumbent, which may affect the level of multihoming and switching costs. The strengths of network externalities are certainly strong at the initial stages of network's growth, both in terms of presence and availability of drivers and riders, but also for their valuable input in terms of data

---

[249] Jullien, *supra*, note 247.

and reviews that can create a more reliable framework for the network. It is possible, however, that network externalities may not be infinitely positive, and that adding marginal users would not be of significant value after a certain threshold. The possibility of decreasing network externalities, together with the coordination and congestion issues on either side of the platform (which can create negative within-group externalities) are all counterforces that can fragment the market. For example, on the supply side, drivers will want to join the larger network with the higher number of potential passengers, but the positive cross-market externalities justifying such decision must be balanced against the potential negative effects of within group externalities that can arise from oversupply of available cars chasing passengers.[250]

Under a pure platform model, a natural monopoly is mostly the result of aggregating network externalities between drivers and passengers and demand over a single network, and less the result of supply-side scale economies. Without direct control over the price charged to passengers, moreover, a pure platform model does not raise concerns over monopoly prices for rides, as independent drivers are free to enter and exit the market and set their own prices in competition with each other. Yet market power could be exercised by a monopoly platform by imposing membership fees or transaction fees at supra-competitive levels.

5.1.2 *One-Sided Models: Drivers vs. Automated Cars*

Where a pure marketplace model is based on matching independent drivers with riders, a one-sided model for on-demand transportation services would involve vertical integration in the form of employed drivers or automated vehicles. A one-sided model lies at the opposite end of the spectrum from a two-sided model. With no relevant indirect network externalities, it can manage its own supply without facing the initial chicken-and-egg problem of coordinating drivers and passengers typical of multisided platforms, but faces higher capital and entry costs than a pure intermediary derived from the cost of employment and/or development of automated vehicles.

In the case of vertical integration by employment, some of the important trade-offs affecting the decision between independent drivers versus employed drivers are that in the employee model there are coordination benefits arising from spillovers across the decisions of individual employees, while in a two-sided market model the benefits are in making professional drivers residual claimants on their individual demand, which can better motivate them to provide unobservable efforts and ensures that they can better adapt their decisions to their private

---

[250] A degree of extra-supply available at each given time may be valuable to keep the network thick. This idle capacity, which is a form of efficiency for passengers, however, creates excessive competition among drivers. As a result, although it would be logical for a driver to join the biggest network, a driver may at the same time want to also join a network with a shortage of drivers, which may not be the largest network. The potential for negative effects created by excessive competition on the driver's side can result in market fragmentation.

information.[251] Moreover, the costs of employment are substantially higher compared to a platform model, but employment contracts may serve an exclusivity-like purpose in a way that makes direct employment attractive for an established network to increase the costs of multihoming.

All in all, employment-based models may be less prone to concentration compared to the pure marketplace, but they reduce the easiness of switching across platforms. A shift from a dominant pure two-sided platform network to a one-sided model based on employment may therefore raise some market power concerns and antitrust questions insofar as the shift implies reduced levels of multihoming and switching among platforms on the drivers' side compared to a scenario with independent drivers who can simultaneously operate on competing networks.

Vertical integration through self-driving cars leads to a different set of consideration. In a hypothetical scenario with automated vehicles, there may be a race between existing ride-sharing platforms and manufacturers of self-driving cars, where successful car manufacturers could eventually undermine the role of established on-demand transportation platforms by establishing their own network and by using their competitive advantage in producing autonomous cars to promote their own ride-sharing network. In this scenario, the importance of data in improving higher safety, predictions, and general reliability of driverless cars is significant,[252] and together with scale economies and efficiency in centralized coordination of a network may lead to further market concentration than a scenario with employed drivers. The likelihood of vertical integration through self-driving cars is high, given that it reduces the cost of labor, which may increase once the regulation of work in the sharing economy obtains more formalization. Many carmakers and tech upstarts, from General Motors to Uber and Alphabet, are investing substantially in autonomous ride-hailing services. Tesla, for instance, has already introduced contractual restrictions that require self-driving cars not to be used for revenue except on the Tesla Network, which is currently being developed, meaning, for example, that Tesla self-driving cars may not be used on Uber's network.[253]

This paradigmatic shift in the provision of on-demand transportation services and the introduction of networks with autonomous vehicles may threaten established platforms; however, vertical integration may allow an established provider to control a large portion of overall supply or capture the entirety of market demand, which may increase antitrust concerns about concentration compared to the current model based on matching passengers with independent drivers.[254] In this scenario, the source of natural monopoly is more closely related to supply-side economies of scale and possibly data, as opposed to network externalities.

[251] Hagiu and Wright, *supra*, note 61.
[252] "The Market for Driverless Cars Will Head Towards Monopoly," *The Economist* (7 June 2018), available at www.economist.com/finance-and-economics/2018/06/07/the-market-for-driverless-cars-will-head-towards-monopoly.
[253] "Autopilot," available at https://www.tesla.com/autopilot.
[254] Federal Trade Commission Report, *supra*, note 66.

5.1.3 *Hybrid Models: The Current Structure of Ride-Hailing*

In reality, sharing economy platforms providing on-demand transportation services have a complex, hybrid structure between the two extremes. They operate as two-sided platforms, but they impose various restrictions over their users in a way that the extent of control can often become significant enough to tilt the structure of the platform away from a pure two-sided marketplace model. In between these two polar extremes, there may be various levels of decentralization of control decisions.

In the prevailing sharing economy model for on-demand transportation services, there are three prevailing central contractual relationships: a direct business relationship agreement between the platform and the driver (although such characterization has been contested by some regulators); an agreement between the platform and the rider; and a third, separate contract between the driver and the rider. With regard to drivers, both Uber and Lyft classify them as independent contractors who are not under an employment relationship with the platform. Moreover, neither Uber nor Lyft imposes explicit exclusivity on drivers, who are allowed to have affiliations with multiple service operators.

According to Uber's contractual conditions, for instance, the service constitutes a technology platform that enables users of Uber's mobile applications or websites to arrange and schedule transportation and/or logistics services "with independent third party providers of such services, including independent third party transportation providers and independent third party logistics providers under the agreement with Uber or certain of Uber's affiliates."[255] Uber's terms of service also clarify that: "Uber does not provide transportation or logistics services or function as a transportation carrier [...] all such transportation or logistics services are provided by independent third party contractors who are not employed by Uber or any of its affiliates."[256] Similarly, according to the Lyft Terms of Service, "the Lyft platform provides a marketplace where persons who seek transportation to certain destinations ('Riders') can be matched with persons driving to or through those destinations ('Drivers')."[257] It adds: "Any decision by a User to offer or accept Services is a decision made in such User's sole discretion. Each transportation Service provided by a Driver to a Rider shall constitute a separate agreement between such persons."[258] Drivers must acknowledge and agree that their provision of transportation services to users creates a direct business relationship between them and the user.[259] The relationship

---

[255] Uber, "Terms and Conditions," (31 December 2017), available at *Legal* https://www.uber.com/en-CA/legal/terms/us/, s 2.
[256] Ibid.
[257] Lyft, "Lyft Terms of Service," (6 February 2018), available at *Lyft* https://www.lyft.com/terms.
[258] Ibid, s 1.
[259] Ibid, s. 19.

between the parties is solely that of independent contracting parties, and not an employment agreement, neither is it a no joint venture, a partnership, or an agency relationship.[260] The platform cannot control drivers in their performance and drivers have complete discretion to provide services or otherwise engage in other business or employment.[261]

There are therefore some elements of a pure two-sided platform model. Drivers remain independent contractors, not affiliated with the platform by an employment relationship, and without exclusivity requirements. Additional rules of affiliation, such as that drivers must maintain a minimum average rating, must comply with license and permits requirements, safety checks of the vehicle, and insurance are all consistent with the degree of necessary control to facilitate transactions, deal with market failures, and comply with regulatory requirements.

One major exception to the platform model is that sharing economy platforms such as Uber and Lyft retain central control of prices instead of delegating pricing decisions to drivers. Both platforms set the level of fares through a price algorithm that detects fluctuations between demand and supply, rather than allowing drivers to set their own fares and to compete on price. Uber characterizes its role as a facilitator of payment of the applicable charges on behalf of the third-party provider and as a limited payment collection agent,[262] but drivers are not allowed to increase or otherwise modify the user charges as calculated through the app for any usage of Uber service.[263] Similarly, Lyft requires that drivers expressly authorize Lyft to set the prices for all charges that apply to the provision of services,[264] and that drivers must agree to pay Lyft a fee based on each transaction.[265]

This form of control introduces hybridity in the two-sided platform model. Drivers must agree to the fare calculation centrally set by the platform. Moreover, both Uber and Lyft exhort in practice a high degree of control over drivers' activity and have programs to reward drivers and induce them to be operative on their specific platform. Lyft has a "Power Driver Bonus" program that rewards drivers with bonuses based on how much they drove in a week, provided that they have an acceptance rate for proposed rides from passengers of 90 percent for the week.[266] Uber has weekly and hourly guarantee programs that provide a set level of gross fares that drivers are guaranteed to earn if they satisfy specific acceptance rates and number of trips.

---

[260] Ibid.
[261] Ibid.
[262] Supra, note 255, s 4.
[263] Ibid.
[264] Supra, note 257, Driver Addendum.
[265] Ibid.
[266] Lyft, "Earnings Guarantee Promotions," available at http://help.lyft.com/hc/en-ca/articles/115012927247-Earnings-Guarantee-promotions.

These incentives programs can create de facto exclusivity during their operation, because they make it impossible for drivers to multihome while they are operative.

The hybridity arising from the control exercised by the platform on its users can itself be the source of conflicting regulatory considerations. For example, a pure two-sided platform model may encourage price competition between drivers, which would give rise to a fully competitive market between independent drivers. However, central control of prices has in this context some efficiency properties because it allows a better coordination of the network and excessive price competition among drivers may undermine the thickness of the market. The choice of centralization keeps transaction costs low and allows more efficient use of dynamic information about supply and demand,[267] which is particularly critical for a homogenous service where coordination and rapid availability of rides are more important than product differentiation. This differs, for instance, from other sharing economy platforms like Airbnb that offer a service with higher level of product heterogeneity where transactions are characterized by a bigger time delay between requests and availability of supply. There is therefore a tension between the benefits of decentralized and centrally set prices. Delegation of prices to drivers resembles the creation of a pure competitive marketplace for independent drivers, but has various downsides including creating more frictions (with drivers frequently readjusting their proposed prices), lack of efficient network coordination, and possibly reduction of output due to incentives for cream skimming and only serve profitable rides compared to a scenario with average cost pricing. On its part, a system of centralized prices allows a superior coordination of the network and better management of fluctuations in supply and demand, but it has a superficial resemblance to a cartel facilitated by the platform if drivers are not employed but independent contractors, and may allow the platform to charge monopoly pricing on either side.

Another plausible form of hybridity that can be the source of competition policy questions is the possibility of partial vertical integration, where a dominant platform directly competes with third-party drivers by becoming a direct supplier on its network. Foreclosure can therefore arise if the platform discriminates in favor of its own various forms of ride service, similarly to what Google and Amazon can do on their own platforms. It is practically harder to conceive how and why such discrimination may occur in the case of on-demand transportation networks, but it cannot be excluded as a form of leverage from one market to another (for instance, Uber may want to expand in various markets related to transportation, delivery, and logistics, including direct provision of taxi and ride-sharing, food delivery, car rentals, driverless cars, and moving services).

---

[267] Einav, Farronato, and Levin, *supra*, note 57.

5.2 ANTITRUST CONCERNS OVER INTER-PLATFORM AND INTRA-PLATFORM COMPETITION

Different business models can have different impacts on concentration, market power, and competition both at the inter-platform and intra-platform level. Some of the central competition policy concerns and cases related to the current structure of ride-hailing networks – in particular, predatory pricing, inducements to exclusivity by drivers, and allegations of collusion among drivers facilitated by a platform – also show the existing tension between concentration and competition at the inter-platform level and between centralization and decentralization at the intra-platform level, with important implications for the possible role of regulation. These issues are discussed in turn.

5.2.1 *Predation*

Ride-hailing platforms have relied on policies of low prices, subsidizing fares, and drivers, especially at the launch of the platform. By operating at a loss, sharing economy platforms prioritized growth over profit in the same way that Amazon did with its online marketplace. The kind of investments made by Uber and Lyft has been for the most part focused on subsidizing the creation and developments of thick networks rather than expanding physical infrastructures. Because every ride-hailing market is necessarily local in nature, for on-demand transportation networks, investing in expansion means expanding on a geographical dimension on an area-by-area basis, rather than entering a variety of new sectors.

Traditional taxi companies have responded to some of these competitive strategies by advancing claims of predation against sharing economy platforms. For instance, Uber has been accused of predatory pricing by a San Francisco taxi company, which alleges that Uber dropped the price of fares to undercut those of traditional cabs, in order to charge supra-competitive prices for ride-hail services after its competition is eliminated.[268] Taxi operators complain that Uber is able to maintain below-cost pricing due to the vast reserves of capital invested with the expectation of reaping extraordinary future returns, supported by large private venture capital funding.

As in the case of Amazon, aggressively low prices show the tension between winner-takes-all market features and competition. Low prices may reflect competition for the market, where gaining dominance may require initial substantial losses to obtain local monopolies in ride-hailing markets, including large initial investments in the development of the network and subsidization of users in order to overcome coordination issues. However, winner-takes-all features do not automatically imply that the race for the market will give rise to a natural monopoly, so the argument that low prices and subsidization of aggregation on a single network may

---

[268]   *Desoto Cab Company, Inc., d.b.a Flywheel Taxi v. Uber Technologies, Inc.*, 2016 District Court Northern District of California San Francisco Division.

be desirable from an efficiency perspective and immune from antitrust scrutiny does not hold without a clear identification of a natural monopoly. In fact, in many geographic areas competing networks are present and appear to be in competition either statically or dynamically. This leaves with an unclear picture as to when and whether concerns over low prices reflect predatory strategies or desirable investments to subsidize the expansion of a more efficient network.

5.2.2 *Exclusivity*

Another dimension of the tension between competition and concentration is offered by exclusivity. Indirect network externalities are a form of scale economies on the demand side, and they can be exploited to induce exclusivity by drivers. Since the elasticity of demand on one side is affected by the value of network externalities arising on the other side of the market, the platform may obtain market power from indirect network externalities that can be exercised on one side of the market. An established user base of riders, perhaps developed by subsidization of fares, may enable a platform to impose direct and indirect forms of exclusivity on drivers, which, in turn, may enhance market power over passengers, possibly reducing interplatform competition. With exclusivity, the platform induces single-homing and increases switching costs, and the gains from exclusivity can be even higher because by having exclusivity on one side of the market the platform can then attract and retain the other side, which reinforces the decision to impose exclusivity.[269]

Incentives to induce exclusivity are therefore higher than in standard markets due to network externalities, and exclusivity can be achieved through a variety of explicit and implicit means. For instance, the platform may require explicit exclusivity agreements with drivers, or impose them as a condition for assuming the entry cost imposed by regulation, such as insurance, safety checks, and so on. As already noted, however, sharing economy platforms explicitly exclude any form of exclusivity in their contractual agreements with drivers. Platforms may also create indirect incentive mechanisms that can practically result in exclusivity during a certain time period. For instance, incentives' programs where the platform ensures a set level of average hourly gross earnings in exchange for supply conditions that make it de facto impossible to multihome among alternative platforms.[270] An example of these indirect forms of exclusivity emerged in a case brought before the District Court for the Northern District of California, where a program proposed by Uber identified drivers who multihomed with Lyft and gave them special bonuses for meeting a certain number of rides per week that practically made multihoming impossible.[271]

---

[269] Mark Armstrong and Julian Wright, "Two-Sided Markets, Competitive Bottlenecks and Exclusive Contracts" (2007) 32, no. 2 Econ Theory, 353.

[270] See, for instance, the program offered by Uber, "Hourly guarantees | Uber," available at www .uber.com/drive/pittsburgh/resources/guarantee-faq/; and Lyft, *supra*, note 257.

[271] See *Michael Gonzales v. Uber Technologies, Inc. et al.*, 2018 California Northern District Court.

Platforms compete on offering better programs to drivers, and bidding for drivers as an input for rides services is another form of price competition.[272] However, their specific design may also have the potential to reduce multihoming and increase switching costs, potentially resulting in barriers to entry for a new platform seeking to enter the market.

Analogous to low prices, some of these forms of induced exclusivity may distort competition among competing networks but can also significantly facilitate the process of efficient concentration toward a natural monopoly. Since it is not easy to clearly identify a natural monopoly, it is not desirable to immunize (as part of an efficiency defense) exclusivity that enhances efficient concentration, but it remains the case that exclusion may, in certain instances, be efficient.

5.2.3 *Collusion Facilitated by the Platform*

Where the treatment of predation and exclusivity reflects the tension between the efficiency of concentration and distortions of competition between platforms (inter-platform competition), antitrust claims of collusion facilitated by the platform through centralized pricing reflect the tension between centralization and decentralization within a platform (intra-platform competition). As it is argued below, these concerns show that a pure marketplace between taxi drivers is undesirable even with the advent of ride-sharing networks.

Broadly speaking, the question of whether drivers should be considered as employees or as independent contractors has been at the centre of the debate surrounding the regulation of the sharing economy. This labor law question has been transposed into the antitrust sphere in the form of a price-fixing investigation against Uber,[273] accused of illegally colluding with drivers in violation of Section 1 of the US Sherman Act by controlling the prices of car rides through Uber's pricing algorithm, and by fixing price surcharges. The case goes to the heart of the two-sided market model because the basis of the claim stems from Uber's argument that drivers are not employees. If drivers are independent contractors, the allegation goes, then they should set their own prices and compete on the level of fares. The fact that the platform is setting prices centrally gives rise to the claim that the pricing algorithm is a mechanism enabling a price-fixing arrangement to increase prices above competitive levels. On the contrary, if Uber drivers were employees, antitrust law would exempt coordination within a firm.

The horizontal conspiracy based on the two-sided market model can be characterized as a per se illegal hub-and-spoke agreement, where an entity at one level of the

---

[272] Ignacio Herrera Anchustegui and Julian Nowag, "Buyer Power in the Big Data and Algorithm Driven World: the Uber and Lyft Example" (2017) CPI Antitrust Chron, available at www .competitionpolicyinternational.com/wp-content/uploads/2017/09/CPI-Anchustegui-Nowag.pdf.

[273] *Meyer v. Kalanick*, 2016 United States District Court, SDNY, available at https://law.justia.com /cases/federal/district-courts/new-york/nysdce/1:2015cv09796/451250/37/).

market structure (the platform) coordinates an agreement among competitors at a different level upstream or downstream (drivers). The hub, for instance, could enter into individual vertical agreements downstream, which allows competitors in the downstream market to collude without evidence that they have entered into an explicit agreement but simply by conscious parallel conduct enabled by the hub. This characterization parallels the e-book price-fixing case *United States v. Apple, Inc.*[274]

An alternative analysis can be framed in terms of a vertical framework under the rule of reason balancing framework, where Uber's pricing mechanism can be seen as a vertical restraint on pricing similar to resale price maintenance. Uber sets a wholesale price (the transaction fee) and imposes a maximum RPM on the retail price collected by the resellers of the service. Passengers pay the retail price set by the platform and drivers earn the difference between the retail price and wholesale price. On the one hand, Uber's algorithm is more than a traditional price floor. Given that discounting is impractical, it de facto determines the exact price of drivers' service. On the other hand, restricting price competition may allow Uber to increase supply, maintain a level of consistency and predictability required by the nature of the service, and better coordination of supply and demand.[275]

One first lesson that can be drawn from this antitrust case is that the hybridity of the business model can give rise to valid competition policy concerns. On the one hand, the claim of collusion seems to rely excessively on the formal characterization of work and business structure of sharing economy platforms. A price-fixing claim would not hold if Uber had a one-sided structure. The allegations of price fixing emerge because Uber refuses to classify drivers as employees and it categorizes its function simply as a matchmaking platform, although it still coordinates prices for the ride services offered by independent drivers. Absent Uber's classification of drivers as independent contractors, the price-fixing claim would not emerge due to the firm exception under antitrust law.

A price-fixing claim would likely not hold if Uber had a pure two-sided market structure either. In such a case, drivers would set their own prices, and prices would reflect market forces rather than Uber's desire to increase its fee by increasing the total price of rides. Moreover, orchestrating a collusive scheme with price-setting

---

[274] *US v. Apple Inc.*, *supra*, note 208; *United States v. Apple, Inc.*, *supra*, note 208 at 28–29. In that case, Apple orchestrated a conspiracy among six publishers to enter the e-books market, where Amazon had been the leader since 2009, among other things by imposing the establishment of an agency model and Most-Favored-Nation (MFN) clauses, which effectively allowed publishers to impose the agency model on Amazon and other retailers as well. The court found that these vertical agreements with Apple were used to facilitate horizontal collusion among publishers, and that this entailed a per se violation of Section 1 of the Sherman Act. In the case of Uber, the legal claim is similar in that the platform is accused of orchestrating price fixing among drivers by making use of its pricing algorithm that drivers must accept when joining the platform, which results in an increase in the price of fares.

[275] See, for example, *Broadcast Music v. Columbia Broadcasting System*, 441 U.S. 1 (1979).

individual drivers would arguably be less plausible. On the other hand, the claim has some validity because the hybrid platform model in combination with the revenue model based on transaction fees adopted by on-demand transportation platforms creates an alignment of interests between Uber's profits and higher fare prices. If Uber extracts 20 percent of the price of a ride from a driver, higher prices mean higher revenue for Uber. By extracting a fraction of the fare that the platform itself has set, a platform's control of prices not only serves the scope of coordinating supply and demand but may also serve to increase platform's profit at the expense of maximizing the network's value. It is not the centralized pricing system alone that creates concerns, but the fact that the fees extracted from drivers in each transaction create incentives to increase the price of rides.

A second, related lesson that emerges from this antitrust case is that centralized pricing has important efficiency properties, and it is plausibly a more efficient mechanism to coordinate supply and demand and reduce search and information costs that afflict taxi markets compared to a purely decentralized platform market-place with independent drivers. Knowing prices in advance reduces information asymmetries, and a central price setter can manage fluctuations of supply and demand or congestion issues more efficiently than decentralized drivers who do not have the ability, incentive, and information to do so. At any given time, there is a possible supply-demand synchronization problem between taxis and passengers, which expands waiting times or leaves taxis empty. As long as the mechanism used to set prices reflects changes in supply and demand, it is a superior form of coordination for on-demand transportation services. Despite the fact that the technology of sharing economy platform could in theory allow the creation of a hypothetical marketplace for competing drivers with the power to set prices (something that was not possible for traditional taxi drivers), the benefits of competition would significantly be outweighed by the losses of not having a centralized price system, especially considering that concerns of collusion via the algorithm could be addressed by imposing different revenue models based on membership fees.[276] The regulatory question, then, is whether the form of price regulation done by a dominant platform can lead to monopoly pricing due to the failure of inter-platform competition between price setting platform that arise with a natural monopoly, requiring substitution of private platform regulation with publicly set rates.

---

[276] The best way to solve possible concerns of collusion or high prices is therefore not to eliminate algorithmic pricing in favor of decentralized price competition among drivers, but to impose a different revenue model. For instance, if Uber hypothetically charged drivers an annual membership fee, rather than a transaction fee from each ride, while retaining control of price setting, efficient centralized pricing would not conflict with the possibility of extracting extra revenue from the price of a ride, which would more closely align with market forces.

5.3 IS ON-DEMAND TRANSPORTATION AND RIDE-HAILING NATURALLY MONOPOLISTIC?

The rationale for the economic regulation of taxi services has been extensively debated in the economic literature. Proponents generally rely on a number of market imperfections that cannot be fixed by unregulated markets: high transaction and search costs for comparison shopping, imperfect information, and risks of price gouging, and various negative externalities, including congestion. Defenders of deregulation instead point to the various economic costs imposed by restrictions on entry, price regulation, lack of incentives to innovate, and regulatory capture.[277]

The technology of sharing economy platforms has reshaped the form of these concerns and the normative rationale of many of the existing regulatory requirements. For example, when looking for a taxi on the street, it may be difficult for customers to evaluate or compare the price of a ride, absent price regulation.[278] This information asymmetry leads to higher transaction costs, and gives drivers the ability to price gouge under certain conditions. This is no longer the case with the advent of ride-sharing platforms, where passengers can know upfront the estimated cost of their trip, and they can also compare prices at a relatively low cost. Similarly, one of the theoretical justifications for entry regulations and restrictions has been to ensure a degree of quality and prevent issues that may arise from other information asymmetries. However, sharing economy platforms have developed highly reliable mechanisms to ensure safety and quality, including rating and reviews, and the ability to track back transactions and users' profiles once a ride is complete.

In the same way that the technological features of sharing economy platforms have challenged many of the assumptions about negative externalities and asymmetric information that previously required regulation, technological change has an impact in the way it changes the assumptions regarding the presence of natural monopolies as a form of market failure in the taxi industry. It is generally accepted that the presence of scale economies did not justify traditional taxicab regulation based on the identification of natural monopoly conditions in taxi markets.[279] While there are some scale economies in the operation of a dispatch system, where larger firms can spread the costs of dispatching at a significant advantage, and may coordinate supply and demand more efficiently than smaller firms,[280] a U-shaped cost curve seems to characterize the provision of taxi services, although it remains

---

[277] For a review, see Adrian T. Moore and Ted Balaker, "Do Economists Reach a Conclusion on Taxi Deregulation?" (2006) 3, no. 2 Econ J Watch, 109.

[278] Robert Cairns and Liston-Heyes Catherine, "Competition and Regulation in the Taxi Industry" (1996) 59, no. 1 J Public Econ, 1.

[279] See Tamer Cetin and Elizabeth Deakin, "Regulation of Taxis and the Rise of Ridesharing" (2017) Transp Policy, available at www.sciencedirect.com/science/article/pii/S0967070X17300409.

[280] Paul Stephen Dempsey, "Taxi Industry Regulation, Deregulation, and Reregulation: The Paradox of Market Failure," SSRN Scholarly Paper ID 2241306 (Rochester, NY: Social Science Research Network, 1996) at 88.

unclear where the minimum efficient scale of operation lies for a taxi network and dispatch system.

As the case study argues, it is plausible that the technology of current sharing economy platforms shifts the point of optimal efficient scale toward larger networks. Demand-side scale in the form of larger and thicker networks appears more important in the ignition phase for a service that is offered on-demand and relies on dramatic reductions of waiting times; fostering a larger network appears more important for the development of mechanisms like ratings and reviews necessary to address asymmetric information problems; data may further contribute to efficiency for the broader purpose of traffic management, and so on. In small urban areas, therefore, the operation of ride-hailing platforms may become more strongly naturally monopolistic, depending on various factors such as the size and density of the population, the importance of alternative methods of transportation, etc. Nonetheless, larger metropolitan areas may still efficiently sustain the presence of competing networks not only in the short term but also in the medium and long run.

Discussed below are the main determinants of concentration that may or may not lead to the emergence of a natural monopoly including: the strength of network externalities between drivers and passengers; the fixed cost – marginal cost ratio in developing and operating the dispatching, and the importance of data for algorithmic routing and planning. In conclusion, the strengths of natural monopoly tendencies for ride-hailing platforms can arguably be placed in between horizontal search and e-commerce marketplaces.

5.3.1 *Network Externalities and Matching: Availability, Waiting Times, and Ratings*

Creating a network relies on important indirect network externalities between drivers and passengers, especially during the initiation phase where a platform faces the classic chicken-and-egg problem between the two users' groups.[281] Undoubtedly, the core function of ride-hailing platforms is matching the two sides of the platforms, and the indirect network externalities between them are significant drivers of market concentration. An additional driver reduces waiting time for passengers, and additional passengers reduce idle times for drivers. The importance of a sufficiently large, thick network of drivers and riders is one of the determinants that may give rise to a natural monopoly. If network externalities are strong and continue to add value even at a large network size, the dominant platform with the larger network will eventually be the most efficient provider and the market will be in the long term able to support only a single network.

The eventuality that network externalities will remain positive indefinitely or for an extent larger than overall market's demand is, however, implausible in the case of

---

[281]   Evans and Schmalensee, *supra*, note 55.

on-demand transportation platforms. Despite the fact that it is necessary to scale and obtain a certain critical mass of drivers and passengers to have a reliable network and to reduce average wait times, increasing the size of the network is likely not as critical after a minimum scale is reached, and marginal reductions of wait times may become insignificant. It is also plausible that a platform may encourage a degree of extra capacity and a number of vacant cabs at any given time, which may induce drivers to be present on multiple platforms, including smaller ones, to increase the chances of obtaining a ride. In such a case, the choice of a multihoming driver does not create a significant advantage for a given network.

The value of network externalities therefore is increasing at first and then becomes negligible after a certain threshold. At first, there is significant value arising from network externalities and expanding the network, so that in the initial phase a larger and fast-growing network benefits from increased availability and reduced waiting times. After a certain size is reached, increasing the number of passengers and drivers does not add substantially to improving availability and wait times. For example, having three or fifteen cars that could match a passenger's request, or reducing the wait time below two or three minutes does not create a substantial difference between networks. Platforms with a significantly smaller share of the market compared to the dominant platform, for example, have often analogous response times and availability. It is therefore unlikely that network externalities, despite being an important driver of concentration, will in themselves necessarily give rise to natural monopoly conditions, because their positive value is likely not infinite and this may leave room for competing networks to coexist depending on the size of demand.

The value of network externalities connects with the importance of data, where additional drivers and passengers add value to the overall network because both generate data that contribute to improving the matching algorithm and to the development of the ratings and reviews system. More data allow more refined and real-time matching, and with more data on users and past rides more reviews become available on the network and transactions become more reliable. For both groups of users, having positive ratings and a richer reviews profile on a specific platform reduce the willingness to switch to another competing platform, where positive ratings and reviews would need to be rebuilt. These scale effects associated with data for both the matching algorithm and review system are significant, possibly extending minimum efficient scale toward larger networks compared to taxis. However, it is plausible that diminishing returns in data collection for the purpose of matching and ratings are likely to occur once a sufficiently large network is established.

5.3.2 Data and the Efficiency of Centralized Algorithmic Routing and Planning

Beyond algorithmic matching between drivers and passengers, the predictive nature of centralized algorithmic routing, ride planning, and traffic management in a given local market may benefit from access to data. From a social perspective, centralized algorithmic routing, coordination of self-driving vehicles,[282] services such as UberPOOL that pair riders headed in the same direction, and traffic management through data analysis may be seen as increasing the efficiency of a single centralized system that optimizes routing and planning in a given geographical area. Thus, data may have additional value beyond the mere matchmaking between drivers and passengers through the platform model, which perhaps may become even more pronounced under integrated models with automated vehicles whose operation and management substantially rely on data. Hence, while there are clear limits to the value of data for the purpose of matching, from an efficiency perspective a single network may be better able to coordinate overall traffic and congestion and operate routing and planning thanks to access to more data.

5.3.3 *Supply-Side Economies of Scale*

There are some economies of scale in dispatch operations for taxicabs.[283] A traditional dispatch system must carry out a range of administrative tasks, handling contracts with licensees, manage ride schedules, bookings, and so on. The fixed costs related to dispatch services can be spread with larger networks, so that economies of scale allow larger dispatch systems to provide better services at a lower price compared to smaller ones. Early empirical studies on economies of scale and costs in the taxicab industry found a U-shaped curve for average costs.[284] A study of the Chicago taxi industry, for example, found that cost per trip drops off rapidly as ridership increased up to 50,000 trips per year, but then costs starts to increase again. With ridership over 50,000, the operator needs more dispatchers and administration and encounters higher coordination costs. As a result, in geographic areas where the number of trips exceeds 100,000 per year, more than one firm can provide services efficiently. Therefore, economies of scale are present but taper off at a certain point, depending among other things on the density of the population, size of the geographic area, and availability of other ways of transportation, with smaller urban areas plausibly served more efficiently by a single provider.[285]

There are also limits to supply-side scale economies that apply in the case of ride-hailing platforms: in fact, fixed costs of entry (for example, developing a ride-hailing app) are not necessarily particularly high, especially compared to horizontal search, and diseconomies of scale may arise at a certain point in broader markets with a larger demand. The major challenge for sustainable entry and competition

[282] For a discussion, see the *Economist, supra*, note 252.
[283] See, for instance, Edward C. Gallick and David E. Sisk, "A Reconsideration of Taxi Regulation" (1987) 3, no. 1 J Law Econ Organ, 117.
[284] Terence Brow, "Economic Analysis of the Taxicab Industry in Pennsylvania: Demand and Cost" (1973) Prepared for U.S. Department of Transportation.
[285] Anthony M. Pagano and Claire E. McKnight, "Economies of Scale in the Taxicab Industry: Some Empirical Evidence from the United States" (1983) 17, no. 3 J Transp Econ Policy, 299.

therefore appears to remain on the demand side, whereby creating an established network of affiliated drivers and passengers in the presence of an established provider, as well as refining algorithmic matching and management of supply and demand,[286] and developing reliable online ratings and reviews may all require a degree of scale through the development of sufficiently large and thick networks.

5.4 A RANGE OF POLICIES BETWEEN COMPETITION AND NATURAL MONOPOLY

Coupling the role of network externalities and data for matching with the potential importance of scale in data for algorithmic prediction of routing and ride management suggest that ride-hailing platforms may be more likely to become natural monopolies than traditional taxicab services. The likelihood depends, among other things, on the extent of demand, size, and density of population in a given geographic area. Especially in smaller areas, the fixed costs of developing the platform and subsidizing participation may be spread in a way that decrease average costs over the entire market demand, while the value of network externalities when adding additional users on the platform may remain increasing over the same range of demand. In larger and denser urban areas, it is possible that the value of network externalities will start decreasing for an established and sufficiently large network, and that average costs may increase to the point where competing multiple networks can coexist.[287] Related, the combination of demand and supply side scale economies characterizing on-demand transportation platforms may also possibly give rise to weak natural monopolies, a scenario that makes entry feasible but not efficient, in that it fragments the market creating wasteful frictions between competing platforms.

Given the ambiguous nature of the forces leading to naturally concentrated ride-hailing markets, there are a number of policy approaches depending on whether the market can sustain effective competition among platforms, whether there is a clearly identified natural monopoly, or whether the market remains poised between the two structures. These policy options are discussed in turn. The first two options, natural monopoly regulation and franchise bidding, gravitate toward the promotion of efficient concentration, while the third option through competition policy intervention underline the beneficial role of competition.

---

[286] Nicolas Garcia Belmonte, "Engineering Intelligence Through Data Visualization at Uber" (May 3, 2016), available at https://eng.uber.com/data-viz-intel/.

[287] With smaller demand, positive network externalities and decreasing average costs may make a single network more efficient than competition, but as demand becomes larger a market may sustain and benefit from fragmentation and the coexistence of competing networks.

5.4.1 *Regulating Ride-Hailing Platforms*

In the case of a ride-hailing natural monopolist, where competition is not feasible and efficiency makes a single provider more desirable, a menu of regulations is required to address the resulting market power. For example, regulation may be desirable because a ride-hailing natural monopolist may exploit its market power by overcharging passengers for the ride and/or extracting an excessive fee from passengers without inducing entry of competing networks. It may also reduce the quality standards of the service, or leverage market power into non-naturally monopolistic segments. In order to evaluate the desirability of concrete and specific regulatory instruments, in particular with regard to price and entry, it will be useful to compare the economic and technological conditions that characterize sharing economy services and that may justify natural monopoly regulation, with the rationales that have permeated and historically justified regulation of traditional taxis.

Price regulation. The first form of desirable intervention entails price regulation of both the fee extracted from drivers, which is the main source of profit for sharing economy platforms, and the price of rides. With competition between platforms, both prices would be expected to adjust to the competitive levels reflecting fluctuations of supply and demand. With a natural platform monopoly, however, the price set by the platform may be a supra-competitive price resulting from an exercise of market power that does not elicit market entry.

The desirability of price regulation for a natural monopoly platform differs from the justifications on which the regulation of taxis has been based, namely, information asymmetries and search costs in particular. In the traditional taxi market, generally, the competitive price of a particular trip will be difficult to estimate in advance.[288] Riders would have to search out offers from multiple drivers before accepting a ride, and drivers would look for the most valuable passengers and lower cost trips. Given that demand in this market is for an immediate service, search costs are extremely high and can be a source of market failure. For passengers, negotiating over the price of a ride would be a wasteful source of transaction costs, and being in a taxi without knowing the price ex ante may create a situational monopoly and hence result in price gauging by drivers. For drivers, the uncertainty about the cost of providing a ride to a passenger (not only distance, but also density and ability to obtain a return ride) may result in cherry picking and drivers excessively competing over the most profitable rides.

Historically, price regulation addressed these sorts of market failure and the inefficiencies of private contracting by establishing average cost pricing, coupled with rules requiring drivers to accept all customers (with average cost pricing some trips are more profitable than others and drivers could otherwise reject unprofitable or less profitable trips), and minimum quality standards that may otherwise be

[288] Gallick and Sisk, *supra*, note 283.

underprovided with regulated prices (drivers may respond by reducing costs in the form of lowering quality). The technological features of the sharing economy phenomenon have changed some of the assumptions on which price regulation is based. The search costs of figuring out prices that affected traditional taxi services have been eliminated by the ability to check estimated prices on the platform. A passenger can know in advance the estimated price of a ride, and therefore does not face the same search costs and asymmetric information. Bearing this in mind, price regulation no longer appears justifiable on the basis of these rationales.

Instead, the rationale for price regulation with a natural monopoly ride-hailing platform is that it may have the ability to charge monopoly prices. Since it operates on the basis of centralized price setting rather than under a pure marketplace model,[289] and thus operates essentially as a price regulator, lack of inter-platform competition may create market power and enable the natural monopolist to charge supra-competitive drivers' fee and passengers' fares. In order to deal with monopoly pricing charged by a ride-hailing network, a regulator might have a number of alternative options. First, it may regulate the fee obtained by drivers, which is the source of revenue obtained from each ride, to provide a normal rate of return to the platform. However, because the fee is a percentage of the fare, it may be necessary to also cap the prices charged to passengers. Alternatively, a regulator may want to separate the source of revenue from the coordination function played by algorithmic pricing. This could entail, for instance, charging drivers a regulated membership fee to join the network, but allowing them to earn the full amount of fares by eliminating the transaction fee from individual rides, leaving to the network control of setting the prices of the latter.

The desirability of price regulation in the case of natural monopoly, as previously discussed in the case of search, depends on the costs and complexity of regulating prices, the magnitude of allocative inefficiency, and whether second-best instruments such as contestability and threat of displacement may act as substitutes to direct regulation of fares and fees. It is not implausible that a dominant and established network may use its price setting power to charge monopoly pricing to either drivers or passengers (or both). On the one hand, direct price regulation of rides and fees at the level of local markets may not be as complex as in the case of regulating search and search advertising prices with a global search engine. On the

---

[289] As explained, there are efficiency reasons why this is desirable. A pure marketplace model would inevitably increase transaction costs, because even though driver and passenger would not negotiate in person, drivers would have to continually adjust their prices on the app. Second, in many cases there would be little social gain from the competitive bids for each trip, which would result in wealth transfers between drivers and passengers more than allocative effects. Third, the platform has the ability to adjust prices and fees to increase the number of matches between drivers and passengers managing overall supply and demand more efficiently. For example, see Edward C. Gallick and David E. Sisk, "Specialized Assets and Taxi Regulation: An Inquiry into The Possible Efficiency Motivation of Regulation," Working Paper No. 119 (Washington, DC: Bureau of Economics, Federal Trade Commission, 1984).

other hand, however, the lower degree of fixed costs and lower entry barriers that characterize ride-hailing compared to search, as well as the availability of regulatory tools such as portability of profiles across networks that can counteract the entry barrier created by network externalities, have the potential to make a natural monopoly position more contestable through the threat of potential entry, possibly reducing, at least to an extent, the necessity of direct price regulation in the presence of a contestable natural monopoly.

Regulation of Entry. The medallion system, as the form of entry restrictions to the taxi industry that prevailed in many jurisdictions, did not find its justification on a natural monopoly framework. One obvious and common explanation is that medallions are the result of attempts to protect and enhance the wealth of member drivers and medallion owners. Other explanations suggest that medallions may have also served as an enforcement tool for the average cost-pricing rule. Gallick and Sisk, for instance, contend that the technological change generated by the advent of the mass-produced automobile, and the resulting enhanced access to car ownership led to the unraveling of average cost price regulation.[290] Medallions served as an enforcement tool against hit-and-run entry that could occur at peak hours and on more profitable routes, which would undercut the regulated average price and possibly undermine the efficiency of price regulation requiring all customers to be served at a uniformed fixed price. On this perspective, the medallion system was imperfect because it inefficiently restricted entry, but it was the most effective way, among alternative tools, to ensure compliance with the average pricing rule.

From the perspective of individual drivers, the technology provided by sharing economy platforms can serve as an alternative system to the medallion system. Because entry and transactions are mediated by platforms, hit-and-run entry by individual drivers is not feasible outside the mediation of the platform, which itself enforces a version of average pricing to which drivers have to comply because the transactions can happen only via the app. The need for medallions as a way to enforce the average pricing rule for each driver loses its significance when the platforms mediate transactions and can therefore enforce compliance with regulated prices, whether or not the platform or local authorities do the regulation.

A different question is instead whether there is any normative rationale to limit entry of competing platforms (as opposed to entry of individual drivers). This is particularly the case with a weak natural monopoly, where a possible rationale for restricting entry is that it undermines the efficiency of concentration, and thus causes higher industry costs and welfare losses.[291] The natural monopolist may not be able to prevent entry by other firms because average costs are increasing and the

[290] Gallick and Sisk, *supra*, note 283.

[291] Douglas Gegax and Kenneth Nowotny, "Competition and the Electric Utility Industry: An Evaluation" (1993) 10, no. 1 Yale J Regul, available at https://digitalcommons.law.yale.edu/yjreg/vol10/iss1/4 at 67.

new firms will excessively compete for the most profitable segments of the market, even though social welfare would be increased with one firm. In such a case, there is a trade-off between inefficient cost duplication and possible dynamic benefits of competition. In the case of ride-hailing networks, the need to restrict entry may make a stronger case for auctioning the market to a single platform through franchise bidding.

Market Power Leveraging. Finally, if a ride-hailing network becomes a natural monopoly and it is vertically integrated, regulation could, in theory, also have to address the problem of market power leveraging from the natural monopoly segment to competitive markets. Hypothetical cases that could emerge from vertical integration, where the natural monopolist and network provider also supplies on the network with its proprietary services, may include, for example, leveraging market power into food and other kinds of delivery service related to urban logistics, such as UberEATS for restaurant deliveries or UberRUSH to dispatch couriers, etc. In the ride-hailing market, however, it remains unclear whether (and in what form) issues of self-preferencing and discrimination will, in fact, take place.

5.4.2 Auctioning the Market to a Single Network

A compelling alternative to the regulation of a natural monopoly is auctioning the market to a single ride-hailing platform. When the local government auctions off a monopoly franchise contract, bidding is a form of competition for the market that replaces competition in the market and the need for natural monopoly regulation, where the bids by firms would be the price at which they are willing to serve the market. If entry is feasible but inefficient, franchise bidding may be an attractive alternative to the regulation of ride-hailing platforms. Unlike universal search and online shopping, on-demand transportation services are local in nature. They are tied to a specific geographic location and its particular features in terms of spatial extension, density, and size of the population. Bidding may therefore be a valid option in a specific area that is likely to create weak natural monopolies, as this would overcome the burden of regulating the market and it would emulate competition for the market.

The major downside of franchise bidding is that it can be optimal from a static perspective, but it is affected by a number of shortcomings from a dynamic point of view related to the inevitable incompleteness of the franchise contract. The contract would require specifications ex ante of how price will change as conditions change, and possibly a periodic review process, which ultimately requires a form of public oversight that is close to natural monopoly regulation. The government will also be exposed to ex post contractual opportunism if it cannot switch suppliers easily, plus incurring the costs of other auctions. Investments in durable and specific assets and human capital whose value exceed the duration of the contract may also increase the costs of switching. All in all, where franchise bidding requires a degree of oversight that is akin to regulation, and implies significant costs of switching at the end of the contract, its advantages may be reduced when compared to regulation.[292]

Moreover, there are market-based solutions to inefficient frictions created by excessive fragmentation that can be delivered by ride-hailing platform aggregators, metaplatforms that aggregate together on the same online map the competing operators and their respective prices, which can substantially reduce frictions and switching costs for both drivers and passengers and can be a valuable pragmatic solution to some of the costs of having multiple networks.[293] Yet it remains the case that auctioning off the market to a single platform remains an attractive option as an alternative to natural monopoly regulation. Its merits will depend more on the specific design of the franchise contract than its theoretical desirability for cases where inefficient entry may distort the efficiency of the market.

5.4.3 *Promoting Inter-Platform Competition*

When a market can effectively sustain in the long term multiple competing ride-hailing networks, the straightforward approach is to promote inter-platform competition. The major benefits of a competitive market are that each platform has more pressure to reduce the price of rides, lower the commission charged to drivers, innovate, and promote competition based on the quality of the service provided to both riders and passengers.

There are a number of competition policy priorities that are pertinent to the ride-sharing market. First, exclusivity inducing mechanisms can increase the costs of switching and multihoming, both of which determine the scope of competition when a market can accommodate multiple competing platforms. For instance, insofar as independent drivers are not exclusive to a specific platform, the ability of both drivers and passengers to be affiliated with multiple competing platform places discipline on platforms' behavior. It may nonetheless be expected that platforms may have incentives to reduce competitive forces by imposing some forms of exclusivity on their users, which can reduce inter-platform competition if a substantial number of drivers become exclusive to the incumbent through direct and indirect means.

Exclusivity can be imposed as a result of indirect network externalities, because the elasticity of demand on one side is affected by the value of network externalities arising on the other side of the market, and the platform can obtain market power

---

[292] See, for instance, Harold Demsetz, "Why Regulate Utilities?" (1968) 11, no. 1 *Journal of Law and Economics*, 55; and critique by Oliver E. Williamson, "Franchise Bidding for Natural Monopolies-in General and with Respect to CATV" (1976) 7, no. 1 Bell J Econ, 73.

[293] See "Wired, Uber and Lyft's Never-Ending Quest to Crush Price Comparison Apps" (November 7, 2018), available at https://www.wired.com/story/uber-and-lyfts-never-ending-quest-to-crush-price-comparison-apps/.

from those indirect network externalities that can be exercised on one side of the market. Enforcement therefore should be particularly strict on explicit forms of exclusivity, but also evaluate the possible exclusivity-inducing effects of various reward programs that may be designed to practically make multihoming impossible. Moreover, tie-ins can be potentially problematic. For example, preinstallation of a given dominant ride-hailing platform on mobile phones, or providing a specific service under a phone plan may all be ways to induce usage of a given platform together with the purchase of mobile devices.

In addition, and given the importance of indirect network externalities for platforms such as Uber and Lyft that rely on developing large and reliable networks, it may be desirable to complement antitrust enforcement with targeted forms of regulation that promote portability of users' profiles across platforms. Because individual ratings and review can be a significant source of entry and switching barriers, portability of individual ratings and reviews is a promising instrument to reduce frictions that users may otherwise face in joining alternative networks, especially new ones. Such regulatory instruments can be powerful tools to ensure that actual and potential competition is at work in the presence of strong network externalities. As a result, the standard antitrust focus on targeting forms of foreclosure may benefit from some complementary ex ante rules like portability that ensure that entry, including potential entry, is an effective competitive threat to the established dominant network, whether naturally monopolistic or not. To be effective, however, these regulatory instruments need to be enforced in a timely manner, arguably faster than a standard antitrust case.

Finally, a further market failure possibly associated with competition between networks that needs to be evaluated is the problem of price skimming. Competition between price-setting platforms may lead to low-cost entrants targeting very profitable and dense areas of a market, leaving less profitable routes underprovided. In the same way that traditional taxis required medallions for the enforcement of average cost pricing, a question may be raised as to whether price competition among platforms may ultimately result in price skimming that undermines transactions. Eric Posner, for example, argues with regard to Uber that without uniform average pricing for all market participants output may be reduced and the market unravel as a result of entry by low-cost platform providers and excessive competition over low-cost and more profitable rides.[294]

Since for ride-sharing platform it is important to ensure reliability of transactions for buyers and expand the size of the network (an incentive that may become even more important with the value of collecting data for self-driving cars), incentives to price skim may be reduced by platforms themselves. In addition, as a proxy to ensure a normal rate of return to drivers facing lower and higher cost trips, it is unclear that average pricing rules is the only or most efficient way to ensure efficient output.

---

[294] Posner, *supra*, note 69.

Matching platforms, for example, use various strategies to elicit efficient matching. One of them is through pricing on each side (the price of the ride and the fee from the driver). Another is coarsening strategic information.[295] In the case of ride-hailing platforms, passenger destination is generally not revealed until after the driver has picked up the passenger. The reason why platforms do not disclose all relevant information is to overcome price skimming by drivers. Hence, platforms have instruments to avoid price skimming, and it remains doubtful whether platform competition may really create problems associated with it.

5.5 CONCLUSION

The rationale for regulating the market for the provision of taxicabs has historically not been based on the presence of natural monopoly conditions. On the contrary, while some form of scale economies is present, especially in the operation of a dispatch system, average costs appear generally to follow a U-shaped curve, which make scale particularly important in small local areas but not for larger geographical markets, where expansion beyond minimum efficient scale is likely to turn into diseconomies after a certain size is reached. In those instances, the market is served more efficiently by multiple networks than a single operator.

Similarly, ride-hailing platforms are not necessarily natural monopolies. Fixed costs of entry are not very high, and the positive effects of network externalities are likely to taper off after a certain critical mass is reached. Especially in larger cities, these factors may leave room for competition between networks, which can create a number of positive effects on prices, fees, and quality of the services. The technological features of ride-hailing platform can, however, increase the chances of natural monopolies compared to the traditional taxi dispatch systems, by pushing the frontier of efficient scale toward larger networks and geographic areas. Moreover, algorithmic matching and predictions for routing and planning in a local area through collection of users' data benefit substantially from increased centralization, possibly making the case for a larger single network serving more efficiently a given local market more compelling from a social welfare perspective.

Some important considerations for the possible role of regulation emerge when bringing together the characteristics of ride-hailing services evaluated in the case study. First, because a pure competitive marketplace between independent drivers remains undesirable even under current technology, platforms remain essentially private market regulators in competition with each other and the local government. Hence, the idea of regulating ride-hailing markets is to an extent a choice between regulatory competition among platforms or public regulation. Second, considering the local nature of the service, and given that in some instances ride-hailing networks

---

[295]   Gleb Romanyuk and Alex Smolin, "Cream Skimming and Information Design in Matching Markets" Am Econ J Microecon, available at www.aeaweb.org/articles?id=10.1257/mic.20170154.

may give rise to weak natural monopoly where entry is feasible but inefficient, the option of awarding contracts through franchise bidding may represent a more desirable solution in the presence of a natural monopoly that price regulation in particular geographical areas. Third, given that matchmaking platforms offering ride-hailing services depend on their ability to create large, thick, and safe networks, the potential objective of promoting inter-platform competition where feasible would benefit from complementary forms of ex ante rules such as portability of user profiles (including ratings and reviews) that reduce switching costs and the barriers created by network externalities. Last, the prospect of autonomous vehicles implies that the market is undergoing an important wave of technological change. Any potential rationale for regulatory intervention for current ride-hailing platforms should also take into account the desirability and timing of intervention in the midst of such technological shifts.

6

The Institutional Dimension of Alternative Policy Options

Building on the application of the natural monopoly framework to the specificities of three case studies, this chapter derives broader and more general policy principles that may be pertinent to digital platform markets at large beyond the three industries evaluated in this book. As seen, digital platform markets are characterized by heterogeneous features and different tendencies toward natural monopoly, calling for case-by-case policy approaches in each industry. At the same time, digital platforms display recurring economic and technological features from which general implications can be derived in order to illuminate common policy principles related to market power and competition. This chapter distills general policy implications for digital platform industries by evaluating and comparing the merit and limits of alternative policy instruments, highlighting, in particular, the concrete institutional costs, complexities, and limitations associated with both ex ante and ex post approaches to market power. The chapter is organized as follows. First, it discusses alternative policy approaches potentially pertinent to digital platform industries, specifically sector-specific regulation, franchise bidding, public ownership, and competition policy. On that basis, it then derives key implications and challenges for the development of policy approaches to address competition and market power, arguing in particular that competition policy and forms of regulatory intervention must be envisioned as complements in digital platform markets.

6.1 SECTOR-SPECIFIC REGULATION

The standard price and entry regulation paradigm is in theory a potential policy response to the emergence of a natural monopoly platform.[296] Regulation would in

---

[296] In the commentary, there have been some calls for public utility regulation and the creation of public regulatory agencies. None of the proposals, however, offers a substantiated analysis of the

most cases be implemented by a new ad hoc industry-specific regulator,[297] or by delegating to existing regulatory agencies the regulation of specific natural monopoly platforms.[298] Although in practice models for the division of labor between competition authorities and industry regulators differ,[299] the ideal division of tasks and institutional comparative advantage favors the model that entails delegating the enforcement of competition laws to competition agencies and courts and remanding to sector-specific agencies the regulation of natural monopoly. Reflecting the advantages of institutional specialization, therefore, the standard regulatory approach to a natural monopoly platform would ideally require delegation to an industry-specific regulator rather than competition agencies.[300]

6.1.1 Price and Entry Regulation

One target of regulatory intervention entails price regulation. As seen, a natural monopolist will be able to charge supra-competitive prices creating an allocative inefficiency problem without inviting market entry. These considerations have generally required regulation of price and output, subject to a fair rate of return on investments and a firm's viability constraints in the absence of government subsidies. In the presence of scale economies, marginal cost pricing will typically not yield sufficient revenues to cover

actual conditions that may or may not give rise to natural monopolies in specific markets, or a proper framework for evaluating available regulatory tools that may be appropriate in particular platform markets. See, for instance, Frank Pasquale and Oren Bracha, "Federal Search Commission? Access, Fairness and Accountability in the Law of Search" (2008) 93 *Cornell Law Review*, 1149; Shalini Nagarajan, "EU Antitrust Chief Keeps Open Threat to Break Up Google: Report," *Reuters* (March 25, 2018), avaliable at www.reuters.com/article/us-eu-google-antitrust-idUSKBN1H110H; Elizabeth Warren, *Reigniting Competition in the American Economy* (2016); *supra*, note 35; Nick Srnicek, "We Need to Nationalise Google, Facebook and Amazon. Here's Why," *The Guardian* (August 30, 2017), available at www.theguardian.com/commentisfree/2017/aug/30/nationalise-google -facebook-amazon-data-monopoly-platform-public-interest.

[297] Natural monopolies have been generally left outside the purview of competition policy and have been subject to sector-specific industry regulation, although, in other cases, natural monopolies have remained outside the purview of industry regulation and been left to competition law, either because they are too small to justify administrative regulation, or because it is often hard to distinguish between natural and nonnatural monopolies.

[298] The number of regulation agencies around the world increased significantly during the 1990s and 2000s. For example, the number of industry regulators in the telecommunication sector increased from twenty to 120, and from ten to seventy in the electricity industry. See, for instance, David Levi-Faur, "The Global Diffusion of Regulatory Capitalism" (2005) 598 *Annals of the American Academy of Political and Social Science*, 12.

[299] The model adopted in jurisdictions such as Australia and New Zealand, for example, is based on a broader aggregation of functions where competition authorities are in charge of both competition law enforcement and forms of economic regulation to specific sectors.

[300] See Edward M. Iacobucci and Michael J. Trebilcock, "The Design of Regulatory Institutions for the Canadian Telecommunications Sector" (2007) Can Public Policy, available at www .utpjournals.press/doi/abs/10.3138/cpp.33.2.127 at 127–145; Phillip Areeda, "Essential Facilities: An Epithet in Need of Limiting Principles" (1989) 58, no. 3 Antitrust Law J, 841.

total costs, and price regulation of natural monopolies is designed to allow the natural monopolist to at least recover its costs and have sufficient financial incentives to provide services to consumers who value the service more than the cost of supplying them.[301] Forms of price regulation have traditionally included rate of return regulation, cost of service, and incentive regulation.

A natural monopoly platform may charge supra-competitive prices either in aggregate, or by exercising market power on one side. As discussed, a ride-sharing platform can raise the total price by increasing the ride charged to passengers and the commission charged to drivers, or it may increase the price one side only, for example, by keeping the price of rides constant while increasing the fee extracted from drivers. A natural monopoly platform may also distort the structure of prices without increasing overall price levels. Price regulation could, therefore, include a cap on the total price charged by the platform, or regulation of specific price structures and prices charged on each side and may also attempt to internalize negative externalities on nonplatform users created by the pass-through of platform fees to both platform and nonplatform consumers. Because the multisided business model is often based on prices at zero on one side of the market, regulatory intervention may also include the imposition of alternative business models on which a platform operates, such as requiring the firm to give a choice between ad-based free services and subscription rates for users without advertising.

Although there is no reason in principle to preclude the ability of a monopoly platform to exercise market power through high prices, concrete implementation of price regulation is likely to be complex in practice and it does not come without costs. Price regulation and rate of return regulation in particular would be highly problematic due to various measurement issues, calculation of the risk entailed in becoming a natural monopolist, the global nature of many digital platforms, and the rapidity of technological change. In general, the case for price regulation rests on a comparison between, on the one hand, the magnitude of allocative inefficiencies resulting from the natural monopoly that price regulation is expected to alleviate, and, on the other hand, the costs of regulation and the availability of second-best responses that may restrain monopoly pricing in lieu of regulation.

In addition to problems of allocative efficiency and pricing, productive inefficiency can also arise from excessive entry of competitors that entail costly duplication of facilities.[302] Inefficient competitors may be attracted by the high profits of the natural monopolist, but their entry would either fail or be inefficient, which may require regulation of entry. Regulation of natural monopoly platforms may therefore

[301] As a result, there is generally a conflict between firm viability constraints and efficient pricing when costs are subadditive.
[302] Absent regulatory constraints on price and entry, the presence of subadditive costs per se does not necessarily lead to the conclusion that a single firm will naturally emerge in equilibrium, which justifies entry regulation in industries with natural monopoly characteristics where multiple firms may inefficiently survive in equilibrium and compete imperfectly.

also include entry restrictions to avoid wasteful network duplication and inefficient fragmentation. For analogous reasons, horizontal break-up is not a desirable policy option with a natural monopoly.[303] On the one hand, there may be some short-term positive effects – for example, breaking up a search engine would offer advertisers a more competitive market and users may indirectly benefit from more competitive conditions (for instance, in the form of higher levels of privacy). On the other hand, various forms of scale would be artificially lost, and fragmentation would ultimately be unsustainable; various forms of economies of scale will eventually recreate a natural monopoly while in the interim foregoing the benefits of aggregation.[304]

6.1.2 *Vertical Integration and Leveraging*

A further problem addressed by regulation is one of market power leveraging by a vertically integrated natural monopoly platform. These concerns have been prominent in network industries in transition from regulation to competition, such as electricity and natural gas, where transmission and distribution segments remained naturally monopolistic and regulated, while competitive segments of the supply chain that moved toward discipline by market forces may still have to rely on access to the natural monopoly segment. Vertical integration can weaken competition in the competitive segments because a natural monopolist that controls a bottleneck facility has economic incentives to exploit market power in noncompetitive segments and extend it by creating artificial advantages for the competitive arm of the integrated firm. There are various ways in which the natural monopolist can accomplish leveraging. For example, the vertically integrated firm may leverage its monopoly power through different forms of discriminatory behavior, by giving its competitive arms interconnection benefits over potential rivals, or by cross-subsidization of the competitive arms, which involves use of profits earned from the natural monopoly market, and is analogous to predation. Tying, exclusivity, and misallocation of costs of its competitive branch to its natural monopoly segment can also achieve the same anticompetitive purpose.

One way to deal with the issue of leveraging by a vertically integrated monopolist is to mandate nondiscriminatory access to the bottleneck essential input. For example, the owner of a railroad may be required to provide nondiscriminatory access to a rival rail operator, or an electricity transmission grid to a competitor in electricity generation. The regulator must set fair and competitive access terms to the bottleneck facility to ensure that competition is at play in the competitive segment and the natural monopolist is not deprived of the benefits of controlling its interconnection facilities more than is necessary. The regulator must also implement ongoing scrutiny of access terms, modifications of the terms of access due to

---

[303] As previously discussed, proposals to break up tech giants are frequently evoked in public debates on digital platforms. See Taplin, *supra*, note 4; Tepper, *supra*, note 39.

[304] Howard A. Shelanski and J. Gregory Sidak, "Antitrust Divestiture in Network Industries" (2001) 68 Univ Chic Law Rev, 1.

the changes in the costs of the operator, and arbitration of interconnection issues. As seen in the case studies, this issue is particularly prominent in the context of hybrid platforms, namely when a platform operator is also supplying on the platform in competition with third-party providers. In general, digitalization expands the feasibility of access remedies because it tends to reduce scarcity constraints. The concrete desirability and feasibility of this kind of behavioral remedy in specific digital industries depends, for the most part, on the institutional ability to identify and address various subtle forms of discrimination through ongoing monitoring, as well as the effectiveness of remedies in light of inputs' shareability.

An alternative to mandated access is provided by vertical deintegration or prophylactic bans. Traditionally, break-up has been the most extreme remedy for excessive concentration and recurring problems of anticompetitive conduct. Famous cases in the history of antitrust occurred with the break-up of Standard Oil in 1911 and the Bell System in 1982,[305] where in the first case, the firm was divided into thirty-four independent companies, and, in the second case, Baby Bells were created to provide local and regional phone services.[306] Vertical separation is premised on durability of market power, repeated attempts to eliminate competition, and of inapplicability of access remedies, where separation forces a platform vertically integrated in adjacent competitive markets to deintegrate or prohibits the monopolist from integrating into downstream or upstream related markets. A prominent supporter of the latter form of prophylactic separation is Wu, who argues for the implementation of a "separation principle" in information industries,[307] which he defines as a constitutional rather than a regulatory approach. The separation principle essentially requires a distance between the major functions in the information economy, the development of information, control of the network infrastructure, and those that control access,[308] which is a per se rule against vertical integration.

Vertical separation offers straightforward clarity and stronger prevention of market power leveraging.[309] Under full divestiture, the natural monopolist has much weaker incentives or opportunities to leverage its monopoly power. There are, however, various costs associated with vertical structural remedies. As discussed in the context of search, this form of intervention increases transaction costs and foregoes efficient integration, reduces economies of scope and other various benefits of coordination. When it takes the form of a prophylactic ban, it can also cause the default elimination of one competitor from a given market (such a remedy practically reduces rather than increases the number of competitors in a given market).

---

[305] See, generally, *Standard Oil Co of NJ v. United Sates*, [1911] 221 US 1 (Supreme Court); *United States v. American Tel and Tel Co.* [1983] 552 F Supp 131 (Dist Court) at 142, n 42; *Maryland v. United States*, [1983] 460 US 1001 (Supreme Court); Wu, *supra*, note 178.

[306] Wu, *supra*, note 178.

[307] Ibid.

[308] Ibid, at 302.

[309] Tim Wu, "Antitrust via Rulemaking: Competition Catalysts," SSRN Scholarly Paper ID 3058114 (Rochester, NY: Social Science Research Network, 2017).

Crucial for digital platforms, it would also not be easy to determine the boundaries between the natural monopoly and other competitive segments. Unlike the case of electricity, for example, where it may be easy to separate wires and the core network activity from generation and supply segments that are potentially competitive, finding a fine-grained separation point in the context of digital platforms would not be as straightforward, given the fluidity between different segments and more generally the rapid speed of technological change. Although access remedies are also imperfect instruments, they are often superior in that they are more flexible and do not undermine synergies arising from integration.

6.1.3 *The Limits of Standard Regulatory Approaches*

While a perfectly designed regulatory regime could in theory represent a first-best response to the emergence of a natural monopoly platform, its concrete application is likely to be highly imperfect and limited by important institutional constraints. As already seen, one first major limit is created by the unavoidable complexity and resulting costs of regulation. Problems of asymmetric information include firm's costs, conditions prevailing in the firm's market, the potential for adopting more efficient technologies, and effects of regulation on incentives and performance. It is unclear how to measure the risk of investments in obtaining a natural monopoly position when regulating prices, how to practically distinguish between competitive and natural monopoly segments, or how to monitor cost misallocations. Firms will have the ability to exploit strategically information asymmetries, and regulators will face substantial limitations in monitoring the regulation of these markets. In the context of global platforms, solutions may also require regulation at a supranational level, adding additional complexities to the task of the regulator. These considerations alone raise some doubts as to whether the costs of standard regulation are justified in relation to the magnitude of market imperfections, and whether identified concerns can, in fact, be effectively mitigated by other instruments.

There are also other critical problems in the standard regulation paradigm that further limit its desirability in practice. A second shortcoming of ex ante regulation is the standard public choice concern with regulatory capture. Public choice as a positive theory that seeks to explain why governments intervene in markets posits that like private actors, politicians and public officials are assumed to be self-interested, and they need to attract support of the electorate in order to remain in power, which requires resources.[310] In the context of regulatory agencies, public choice theory has suggested that regulatory capture can occur through the control of a regulatory body by special interest groups that operate in the regulated sector,[311]

---

[310] Steven P. Croley, *Regulation and Public Interests: The Possibility of Good Regulatory Government* (Cambridge, MA: Princeton University Press, 2009).

[311] Sam Peltzman, "Toward a More General Theory of Regulation" (1976) 19, no. 2 J Law Econ, 211; George Stigler, "The Theory of Economic Regulation" (1971) 2, no. 1 Bell J Econ, 3.

and empirical evidence confirms that the practice of regulation is not always consistent with the goals of improving welfare. Since a regulatory agency can never be completely independent of political influences, its mandate can shift from providing a solution to market failures, to becoming an instrument for the protection of incumbents, creating a barrier to entry protecting the market position of regulated firms.

The debate on platforms is already politically shaped, with European enforcers accused of being excessively interventionist against foreign-owned platforms, and jurisdictions where such platforms originate being excessively permissive. Debates in competition policy scholarship are also increasingly questioning the desirability of corporate funding for academic research, especially by large tech platforms.[312] Political economy problems, in particular the prospect of creating sector-specific regulators, are likely to be further exacerbated by domestic regulatory initiatives in a context where services are often supra-national in scope.

A final limit, and perhaps the most critical shortcoming of regulation, is one of dynamic performance. As in standard network utilities, regulation can become a form of barrier against technological change that may create inefficient path dependence and reduce dynamic competition. Platforms will have a strong incentive, once regulated and institutionalized, to defend the status quo. This is even more pernicious in technologically dynamic sectors where established market positions can potentially be made more contestable, at least in some markets, and where the adopted regulations may become outdated and eventually invoked by the regulated firm to protect against entry and technological displacement.

As a result, and unlike an idealized version of regulatory intervention, which would appear in theory almost always superior to the shortcoming of market-based outcomes and the inefficiencies associated with market power,[313] these identified institutional limitations of standard ex ante regulation are likely to reduce substantially its desirability in most digital platform industries.

6.2 FRANCHISE BIDDING: AUCTIONING THE MARKET TO A SINGLE PLATFORM

An alternative to the economic regulation of a natural monopoly is auctioning a given market to a single platform provider.[314] In its general form, the state contracts out the provision of a service to a private firm. The government offers a contract for a particular service on the open market, where firms make offers and the government choses the best offer based on selected criteria. Such process is a form of publicly

---

[312]   Denis Waelbroeck and Professor Ioannis Lianos, *Panel Debate: Corporate (and Other) Sponsorship of Academic Research in Competition Law* (UCL Centre for Law, Economics, & Society, 2018).

[313]   Harold Demsetz, "Information and Efficiency: Another Viewpoint" (1969) 12 J Law Econ, 1.

[314]   See Demsetz, *supra*, note 292. And critique by Oliver E. Williamson, "Franchise Bidding for Natural Monopolies-in General and with Respect to CATV" (1976) 7, no. 1 Bell J Econ, 73.

induced competition for the market. The bidder offering the lowest price is awarded the franchise. Contractors have incentives to lower costs and introduce new and innovative services to win the market, and if they fail to provide the expected service, they may face actions for contract breach or nonrenewal of the contract, which maintains in place both the ownership and competition effects of markets while also benefiting from economies of scale and avoiding socially inefficient entry.

The major virtue of this form of market regulation is that it provides maximum protection against fragmentation, and initiates a competition for the market that is expected to aid the selection of the best provider or network that offers to supply the service at the lowest price and more efficiently without the need for regulation.[315] Because this policy option attempts to replicate the outcomes that would emerge in a perfectly contestable market, the power of competitive markets can still be harnessed ex ante during the franchising bidding process even though ex post there is only a single firm in the market. Ex post, regulation takes place via terms and conditions of the contract. Franchise bidding reduces the information asymmetries of economic regulation, mitigates issues of investment incentives, and provides incentives for cost savings. The idea is associated mainly with Demsetz, who argued that even though scale economies may lead to monopoly there may be no need to have regulation if the bidding process could be used to ensure an outcome that mimics competition for the market, especially when there is little risk of collusion among bidders, and the number of bidders is high.[316]

As with any other form of intervention, franchise bidding is, however, an imperfect way to address the natural monopoly problem. Williamson, in particular, has pointed to a number of problems that can undermine the desirability of franchise bidding as an alternative for regulation. For example, the initial award criteria and the duration of the contract must be specified. Long-term contracts have the advantage of security for the franchisee, who may then be more willing to invest in durable investments. However, consumers need mechanisms to punish misbehavior. This implies some mechanisms to monitor behavior or short-term contracts that however can undermine incentives to invest. Criteria for establishing prices, mark-ups over cost, limits on profits or rate of return will also need to be established and modified due to possible changes in technology, shifts in demand, and so on. These considerations imply some degree of ongoing scrutiny.[317]

Moreover, it cannot be assumed that ex ante competition will be strong, as there must be an adequate number of ex ante competitors and they must act independently (without collusion). Switching costs will also be high once the contract expires.[318]

---

[315] Demsetz, *supra*, note 292.
[316] Ibid. As pointed out by Goldberg, however, franchise bidding nonetheless may still imply the need to monitor and enforce the terms of the contract, which is akin to regulation. See Victor P. Goldberg, "Regulation and Administered Contracts" (1976) 7, no. 2 Bell J Econ, 426.
[317] See Goldberg, *supra*, note 316.
[318] Williamson, *supra*, note 314.

Among other things, incumbent contract holders will likely have a significant advantage at renewal time, and new entrants will face substantial learning costs that the incumbent will not face given the acquired knowledge and information about a given market. Public agencies may be less inclined to switch given such costs, likely giving rise to de facto inefficient monopolies beyond the duration of the contract and more generally creating risks of political capture. In the context of platforms, an additional limitation that makes franchise bidding unattractive is the global and digital nature of the services provided.

As seen in the third case study on ride-hailing platforms, awarding a market to a single platform may theoretically be an option for a natural monopoly platform offering services that are local in nature, and where there are additional market failures that may in any event require various kinds of regulatory intervention. Hence, an example where this policy option should not be automatically ruled out is on-demand transportation services, where there may be virtues in centralizing algorithmic routing and matching on a single network and discouraging inefficient entry of alternative platform networks. Auctioning the market to a single platform would solve the inefficiencies of fragmentation and lack of coordination across platforms that could emerge with platform competition, and could allow the application of uniform regulatory requirements such as background checks, insurance requirements, caps on maximum price surcharges, and even facilitate the development of a rating system where reviews could belong to individual drivers and passengers rather than a specific platform.

In sum, franchise bidding can in a limited set of circumstances offer an alternative approach to regulation. Its main advantage is that auctioning a market to a given platform offers major benefits in terms of efficient concentration and reduced fragmentation, while remaining to some extent compatible with competition for the market, by retaining a form of ex ante race for the market. Moreover, since the market is auctioned only for a predefined time period, franchise bidding does not entail the same level of monopoly entrenchment risks that are implicit in ex ante regulation. These virtues need to be qualified, however, as they do not represent a panacea for a natural monopoly platform. Among other things, market forces may themselves offer less costly responses to overfragmentation even in the presence of competing platforms;[319] switching costs, and risks of frictions at the time of renewal at the end of the contract may often be substantial; and in many contexts, franchise bidding may not be a feasible solution at all, due to low number of bidders or the global nature of the service.

6.3 PUBLIC OWNERSHIP

Another alternative to the regulation of private monopolies is public monopoly, based on the idea that a public firm will be motivated to act in socially desirable ways

---

[319] For example, through price-comparison platforms for ride-hailing services.

rather than simply following profit maximization. The issue of the relative costs and benefits of public ownership vis-à-vis private ownership raises a host of contentious political and social debates about the relative merits of free markets and collective forms of ownership, and from a policy perspective this method of dealing with natural monopolies and public utilities, while common in various industries in various countries, has lost its appeal beginning in the 1980s, in favor of privatization.[320]

There are economic reasons based on principal-agent models why public owner-ship of a firm is usually less efficient than privately owned firms. The ownership structure affects incentives of managers and performance because it is difficult to align the interests of managers with those of the public. While in the private own-ership model shareholders have several tools to align managers and shareholders' interests, and market forces discipline poor performance by managers, public agencies are not constrained by profit maximization, and do not face the threat of competition imposed by the market or bankruptcy. Public interest as an objective is also vague and may include multiple conflicting goals, increasing the risk of politically self-interested choices as suggested by public choice theory. These costs, however, need to be compared with the cost of monitoring private firms that economic regulation generally entails, which, in certain instances, may be large enough to justify government control.

The idea of turning natural monopoly platforms into public entities appears in most cases highly unrealistic and therefore does not warrant much further elabora-tion. However, it must be said that calls to nationalize some of the prominent digital platforms have been part of the public debate on digital platforms. Some commen-tators, for example, have suggested the need for public ownership of the digital infrastructure controlled by digital firms such as Facebook, Google, and Amazon. Weyl, in particular, is a prominent supporter of the nationalization of Facebook and Uber.[321]

---

[320] See B. Bortolotti, M. Fantini, and D. Siniscalco, "Privatisation Around the World: Evidence from Panel Data" (2004) 88, no.1–2 J Public Econ, 305; V. V. Ramanadham, *The Economics of Public Enterprise* (London: Routledge, 1991); John Vickers and George K. Yarrow, *Privatization: An Economic Analysis*, MIT Press series on the regulation of economic activity 18 (Cambridge, MA: MIT Press, 1988); Jeffry M. Netter and William L. Megginson, "From State to Market: A Survey of Empirical Studies on Privatization" (2001) 39, no. 2 J Econ Lit, 321; D. Andrew, C. Smith, and Michael J. Trebilcock, "State-Owned Enterprises in Less Developed Countries: Privatization and Alternative Reform Strategies" (2001) 12, no. 3 Eur J Law Econ, 217; Andrei Shleifer, "State versus Private Ownership" (1998) 12, no. 4 J Econ Perspect, 133; Edward Iacobucci and Michael Trebilcock, "The Role of Crown Corporations in the Canadian Economy: An Analytical Framework" (2012), available at https://tspace .library.utoronto.ca/handle/1807/89449.

[321] Asher Schechter, "Glen Weyl: 'The Very Structure of Capitalism Is Inherently Monopolistic'" (May 3, 2018), available at https://promarket.org/glen-weyl-structure-capitalism-inherently-monopolistic/.

6.4 RELIANCE ON COMPETITION POLICY AND SCHUMPETERIAN COMPETITION

The recurring features of digital platform markets reduce the importance of static competition between platforms and excessively concentrated market structures, and, in contrast, shift the focus of ex post intervention toward the promotion of market contestability, potential competition, and entry for displacement. A Schumpeterian approach, authoritatively endorsed among others by Jean Tirole, is, in principle, a refinement of the laissez-faire approach – which believes that monopoly power in tech sectors will eventually be eroded by innovative competitors – that instead favors various degrees of competition policy intervention to ensure that displacement of established monopolies in fact occurs and occurs more quickly than it would without intervention.

This section evaluates the contours of a Schumpeterian framework based on competition policy intervention, from both a substantive and an institutional perspective. Substantively, it highlights how the features of digital platforms make concerns about small competitors, discriminatory behavior, and exploitative exercises of market power potentially more compatible with an efficiency and consumer welfare orientation. Institutionally, it shows that many forms of intervention dictated by a Schumpeterian framework necessarily gravitate toward approaches that are quasi-regulatory in nature, raising significant institutional challenges for ex post intervention based on competition policy.

6.4.1 *Promoting Monopoly Displacement and Potential Competition: A Substantive Perspective*

The feasibility of a competition policy framework based on monopoly displacement and potential competition depends in part on the normative and substantive features of a specific competition policy regime. From a normative perspective, goals of intervention as often reflected in the legislative history of various competition policy regimes can vary substantially, possibly including efficiency and total welfare, consumer welfare, the protection of specific market structures,[322] and a mix of fairness concerns toward consumers, small businesses, economic growth, inequality, and reducing undue political influence by large firms.[323]

For example, the Canadian Competition Act explicitly identifies in Section 1.1 four explicit goals that are theoretically pursued simultaneously: enhancing economic efficiency; participation in global markets; fairness toward small and medium

---

[322] For recent discussions on the goals of antitrust, see, for instance, Wu, *supra*, note 243; Tepper, *supra*, 39.

[323] Eleanor M. Fox and Michael J. Trebilcock, *The Design of Competition Law Institutions, Global Norms, Local Choices* (Oxford: Oxford University Press, 2013). See also discussion in Francesco Ducci and Michael Trebilcock. "The Revival of Fairness Discourse in Competition Policy" (2019) 64 *Antitrust Bulletin*, 79–104.

sized businesses; and consumer welfare.[324] Other jurisdictions follow a similar pattern. South Africa's competition laws set as goals promoting participation of all citizens in the economy and promoting the fair distribution of ownership and control of markets among different racial groups and balancing the interests of workers, owners, and consumers. The objectives of China's anti-monopoly law are to promote efficiency, while safeguarding healthy development of a socialist market economy and the public interest, protecting the state-owned economy and small business, encouraging the expansion of domestic enterprises, and scrutinizing foreign takeovers. Japan promotes consumer welfare, but it also seeks to protect small and medium sized businesses and devotes significant attention to policing low prices in Japan's economy. The European Union places particular emphasis on distortions within the internal common market and has historically devoted particular attention to the protection of smaller competitors, in addition to pursuing the maximization of consumer welfare and the efficiency of markets. There are significant trade-offs between these goals, whether it is between total surplus and consumer surplus, or between efficiency and the protection of small and medium sized businesses. How to balance possible conflicts between goals is often left unresolved in the legislative text.

These differences in terms of the normative reach and goals of enforcement influence the scope of ex post intervention in the context of unregulated digital platforms. First, a Schumpeterian approach is efficiency oriented, and thus sees concentration as desirable insofar as various forms of scale entail positive efficiency properties. Pushing this perspective to its extreme, in theory this may, for instance, entail that the greater realization of network effects due to the elimination of rival networks and the consequent aggregation of all users on the same network should be considered efficient. For example, Armstrong and Wright show in a model of competition between undifferentiated platforms that exclusivity can be used to eliminate a rival but that exclusion is efficient.[325] Lee's empirical work on the video game industry, showing that exclusivity agreements can help smaller firms enter the market, also suggests that such entry may not necessarily be efficient.[326] According to Weyl and White, enforcement policy should be tilted in platform markets to encourage exclusionary behavior that reduces the sorting-out phase toward monopoly.[327]

This competition policy approach, however, is less compatible with regimes that include broader concerns and noneconomic goals beyond economic efficiency.[328]

---

[324] Ibid.

[325] Armstrong and Wright, *supra*, note 269.

[326] Robin S. Lee, "Vertical Integration and Exclusivity in Platform and Two-Sided Markets" (2013) 103, no. 7 Am Econ Rev, 2960.

[327] Glen Weyl and Alexander White, "Let the Right 'One' Win: Policy Lessons from the New Economics of · Platforms" (2014) Coase-Sandor Working Paper Series in Law and Economics No. 709-2014.

[328] Including fragmentation of economic power for the sake of preventing aggregation of political power, small businesses, redistributive goals, and other social and political values. These broader objectives highlight the friction between efficient concentration and noneconomic goals.

Considerations of fairness, excessive concentration, and normative views that favor strict approaches to single-firm dominance would condemn forms of conduct leading to concentration despite the presence of efficiencies, and are likely to clash, at least to some extent, with approaches based on the efficiency of highly concentrated or monopolistic markets. Since a competition policy based on efficient market concentration and contestability is plausibly more controversial in jurisdictions that pursue goals beyond efficiency, the normative foundations of an antitrust regime put important limits on the feasibility of a Schumpeterian framework.

In addition to these normative considerations, the substantive features of a regime also dictate the scope of ex post intervention. For example, while most jurisdictions have provisions that deal with abuses of a dominant position with exclusionary effects, the scope of single-firm "abuse" can vary substantially across jurisdictions. In particular, although the predominant welfare-based approach is narrowly concerned with anticompetitive exclusion of efficient competitors, notions of abuse can be broader in some regimes possibly covering issues of exploitative exercises of market power, concerns for smaller competitors, or discriminatory behavior by a dominant firm. These differences play out in important, and at times counter-intuitive ways, in the context of digital platform markets.

For instance, competitor-oriented approaches toward single-firm conduct have largely been abandoned in mature jurisdictions in favor of consumer and economic welfare. Nonetheless, because the target of exclusion under a Schumpeterian framework will often be small, nascent competitors that have the potential to grow and become substitutes for a dominant platform in the future, the promotion of niche entry and potential competitors becomes consistent both with an efficiency framework oriented at dynamic competition, as well as the protection of a specific kind of small competitors. As a result, a Schumpeterian framework brings these contrasting objectives closer together, but faces the challenge of protecting small efficient competitors that have the potential to become substitutes for an incumbent platform under an efficiency paradigm.

Likewise, tendencies toward natural monopolies and a focus on monopoly displacement potentially increase in certain contexts the relevance of various forms of exploitative exercise of market power. The reason is that while prices above marginal costs or nonprice forms of exploitative conduct may indirectly be disciplined by contestability in some cases, in markets where contestability is low and market power more durable, exploitative conduct may become more problematic due to the weakness of market forces. From an economic perspective, addressing exploitative abuses through competition law is seen unfavorably. High prices are often seen as a legitimate reward for investments and an important market signal to encourage entry. Likewise, the questions of whether and how competition authorities and courts should address excessive pricing remains a highly contested issue from a competition policy perspective. Indeed, various jurisdictions do not condemn exploitative abuses, and even when they include them within single-firm conduct, competition authorities and courts are generally seen as lacking expertise or authority to regulate prices. Nonetheless, because exploitative abuses of market power become potentially more prominent in digital industries with low entry and contestability, jurisdictions that address exploitative abuses through competition laws have, in theory at least, the substantive tools to intervene against excessive pricing or equivalent nonprice abuses. These forms of market power exercise, generally justified by a fairness rationale within the competition policy domain, become in digital industries potentially more consistent with efficiency, insofar as market forces' responses to exploitative exercises of market power are expected to be weak and slow.

Moreover, the potential for dealing with repetitive discriminatory behavior by a vertically integrated platform depends on the presence and scope of legal tools and doctrines that deal with mandated access to essential inputs, such as the essential facilities doctrine and refusal to deal provisions. In general, provisions that mandate access entail various problems. Among other things, they interfere with property rights and undermine incentives to invest, and they raise challenging issues when dealing with the terms of access and ongoing monitoring. Since digital platforms can structurally give rise to bottleneck or essential inputs, however, competition law doctrines and provisions that deal with a duty to provide access become particularly relevant.

In sum, the prospect of a Schumpeterian framework focused on dynamic competition, control of market power through the threat of entry, and contestability depends to a large extent on the specific normative orientation and substantive characteristics of a competition policy regime. While, on the one hand, such a paradigm is consistent with an efficiency and consumer welfare orientation, on the other hand, various facets of single-firm conduct that are generally seen as more formalistic or fairness oriented (such as protection of small businesses, exploitative abuses, or concerns with discriminatory conduct and refusal to deal by a dominant firm) become, to an extent, more consistent with an efficiency paradigm. Having identified the general features of a competition law regime that may make it more or less compatible with efficient concentration and a contestability-based approach, the chapter now turns to a more concrete identification of areas of intervention that become important under such a Schumpeterian framework: (A) protecting potential competitors; (B) tackling exploitative exercises of market power; (C) addressing discriminatory conduct by hybrid, vertically integrated platforms.

A. Protecting Potential Competitors

Various forms of foreclosure have been observed in platform markets. For example, the use of exclusivity inducing mechanisms that "steer" customers to a specific platform has been a particularly prominent example. Steering involves a platform's restrictions on one side of the platform that restrict inter-platform competition on that side and often includes a shift of those rents in terms of subsidies to users on the other side of the market. Examples include "no-surcharge" rules imposed by credit card companies on merchants that restrict their ability to steer customers to other methods of payment, or MFN clauses imposed by reservation and price-comparison platforms that restrict the ability of providers to price at a lower price on other platforms or on their own websites. Such restrictions induce exclusivity by subsidizing participation on one side and then exploiting indirect network externalities on the other side where the restriction was imposed, potentially reducing inter-platform competition. Such clauses and generally "contracts that reference rivals" have also been shown to give rise to excessive intermediation by platforms.[329]

In digital platform markets that tend toward monopoly or tight oligopolies, however, the main exclusionary concern is usually oriented at the exclusion of *potential* competitors that threaten to displace the monopolist, as opposed to existing competitors. Nascent firms often enter what is niche or small segments of a market and may eventually threaten the incumbent established platform, and this entry from adjacent markets can give rise to the kind of unexpected market disruptions that may ultimately turn to the entrant into a head-to-head competitor in the primary market. For example, Amazon started with the narrow sale of books before expanding to online shopping, cloud computing, and so on. Google started with a technology to better use hyperlinks on the web before expanding into various other markets. Expansion often starts from small segments, where embryonic and potential competition from these small segments works its way into dominance by displacing incumbents.[330] The goal of intervention against exclusion, as a result, should be focused on various harms that create barriers or delays against monopoly displacement by potential competitors. Two prominent examples are provided by (i) defensive tying and (ii) and preemptive mergers, two mirror strategies that often target small, nascent firms in an attempt to preempt their possible growth into substitutes for an established platform.

(i) Defensive Tying to Protect the Original Market. The relevance of tying and market power leveraging in platform industries has a prominent history. In 1991, the United States opened an investigation against Microsoft for a number of anticompetitive practices related to its operating systems, which was concluded with a settlement that made changes to, among other things, certain licensing rules.[331] Later, Microsoft was accused of unlawful monopoly maintenance in the operating system market by seeking to eliminate the nascent threat posed by web browsers to

---

[329]   This is because they "tax" nonplatform customers due to the cost externalization that platform users will spread across all consumers, such as cash consumers bearing the costs of credit cards when merchants pass some of them by increasing the prices of goods or services. See Benjamin G. Edelman & Julian Wright, "Price Coherence and Excessive Intermediation," SSRN Scholarly Paper ID 2513513 (Rochester, NY: Social Science Research Network, 2015).

[330]   See the discussion in the case studies of this book.

[331]   See *United States v. Microsoft Corp.*, 56 F 3d 1448 (Dist of Columbia Circuit 1995).

operating systems. The strategy to protect its position was an attempt to leverage market power into the new emerging browser market, where the entry of Netscape posed a serious threat to Microsoft's position in the market for operating systems.[332]

The DOJ argued (and the District Court accepted) that Microsoft's added browser functionality for Windows was an attempt to marginalize Netscape, because Netscape posed a potential competitive threat to the Windows operating system. Since Netscape could be run on a number of operating systems, DOJ alleged that Netscape could erode the market power of Windows and Microsoft's response was to give away Internet Explorer and integrate it into Windows so that Netscape would not become a platform that would compete with Windows. Thus, DOJ alleged that Microsoft's free distribution of IE, its bundling with Windows, and its attempts to win the browser wars were *defensive* moves by Microsoft to protect its Windows monopoly, where Netscape was not necessarily an immediate threat but its growth and the addition of new functionalities may have reduced the centrality of operating systems.[333] The concern was not that leveraging would distort competitive conditions in the market for internet browsers, but that it would protect against the risk of displacement in the primary market for operating systems. The EU then also initiated a complaint against Microsoft for tying Windows Media Player to Windows, where, however, the concern was more with monopolization of the tied markets, rather than defensive tying.[334]

The literature on tying has for the most part focused on the ability of tying to achieve price discrimination or foreclose competition in the tied, competitive market. In general, when tying occurs a product is offered by a seller under the condition that another product is also bought, such as shoes and shoelaces. Tying and bundling can involve packaging goods together where different goods are sold in fixed proportions, but also include requirement tying where two goods are sold together in variable proportions and the seller requires the buyer to purchase all the units of the tied good. Tying often has efficiency rationales: it can reduce transaction costs and search costs, exploiting division of labor economies of scale, such as assembling a car or selling right and left shoes together. Tying can also solve problems of asymmetric information and quality externalities.[335]

When not clearly used for efficiency purposes, the effects on welfare are generally ambiguous. Tying can, for example, be used as a demand-metering device. With heterogeneous consumers consuming different proportion of a tied good B, tying good A to good B and charging a supra-competitive price on price B enables a firm to extract more surplus from inelastic consumers, with ambiguous welfare effects

---

[332] See *United States v. Microsoft Corp.*, 253 F 3d 34 (Dist of Columbia Circuit 2001); *United States v. Microsoft Corp.*, 147 F 3d 935 (Dist of Columbia Circuit 1998).

[333] Ibid.

[334] European Commission, *Commission Initiates Additional Proceedings Against Microsoft*, Press Release IP/01/1232 (Brussels: European Commission, 2001).

[335] Edward Iacobucci, "Tying as Quality Control: A Legal and Economic Analysis," SSRN Scholarly Paper ID 293602 (Rochester, NY: Social Science Research Network, 2001).

overall and possibly enabling some consumers that would otherwise be priced out of the market to buy the bundled goods. Chicago School thinkers also discounted the scope of exclusionary effects created by tying, based on the single monopoly profit theorem.[336] Because a seller can extract only one monopoly surplus, it may not have the incentive to extend market power in a secondary market because the seller is not better off with or without a tie. The theory and the validity of its assumptions have been challenged by post-Chicago scholarship, which showed that, in fact, tying may be anticompetitive, mostly focusing on the ability of a seller to deny scale to potential competitors in the tied good. Whinston, for example, has shown that without perfect information and constant returns to scale in the tied market, tying can be used to induce exit in the tied market.[337]

Although not as prominent as such theories, some literature has also recognized the ability of trying to influence competition in the tying market by deterring the emergence of substitutes in the tying good in line with the framework that emerged in the Microsoft Netscape investigation – an anticompetitive strategy that is arguably central in future platform cases. Carlton and Waldman concentrate on the monopolist's ability to use tying and foreclosure to increase future profits by deterring entry of efficient firms into the monopolist's primary market and newly emerging markets.[338] The strategic use of tying can deter entry in the tying good. First, it can deter the alternative producer from ever entering the complementary market by eliminating the profits associated with the alternative producer selling complementary units in the first period, thereby making it impossible to cover the fixed costs of entry. When tying prevents the alternative producer from entering the complementary market, it also prevents the rival from entering the primary market. Tying prevents the alternative producer from earning profits from sales of complementary units before primary-market entry is possible, and this serves to lower the alternative producer's return to ever entering the complementary market. Network externalities can exacerbate the costs of complementary-market entry and the disadvantages associated with having to simultaneously enter two markets rather than one. Similarly, Williamson suggests that the probability of entry may be reduced if the potential entrant only has experience relevant for producing one of the goods.[339] If the potential entrant lacks experience in one of the products, then tying can inhibit entry because it forces the firm to enter both markets. Tying appears a suitable candidate for anticompetitive conduct that a dominant firm can use to remain dominant in markets undergoing rapid technological change, and preserve and create market power in the tying market and newly emerging markets.

---

[336]   Robert H. Bork, *The Antitrust Paradox*, 2nd ed. (New York: Free Press, 1993).

[337]   Michael Whinston, "Tying, Foreclosure, and Exclusion" (1990) 80, no. 4 Am Econ Rev, 837.

[338]   Dennis W. Carlton and Michael Waldman, "The Strategic Use of Tying to Preserve and Create Market Power in Evolving Industries" (2002) 33, no.2 RAND J Econ, 194.

[339]   Oliver E. Williamson, "Assessing Vertical Market Restrictions: Antitrust Ramifications of the Transaction Cost Approach" (1979) 127, no. 4 Univ Pa Law Rev, 953 at 953–993.

The Microsoft Netscape case and tying as a defensive strategy is arguably a primer for the application of competition policy in current platform markets, where attempts to thwart nascent potential competition and market power leveraging to protect against displacement in the original market are likely to be the most pernicious forms of anticompetitive harm. This form of conduct in a way also resembles the *Loraine Journal* case, where a dominant newspaper refused to sell ad space to any merchant who also purchased advertising from a competing new radio station, which meant that advertisers could buy radio or newspaper advertising but not both. Because many businesses considered newspapers advertising essential for the promotion of sales,[340] the behavior attempted to destroy, among other things, the nascent competition from the emerging radio station.[341]

(ii) **Blocking Mergers of Potential Substitutes**. A parallel strategy to eliminate the threat of entry from adjacent markets by defensively leveraging market power is the acquisition of *potential* competitors. In this case, the dominant platform is attempting to merge with smaller competitors that are present in related markets that at the time of the acquisition may possess some degree of complementarity with the incumbent. The goal of the incumbent is to prevent such partial complements from becoming possible substitutes.

Possible examples of mergers that may fall into this framework are numerous.[342] They may include Google's acquisition of DoubleClick, a firm operating in internet ad services; Google acquisition of GPS navigation and map software Waze, one of the few competitors in the mobile mapping sector to Google Maps; Google's merger with YouTube; Microsoft's acquisition of Skype, which may have competed in the future with other Microsoft products for business, or LinkedIn; Amazon's acquisition of Quidsi, which in 2008 was one of the emerging e-commerce firms; the merger of Facebook with Instagram, WhatsApp, and the emerging social media app tbh, all of which may have threatened Facebook's dominant social network through mobile photo sharing and different models of mobile chats.

Various commentators have acknowledged that mergers of potential competitors should be more vigorously reviewed, and that the lack thereof may be a major shortcoming of antitrust intervention in platform markets. Shapiro, for example, suggests stricter merger enforcement in general, including a stronger emphasis on

---

[340] *Lorain Journal Co. v. United States*, [1951] 342 US 143 (US Supreme Court).
[341] The importance of tying in platform markets is also supported by the findings of more recent literature showing how tying may have additional anticompetitive effects in two-sided markets. Choi and Jeon focus on the anticompetitive use of tying in order to overcome price constraints and the impossibility of charging negative prices and being a substitute for predation. See Choi and Jeon, *supra*, note 113. Likewise, tying one platform to a second platform leads to the failure of the single monopoly profit theorem because tying on one side of the market enables the platform to steer additional users on the other side of the market with whom it would have not dealt otherwise. See Iacobucci and Ducci, *supra*, note 169. See also Amelio, Karlinger, and Valletti, *supra*, note 112.
[342] See Tepper, *supra*, note 39.

mergers that may lessen competition in the future.[343] Similarly, Weyl and White include excessive entry for buyouts as one of the many concerns in platform markets leading to overfragmentation.[344] A more prophylactic approach to mergers of potential competitors avoids the need to break up the merged entities if the merger results problematic post-acquisition,[345] where separating the two entities post-merger may be costlier than preventing the merger in the first place and may in any case do little to protect potential competition. At the same time, enforcement against preemptive mergers, as in the case of defensive tying, is targeted at *potential* rather than actual competition that may be small at the time of the acquisition – hence, it entails a highly speculative analysis and it is constrained by the limits imposed by merger thresholds. Various substantive changes to merger review have as a result been suggested in order to better address the issue of killer acquisitions and fill the gaps of merger policy in this area.[346]

B. Exploitative Abuses

The prospect of platform competition based on cycles of monopolies is premised on the idea that contestability can constraint the exercise of market power such as excessive pricing without the need to directly intervene. While this may be true in markets with sufficiently high levels of contestability, and given that digital platform industries are likely to possess different degrees of natural monopoly features and contestability, exploitative exercises of market power can, however, become more problematic in contexts where market power is more durable and the threat of entry weak. In such cases, pricing above marginal cost as well as forms of nonprice exploitation (such as misuse of data or quality reductions) may not be disciplined effectively by market forces and by the threat of monopoly displacement.

Substantively, jurisdictions covering exploitative abuses under competition law provisions may have some room for intervention against certain forms of platform pricing and equivalent nonprice abuses that may cover a gap resulting from the absence of direct regulation. Brazil, Chile, China, India, Israel, and South Africa, for example, condemn high prices as an undue exercise of market power.[347]

---

[343] Shapiro, *supra*, note 10.

[344] Weyl and White, *supra*, note 327.

[345] See, for instance, European Commission, *Mergers: Commission Alleges Facebook Provided Misleading Information About WhatsApp Takeover*, Press Release (Brussels: European Commission, 2016). European Commission, *Mergers: Commission Fines Facebook €110 Million for Providing Misleading Information About WhatsApp Takeover*, Press Release (Brussels: European Commission, 2017).

[346] Tepper, *supra*, note 39. See also discussion in UK Report of the Digital Competition Expert Panel, *supra*, note 12. For a broader discussion, see also Tommaso M. Valletti and Hans, Zenger, "Increasing Market Power and Merger Control" (May 14, 2019) *Competition Law & Policy Debate*, 5, no. 1, 26–35, available at https://ssrn.com/abstract=3387999; Shapiro, *supra*, note 10.

[347] Einer Elhauge and Damien Geradin, *Global Antitrust Law and Economics*, 2nd ed. University Casebook Series (New York: Foundation Press Thomson/West, 2011), p. 448.

Substantive provisions on exploitative abuses may in theory cover a platform charging supra-competitive prices in total, a platform charging a price to one side that may be considered exploitative, or nonprice abuses such as quality reductions, reduction of privacy standards, or misuse of users' data.

Institutionally, the ability of institutions in charge of competition policy enforcement to address these types of behavior remains nonetheless limited. This partially explains why the general consensus in mature competition law regimes is that high and excessive prices should be viewed as outside the scope of competition policy intervention, and why even jurisdictions that condemn in theory high prices as an abuse of dominance, rarely enforce these provisions – for example, although in Europe Article 102 TFEU explicitly includes exploitative conduct and "directly or indirectly imposing unfair purchase or selling prices" by a dominant firm as a violation of competition law, such provision is rarely enforced. The limited desirability of price regulation by competition law comes in particular from the fact that competition authorities generally lack the required institutional expertise required to identify an excessive price and the appropriate remedy – questions that are instead generally delegated to specialized industry-specific regulators.

There is no easy answer to the issue of exploitative exercises of market power in digital markets displaying low contestability and naturally monopolist features. As previously seen in this chapter, the obvious policy approach entails price regulation by a sector-specific regulator, but its many shortcomings are likely to reduce its desirability in practice. In its absence, competition policy can address market power exercises of exploitative nature in two ways: either through abuse of dominance provisions, or, indirectly, through policies that promote contestability. The former can directly address excessive pricing but entails a set of institutional capabilities generally beyond the reach of ex post enforcement; the latter approach is less burdensome but encounter limitations in markets with low contestability where the ability to exercise market power can be expected to remain durable and unchallenged. The pendulum between these options will depend on the magnitude of harm in the absence of intervention and the cost and benefits of alternative forms of intervention, based on the specific features of each digital industry.

C. Discrimination by Hybrid Vertically Integrated Platforms

The focus on dynamic *inter*-platform competition is only one side of a desirable enforcement policy. From the perspective of *intra*-platform competition, intervention needs to address issues of discrimination and leveraging by hybrid platforms that are vertically integrated in adjacent segments, where access to bottleneck inputs may be desirable due to the structural features of some digital industries. As seen in the case studies, market power leveraging in adjacent markets and discriminatory conduct have been a prominent issue in various platform markets. Most jurisdictions have a number of provisions related to abuse of dominance that may in theory cover

specific issues of leveraging by a natural monopolist, for example, tying and bundling provisions can address anticompetitive strategies that attach as conditions for
access and interconnection acquisitions of other products or services from the
natural monopolist; margin squeezing provisions can address specific forms of
discriminatory behavior; rules on predatory pricing can in theory deal with various
issues of cross-subsidization and cost miscalculation, and refusal to deal provisions as
part of single-firm conduct.

The most critical antitrust provision for issues of discrimination, and one upon
which significant reliance would be expected in the context of a natural platform
monopoly, however, is the essential facilities doctrine.[348] The doctrine is usually part
of abuse of dominance or monopolization claims in the form of refusals to grant
access to facilities that are deemed essential and can be shared. Its most common
purpose is application to a vertically integrated monopolist that has the ability to
refuse to supply, delay the supply of essential bottleneck inputs (access to a network),
or attach discriminatory conditions to advantage its competitive arm vis-à-vis competitors. Problems of access to bottleneck facilities can emerge from refusal to deal
by a single firm, or by a joint venture and group boycott. At the core of the essential
facilities doctrine,[349] there is a balance between taking advantages of synergies and
economics of scale and the need to ensure competition in a vertically

---

[348]   The essential facilities doctrine has been invoked in different platform contexts. For instance,
Google's general search result listings and Amazon's various businesses, in particular its e-commerce
marketplace, have been suggested as possible candidates for the application of the essential facilities
doctrine. Various official reports also mention the essential facilities doctrine in the context of digital
markets. The French and German antitrust authorities' study on the interaction between competition law and big data concludes, for example, that big data could qualify as an essential facility and
that the failure to share them with a competitor could therefore be an abusive practice. A white paper
recently published by the Canadian Competition Bureau on big data and innovation also suggests
that making data available to competitors for use as an input, for example, through the compulsory
licensing of intellectual property, and considering data as an "essential facility," may be an appropriate quasi-structural remedy to increase downstream competition and reduce barriers to entry.
Similarly, the European Commission, in a recent publication on "Building a European Data
Economy," has confirmed that data-driven business models may give rise to various claims of access
to data held by one economic operator. See, respectively, Autorité de la Concurrence and
Bundeskartellamt (2016) *supra*, note 65; Competition Bureau of Canada (2017) *supra*, note 65;
European Commission, *Staff Working Document on the Free Flow of Data and Emerging Issues of
the European Data Economy*, Working Document (Brussels: European Commission, 2017).

[349]   For literature on the essential facilities doctrine, see Areeda, *supra*, note 300; Robert Pitofsky,
Donna Patterson, and Jonathan Hooks, "The Essential Facilities Doctrine Under United States
Antitrust Law" (2002) 70 Georget Law Fac Publ Works, 443; Abbott B. Jr Lipsky and J. Gregory Sidak,
"Essential Facilities" (1998) 51 Stanford Law Rev, 1187; Spencer Waller and Brett Frischmann,
"Revitalizing Essential Facilities" (2008) 74, no. 1 Fac Publ Works, available at https://lawcommons
.luc.edu/facpubs/72; Gregory J. Werden, "The Law and Economics of the Essential Facility
Doctrine" (1987) 32 St Louis Univ Law J, 433 at 434–436; Marina Lao, "Networks, Access, and
Essential Facilities: From Terminal Railroad to Microsoft" (2009) 62 SMU Law Rev, 557;
Stephen M. Maurer and Suzanne Scotchmer, "The Essential Facilities Doctrine: The Lost
Message of Terminal Railroad," SSRN Scholarly Paper ID 2407071 (Rochester, NY: Social
Science Research Network, 2014); Spencer Weber Waller, "Areeda, Epithets, and Essential
Facilities," 2008 Wis L Rev, 359–386.

interconnected market through mandated access, while ensuring that intervention does not excessively interfere with investment incentives. While its scope remains more an epithet for some commentators,[350] and goes against the general antitrust principle that preserves firms' freedom to decide with whom to deal, many jurisdictions possess a version of the doctrine.

The essential facilities doctrine has its origins under US antitrust law, where its foundations were established in the *Terminal Railroad* case.[351] There, a joint venture controlling all the routes of rail access to and from St. Louis was required to permit railroads not part of the joint venture to use the facilities on nondiscriminatory terms so as to place "every such company upon as nearly an equal plane ... as that occupied by the proprietary companies."[352] The Court recognized, on the one hand, the efficiency properties of combining terminal systems, but, on the other, also that by becoming a bottleneck facility, competitors needed access on reasonable, nondiscriminatory terms. The remedy was to impose admission of any existing or future railroad to the joint ownership and control of the combined terminal properties upon just and reasonable terms, and use of the terminal facilities by any other railroad not electing to become a joint owner. Such remedy was preferred to a structural relief that would have restored competition, but sacrificed important efficiencies arising from aggregation of assets.

In a subsequent case, *Associated Press*, the publisher of a large number of newspapers' members of a cooperative association active in the collection and distribution of news, set up bylaws that prohibited all members from selling news to nonmembers, and which granted power to block its nonmember competitors from membership. The bylaws were found to be in breach of Section 1 of the Sherman Act by restricting admission to AP membership to competitors, with the effect of blocking all newspaper nonmembers from any opportunity to buy news from AP or any of its publisher members. The reasoning in the case was that although AP did not have a complete monopoly,[353] the inability to buy news form the largest news agency had negative effects on the publication of competing newspapers, as it was "practically impossible for any one newspaper alone to establish or maintain the organization requisite for collecting all of the news of the world, or any substantial part thereof." Based on the reasoning of the court, aside from the administrative and organization difficulties thereof, the financial cost was considered so great that no single newspaper acting alone would sustain it. This was held in spite of some competing newspapers having managed without AP news, and in spite of the fact that AP

[350] Areeda, *supra*, note 300.
[351] *United States v. Terminal Railroad Assn of St. Louis* (1912) 224 US 383 (US Supreme Court).
[352] Ibid, at 411.
[353] The exclusive right to publish news in a given field, furnished by AP and all of its members, would give many newspapers an insurmountable competitive advantage over their rivals. Hence, in the case the fact that an agreement to restrain trade did not inhibit competition in all of the aspects of that trade could not save it from condemnation from the Sherman Act. See *Associated Press v. United States; Tribune Company v. United States; United States v. Associated Press* 326 U.S. 1 (1945).

made its news generally available by supplying it to a limited and selected group of publishers in the various cities.

Both *Terminal Railroads* and *Associated Press* involved a form of refusal to deal in the form of group boycott where the cooperating competitors were required to admit rivals on nondiscriminatory terms. It was only in *Gamco* that the access to bottleneck inputs was for the first time imposed as part of unilateral conduct. The defendant owned and provided facilities for fresh fruit and vegetable wholesalers. Gamco, one of the tenants, after transferring stock to an out-of-state person in violation of the lease, was then refused renewal of its lease. The essential facility involved the building that served as a centralized market for wholesaling of fresh produce in Providence, Rhode Island. In the determination of anticompetitive exclusion from access to a scarce facility that was impracticable to replicate, it was particularly important that its control granted monopoly power, involved clear efficiencies from aggregation into a centralized market, and the central function of the warehouse was to serve all dealers in Rhode Island.

While these cases were decided on the logic of the essential facilities, the doctrine was only made explicit in *Hecht*, a case in which the plaintiff sought access to a football stadium, which was deemed essential. Access was imposed based on the fact that it involved a government-controlled facility that could accommodate two professional team franchises due to clear excess capacity. The doctrine's application to unilateral refusals then took full force in *Otter Trail*, where an integrated electric utility in Minnesota refused to provide access to municipal utilities in its service area when they attempted to enter the electric power distribution market. Otter Trail refused to sell or transmit wholesale power to the municipal utilities and this was found to be an attempt to monopolize the market for retail distribution of electric power in its service area.[354] The US Supreme Court relied on the fact that Otter Trail intended to exclude rivals in order to maintain control over power distribution (probably a natural monopoly).

The boundaries of the doctrine remained controversial in a number of lower courts cases and were eventually refined in *MCI Communications Corp. v. AT&T*.[355] In *MCI*, the plaintiff argued that AT&T improperly refused to allow it to connect its telephone lines with AT&T's nationwide telephone network and that such interconnection was essential for MCI to compete against AT&T in the long-distance market. The Seventh Circuit identified four necessary elements for the application of the essential facilities doctrine: (1) control of the essential facility by a monopolist; (2) inability to practically or reasonably duplicate the facility by a competitor; (3) denial of use; (4) feasibility of providing the facility.

---

[354] *Otter Tail Power Co. v. United States* [1972] 410 US 366 (Supreme Court) at 368.
[355] *MCI Communications v. American Tel & Tel Co.* [1983] 708 F 2d 1081 (Court of Appeals, 7th Circuit).

While these constitute the basic elements of the doctrine in US law, its exact scope has been further shaped in *Aspen*[356] and *Trinko*.[357] *Aspen* is somewhat an outlier in the sense that the infringement of Section 2 of the Sherman Act was based on ending a preexisting business relationship. In that case, the US Supreme Court upheld a monopolization claim against a defendant that controlled access to three of the four ski hills in Aspen, Colorado. The plaintiff, who controlled the fourth, complained that the defendant precipitously refused the joint ski pass that had been offered for some time and also stopped selling plaintiff's tickets at all. The Court based its decision on the lack of business justification for the change of behavior and emphasized the importance of the preexisting relationship between the plaintiff and defendant as an indicator of exclusionary intent to monopolize through refusal to deal.[358] Finally, the reach of the doctrine was later significantly narrowed in *Trinko*, where the US Supreme Court restricted the scope of duty to deal with rivals[359] and described the doctrine as being "crafted by some lower courts."[360] However, the Supreme Court refused to either embrace it or to repudiate it.

Variations of the underlying principles of the doctrine have been applied in many jurisdictions, although not always by explicitly recognizing it as an essential facility doctrine. In Canada, where the doctrine has not been explicitly adopted, there are various sections of the Competition Act that address essential facility-like type of access. Section 75 addresses refusal to deal cases by imposing a duty on suppliers to accept customers when they are unable to obtain adequate supplies of a product anywhere in a market on usual trade terms. Section 78(e) on abuse of dominant position under section 79 explicitly mentions as an anticompetitive act preemption of scarce facilities or resources required by a competitor for the operation of a business, with the object of withholding the facilities or resources from a market. Section 78(a) identifies squeezing by a vertically integrated supplier of the margin available to an unintegrated customer who competes with the supplier for the purposes of impeding or preventing the customer's entry or expansion into a market. The central case involving essential facilities is *Interac*, where members of a major financial institution structured as a joint venture imposed rules for admission of new members where it refused to admit any new member with voting rights, and increased dramatically the fees for other new members – practices that were terminated after a consent order imposed access to the network and amendments to the governance structure and rules related to pricing and new services. Australian courts have declined to explicitly adopt the doctrine under competition statutes, but Australian authorities have adopted a statutory and regulatory scheme to

---

356 *Aspen Highlands Skiing Corp. v. Aspen Skiing Co.* [1984] 738 F 2d 1509 (Court of Appeals, 10th Circuit).
357 *Verizon Communications Inc. v. Law Offices of Curtis V. Trinko, LLP* [2003] 540 US 398 (Supreme Court).
358 *Aspen Skiing Co. v. Aspen Highlands Skiing Corp* [1985] 472 US 585 (Supreme Court).
359 *Verizon Communications Inc. v. Law Offices of Curtis V. Trinko, LLP, supra*, note 357.
360 Ibid, at 410.

regulate essential facilities called National Access Regime, which grants power to state and federal agencies to compel owners of essential facilities to deal with competitors on fair and nondiscriminatory terms, and a number of industry-specific equivalent regimes. South Africa has adopted a two-pronged approach to unilateral refusals to deal by dominant firms. Section 8(b) of the South African Competition Act prohibits dominant firms from "refusing to give a competitor access to an essential facility when it is economically feasible."[361] The Act defines an essential facility as "an infrastructure or resource that cannot reasonably be duplicated, and without access to which competitors cannot reasonably provide goods or services to their customers."[362] In European competition law, a unilateral refusal to grant access to an essential facility is part of refusal to deal under Article 102 TFEU.[363] A notable feature of the European version of the doctrine is the way in which it has expanded in cases involving intellectual property rights and intangible assets, where European Union courts have taken the position that refusal to provide a license of intellectual property rights may be abusive in exceptional circumstances, in particular when the refusal prevents the emergence of a new product for which there is a potential consumer demand, the refusal is not justified by an objective justification, and the refusal will exclude any or all competition or will eliminate any or all competition in a secondary market.[364]

---

[361]   *Competition Act*, 1998 [*Competition Act*], s 8(a) S. Afr.

[362]   Ibid, s 1(viii) S. Afr.

[363]   Commercial Solvents is the first important essential facilities case, where a dominant firm in the production of ethambutol ceased serving a manufacturer by refusing to supply raw materials to downstream competitors while becoming active in the downstream market through a subsidiary. The European Court of Justice held this to be an abuse of dominance, on grounds that the manufacturer had no feasible alternatives and that supplying its own raw material would have been prohibitively expensive. See *Istituto Chemioterapico Italiano S.p.A and Commercial Solvents Corporation v. Commission of the European Communities*, 1974 European Court of Justice. Another important case is *Sea Containers v. Stena Sealink*, where the owner and operator of a port was forced to grant access to third parties based on the fact that it had a dominant position in the provision of an essential facility and infringed Article 102 TFEU by using the facility while refusing other companies access. The *Oscar Bronner* case established the outer limits of the doctrine under European law. In this case, a regional newspaper demanded access to a national newspaper's distribution network. Denial of access to the home delivery scheme was justified as legitimate because the service was not indispensable to the newspaper's business and many methods of distributing daily newspapers through post, shops, kiosks, etc., were available, even if they were less advantageous than the home delivery scheme in question. *Oscar Bronner GmbH & Co. KG v. Mediaprint Zeitungs- und Zeitschriftenverlag GmbH & Co. KG, Mediaprint Zeitungsvertriebsgesellschaft mbH & Co. KG and Mediaprint Anzeigengesellschaft mbH & Co. KG* [1998] European Court Reports (European Court of Justice (Sixth Chamber)).

[364]   In *Magill*, the bottleneck facility concerned not a physical infrastructure but program listings of three television broadcasters in Ireland, where the refusal impeded the emergence of a comprehensive weekly TV guide giving details of all programs available to viewers in Ireland. *Magill* C-241/91 P & C-242/91 *Radio Telefis Eireann (RTE) and Independent Television Publications Ltd (ITP) v. Commission of the European Communities* [1995] 1995 I-00743 (European Court of Justice). See also *Oscar Bronner GmbH & Co. KG v. Mediaprint Zeitungs- und Zeitschriftenverlag GmbH & Co. KG, Mediaprint Zeitungsvertriebsgesellschaft mbH & Co. KG and Mediaprint*

The reason why the essential facilities doctrine is the most important competition law tool to deal with discriminatory conduct in the context of a vertically integrated digital platform that competes with third parties on its own platform is that repeated discriminatory treatment of competitors in this vertically integrated setting can be seen as a denial of access to bottleneck facilities that the doctrine can remedy. As seen, approaches toward mandated access remedies through competition laws vary across jurisdictions, but the core economic principles at the basis of the doctrine's variants (essentiality, denial of access, shareability) appear to have plausible pertinence in digital sectors that are structurally very concentrated. Essentiality is not impossible to determine in the case of a natural monopoly platform as well as highly concentrated industries where bottleneck inputs are necessary for downstream competition, even if fringe competitors are present.[365] Denial of access can be identified in various direct and indirect forms, for example, refusal to provide access to the platform through biases in results, demotion of particular competitors in search rankings, and exploitation of artificial scarcity to favor vertically integrated proprietary services.[366] As discussed in the first case study in the context of Google search results, shareability constraints, in terms of underutilized capacity or artificial scarcity, are also often alleviated in the context of digital platforms.[367] Unlike physical platforms like shopping malls that can accommodate only a limited number of retailers, or newspapers with limited advertising space, digital personal

---

Anzeigengesellschaft mbH & Co. KG, supra, note 363. In *IMS Health,* a market research company that provided regional data-reporting services to pharmaceutical companies, which were checked and formatted according to a brick structure, was ordered by the Commission to license the brick structure, finding that it had become the de facto industry standard. See *IMS Health GmbH & Co. OHG v. NDC Health GmbH & Co. KG* [2004] 2004 I-05039 (European Court of Justice (Fifth Chamber)). Similarly, in *Microsoft,* the illegal refusal involved information necessary for non-Microsoft work group server operating systems to communicate with Windows' operating system. The Commission ordered Microsoft to provide its information to competitors on "reasonable and non-discriminatory terms." See *Microsoft v. Commission* [2007] 3619 ECR II (Court of Justice of the European Union First Instance). In the 2008 Guidance Paper on enforcement priorities in applying Article 102, the Commission indicates that refusal to deal may infringe competition law when: 1) refusal relates to a product or service that is objectively necessary to be able to compete effectively on a downstream market; 2) the refusal is likely to lead to the elimination of effective competition on the downstream market; 3) the refusal is likely to lead to consumer harm. See *Communication from the Commission – Guidance on the Commission's Enforcement Priorities in Applying Article 82 of the EC Treaty to Abusive Exclusionary Conduct by Dominant Undertakings,* Guidance Document OJ C 45, 24.2.2009 (Brussels: European Commission, 2009).

[365] Some cases show that the absence of alternatives is not perfectly correlated with findings of essentiality, and vice versa. For example, in the US case *Associated Press,* the conclusion was that Associated Press could not be duplicated even though partial substitutes were available; in the European case *Oscar Brunner,* access was instead denied to a facility even when there were no alternatives home delivery scheme available. See, respectively, *supra,* notes 353 and 363.

[366] In *Associated Press,* for example, the US Supreme Court held it to be a violation of the Sherman Act for the Associated Press to discriminate against competitors in its admission policy. However, the remedy was to preclude such discrimination, and not that it was obliged to admit everyone (*supra,* note 353).

[367] Lao, *supra,* note 349 at 9; Lao, *supra,* note 184.

assistants, search engines, or e-commerce marketplaces have more room to share scarce inputs due to digitalization (for example, on a rotational basis).[368]

Two important factors, however, determine the effectiveness and desirability of imposing access to digital bottlenecks. First, the substantive reach of jurisdiction-specific legal doctrines. These may often reflect different views on property rights, how best to exploit a technology once created, and how to create optimal incentives for innovation and investment. The interplay of these factors may in some instances lead to a degree of hostility toward duty to deal that is not necessarily and fully consistent with an economic perspective. Second, the institutional ability to enforce and administer access remedies. The costs and complexities associated with such behavioral remedies arguably represent the most challenging concrete obstacle for enforcement in the absence of an industry regulator.

6.4.2 *The Institutional Limits of Ex Post Enforcement*

From an institutional perspective, the virtues of the just described Schumpeterian competition policy framework are various, especially compared to standard ex ante regulation. It avoids the costs of setting up industry-specific regulators; it avoids the need to directly regulate prices; and it fosters contestability, innovation, and cycles of monopoly displacement rather than the negative effect of undermining incentives to technological change and innovation that regulation necessarily entails. At the same time, the institutional dimension of ex post intervention through competition law enforcement also sets the limits of this ex post policy approach. In particular, even if the case for standard ex ante regulation remains weak, a Schumpeterian paradigm entails forms of intervention that are quasi-regulatory in nature and that are often beyond the reach of many antitrust agencies and courts. Thus, taking seriously the institutional dimension of ex post approaches reveals the need to fill the gaps of standard enforcement and strengthen antitrust institutions' capabilities to address these quasi-regulatory market power concerns at play in digital industries.

First, a framework of contestability and the resulting emphasis on potential competitors require much more expeditious and prophylactic approaches. The major institutional issue when dealing with defensive leveraging, for example, is one of timing and effectiveness of remedies. Since the objective is not simply to restore a distortion of competition, but rather to prevent exclusion of small potential competitors that can in the future threaten an established position, a finding of anticompetitive exclusion may do little to preserve potential competition and dis-placement if a decision occurs too late and the source of competitive threat has already been eliminated. Thus, approaches toward exclusionary conduct entail faster and more preemptive forms of intervention than a standard antitrust case.

---

[368] As argued in the first case study on horizontal search, access could be provided by rotating different results across equivalent search queries on a probabilistic basis.

Likewise, merger policy in the case of small potential competitors raises challenges beyond the need to fill possible substantive gaps, as it will necessarily entail a great deal of uncertainty and willingness to embark in more speculative analysis that may increase false positives. Moreover, substantive changes are in themselves problematic insofar as they would carve exceptions and ad hoc approaches for the digital economy within a legislative text that applies to all sectors and has a generalist aspiration. Given that acquisition of small competitors become for the most part problematic in specific digital platforms industries with distinct structural features, it may be more desirable to adopt ad hoc oversight and quasi-structural approaches that gravitate toward per se rules for specific markets outside and beyond the general merger review process.

Second, the promise of a competition policy approach oriented at contestability often depends on the complementary presence of targeted forms of regulation that impose various forms of mandated portability across platforms. This is particularly relevant when platforms derive their competitive advantage from a large and established network of users, and where an installed base can represent a barrier to entry for competitors that rely on developing a large network to make entry feasible and profitable. Portability of reviews and users' profiles can be an effective way to promote entry, contestability, and competition – for example, a driver or a seller requesting portability of reviews obtained on a specific platform to another platform, or users of a social network requesting portability of their profiles and social graphs to alternative platforms. The desirability of specific forms of regulatory intervention is highly context specific. In the case of network externalities, these remedies can be very effective at a low cost. In other cases, for example in the context of data,[369] the complexity and costs associated with portability instruments appear much higher, raising doubts on their desirability and applicability in practice. In either case, the effectiveness and timeliness of portability rules is key, and likely beyond the framework of standard antitrust cases.

Third, enforcement against exploitative abuses remains institutionally problematic even when these kinds of market power exercise fall substantively within provisions dealing with single-firm conduct. As seen, while control of high prices can, in theory, be dealt with through competition law and ex post enforcement, in practice competition authorities or courts generally lack the necessary institutional expertise to deal with this type of issues, which gravitate toward the domain of price regulation. Likewise, it remains unclear when dealing with nonprice exploitative abuses where the various thresholds triggering abuse should be located, especially in the absence of a defined regulatory standard. Contestability, on its part, can address

---

[369] It has been suggested, for instance, that compulsory access to data may foster competition, such as forcing a dominant general-purpose search engine to grant access to data to competing general-purpose search engines. Argenton and Prüfer, in particular, argue that all search engines should be required through regulation to share their anonymized data on clicking behavior of users following previous research queries. See Argenton and Prüfer, *supra*, note 177.

exploitative abuses indirectly, but its feasibility depends on how realistically a given market can be made contestable in the short term. Digital industries where market forces are particularly weak and market power expected to be durable represent therefore another constraint for an ex post policy framework.

Fourth, there are major institutional problems related to discriminatory behavior and access to bottleneck inputs. In particular, mandated access to an essential facility implies as a prerequisite the institutional ability to set and adjust access terms, to carry out ongoing monitoring of access, and arbitrate disputes in a timely manner, all of which are also generally outside the expertise of competition law agencies and courts. Antitrust laws are enforced on a case-by-case basis, either by public or private enforcers harmed by an antitrust violation. Disputes are costly and lengthy due to the legal and economic complexities at stake. Hence, competition laws may be underenforced when discrimination is subtle, or when the harm is not substantial from a case-by-case perspective, which may reduce the deterrent effect of enforcement. Instead of lengthy and demanding procedures, administrable access rules in some digital sectors may require less complex legal and economic analysis than the typical balancing of anticompetitive effects and efficiencies, as well as more timely procedures and ongoing monitoring closer to regulatory oversight. A Schumpeterian framework may require enhancing the institutional ability of competition agencies to operationalize access to digital bottleneck in specific digital sectors.

6.5 RETHINKING THE INTERFACE BETWEEN COMPETITION POLICY AND REGULATION

As discussed in previous chapters, policies that are consistent with various degrees of concentration are in general more desirable in digital platform industries. That is why horizontal break-ups are likely to be counterproductive, and why competition law enforcement's role in fragmenting markets may be of limited utility. However, identifying a principled policy approach consistent with different degrees of natural monopoly features and contestability is not an easy task. As in any market, no single instrument is perfect, and policy approaches will entail a comparison between the relative costs and benefits of imperfect forms of intervention that can often involve second-best policy responses. What in particular emerges from the discussion in this chapter is the way in which the features of digital platform markets challenge the institutional limits of alternative forms of intervention, and how the identified institutional shortcomings of available policy options make the case for increased complementarity between ex ante and ex post forms of intervention.

On the one hand, the unavoidable institutional problems associated with economic regulation reduce its desirability and scope in practice. As seen, in some cases franchise bidding may provide an alternative solution to a natural monopoly platform, but this alternative form of intervention is applicable in a limited set of circumstances and not immune from institutional costs, insofar as administering the bidding process and the conditions for the temporary monopoly position can make franchise bidding to some degree akin to regulation. Hence, competition policy appears in most, if not all cases, the most plausible policy approach to market power in digital platform markets.

On the other hand, because the features of digital industries demand a competition policy framework oriented at promoting forms of Schumpeterian competition and addressing market power issues that are often quasi-regulatory in nature, critical institutional constraints also limit the strengths of ex post intervention. Among other things, competition authorities and courts lack expertise in price regulation; the promotion of contestability may require faster enforcement as well as targeted remedies such as mandated portability that are regulatory in nature; and relying on competition law to deal with access issues will inevitably lead to a slippery slope to regulation due to the need to impose access terms on market participants and supervise them continuously – tasks that a competition agency or court is generally not equipped to deal with.

Some may take the identified institutional considerations of antitrust enforcement to their extreme conclusion, and advocate delegation of these market power concerns either to industry-specific regulators or to a new hypothetical body in charge of regulating the digital economy[370] as a superior solution to competition policy. This book, however, does not see the identified institutional limitations of competition policy as fatal constraints on an ex post approach to market power in digital platform markets. Rather, it suggests that the case in favor of a Schumpeterian policy framework will inevitably require a more complementary role between competition policy and novel forms of regulatory intervention, through an optimal mix of ex post and ex ante rules that may mitigate the institutional limitations of standard competition policy enforcement. For these reasons, as well as political economy considerations related to institutional design, empowering existing competition agencies with more power and institutional ability to deal with the kind of market power and competition issues raised by the structural features of some digital platform industries may be a more promising route, as well as a more feasible task for real-world institutions.

6.6 CONCLUSION

The economic and technological features of digital platform markets overall challenge the institutional limitations of standard ex ante and ex post approaches to market power. As a result, while each platform market is likely to raise specific

---

[370] See, for instance, George Stigler Center for the Study of the Economy and the State – University of Chicago Booth School of Business (2019), *supra*, note 12.

competition and market power issues on its own, this chapter has suggested that the major general policy challenge in digital platform industries is developing a principled policy approach to market power that can mitigate the institutional limits of ex post enforcement, possibly through a form of competition policy intervention that can address various market power issues that are more or quasi-regulatory in nature.

7

Conclusion

This book has sought to evaluate digital platform competition and approaches to market power through the lens of the natural monopoly framework. On the basis of three case studies, it has showed that technological change makes natural monopolies more plausible compared to older, physical predecessors of current platform markets, although natural concentration is often a function of a heterogeneity of factors related to technology that vary across industries and do not necessarily depend on the platform model and multisided externalities alone. The implications and conclusions derived from the evaluation of the natural monopoly framework are that neither laissez-faire arguments, based on the claim that market forces and new cycles of monopolies will erode high profits and market power without the need for intervention,[371] nor arguments in favor of aggressive intervention to reduce concentration, such as horizontal break-ups or protecting decentralized markets structures,[372] are justifiable.

In contrast, the book has argued that policies that address market power while accepting various degrees of efficient concentration become as a whole more desirable, but it has also highlighted how the search for a fine-grained approach based on the identified economic and technological features of digital industries is influenced by important institutional considerations. In particular, this book concluded that the higher likelihood of natural monopolies, simultaneously taking seriously the institutional dimension of intervention, will require a more complementary role between competition policy enforcement and regulatory instruments, as opposed to clear-cut alternative choices between the two paradigmatic forms of ex post and ex ante intervention.

These arguments and conclusion have been addressed and developed throughout this book building on the following steps and structure. Beginning in Chapter 2, the book first discussed how technological change has generated a new generation of platform markets where natural tendencies toward efficient monopoly are more

---

[371] See, for instance, David Evans, "Why the Dynamics of Competition for Online Platforms Leads to Sleepless Nights but Not Sleepy Monopolies" (2017), available at https://ssrn.com/abstract=3009438.
[372] See Lina M. Khan, *supra*, note 2.

pronounced than older physical predecessors of digital platforms. On that basis, the chapter adopted natural monopoly regulation as opposed to competition as a more suitable theoretical starting point of analysis for market power in digital platform markets, and it then attempted to trace the general boundaries and limitations of such a framework in the digital platform context.

On the basis of three case studies – horizontal search engines (Chapter 3), e-commerce marketplaces (Chapter 4), and ride-hailing platforms (Chapter 5) – the book then sought to shed light on the specific conditions that may give rise to natural monopoly platforms in different industries, and then derived general policy principles that may be pertinent to digital platforms as a whole. In Chapter 6, in particular, it suggested that while policies that accept various degrees of efficient concentration generally become more desirable, the exact design of a principled policy approach is affected by specific trade-offs imposed by the institutional dimensions of alternative and highly imperfect forms of intervention. As a consequence, ex post competition policy enforcement and ex ante regulatory instruments need to be seen as complements in digital platform markets.

7.1 LESSONS AND OPEN QUESTIONS

The evaluation of the natural monopoly framework to the three case studies, as well as the discussion of alternative policy approaches, offer a number of key implications with regard to market power and competition in digital platform industries. This concluding chapter summarizes some of the central lessons and open questions that have arisen throughout the book.

7.1.1 *Natural Monopolies and Digital Platforms*

Natural monopolies are generally associated with subadditivity and supply-sided scale economies, where high fixed costs and low marginal costs make a single provider more efficient than competing firms. In the context of digital platforms, the book has shown that there are other critical factors that add to standard supply-side scale economies and that may be associated with natural monopolies. As explained in Chapter 2, positive returns to data collection and analysis and demand-side efficiencies in aggregating direct and/or indirect network externalities on a single network are potential drivers of natural concentration, which add to the efficiency generated by supply-side economics of scale (which can be particularly pronounced in some markets due to large fixed costs and virtually zero marginal costs enabled by digitalization). As highlighted in the case studies, evaluating the magnitude of scale on the supply side, the demand side, or data collection entails an empirical determination, but the answer is likely to differ across platform markets, showing the highly heterogeneous role of these factors in each market, as well as important constraints that may militate against natural concentration in some contexts.

The case of horizontal search engines, for example, shows paradigmatically how the technological forces that drive the present wave of platform markets increase the likelihood of natural monopolies. First, search engines have large fixed costs necessary to develop the search algorithm and infrastructure to store and analyze large amounts of data. Once the algorithm is developed and investments are made, marginal costs to serve users' eyeballs with search results or advertisers that want to be present on the general search page are instead very low. In fact, the costs of serving additional users on both sides may be close to zero, creating a large degree of supply-side scale economies due to the digital nature of the service. Second, more users performing searches and using a search engine generate more data. This creates an additional form of economies of scale and scope and a critical efficiency advantage in terms of quality-adjusted costs associated with the predictive and universal dimensions of horizontal search. As a result, the combination of large economies of scale on the supply side and the importance of data make horizontal search prone to natural monopoly.

The second case study on e-commerce marketplaces, in contrast, highlights the limits of natural concentration in the context of digital platforms. In particular, it concluded that e-commerce platforms such as Amazon Marketplace lack the features of natural monopolies despite being characterized by a significant degree of network effects and scale economies. Buyers benefit from the presence of more sellers on the other side of the platform, and sellers, in turn, want to join a platform where a large pool of buyers can be reached. These network externalities create concentrating forces that lead to large platforms. Developing the online interface and the infrastructure sustaining online shopping also benefits from economies of scale on the supply side, which contribute to concentrated market structures. Yet neither force is strong enough to make a single platform the most efficient market outcome. Not only does the value of network effects at a certain point decrease once a critical mass of users is reached; there is also a strong dimension of product differentiation and demand heterogeneity at play in e-commerce, which goes against the efficiency of aggregating users over a single network and makes the presence of niche, specialized e-commerce platforms viable and desirable with heterogeneous demand. With regard to supply-side scale economies, there are important fixed costs in developing an e-commerce infrastructure, but marginal costs are not small and scale economies are likely not sufficiently large compared to demand, possibly leading to diseconomies of scale at large dimensions. Similarly, because for e-commerce marketplaces matching is more important than prediction, data do not have the same critical value that they has in horizontal search. The plausible explanation of dominance of online commerce platforms such as Amazon is not natural monopoly features but instead superior investments in developing an efficient logistics and delivery infrastructure and coupling it with a large online marketplace.

More ambiguous conclusions are reached with regard to the natural monopoly features of ride-hailing platforms, Uber for example, which are located in between horizontal search and e-commerce platforms. On the one hand, ride-hailing service providers rely on efficiently matching large networks of affiliated passengers and drivers. These indirect network externalities drive concentration and can thereby be a possible source of natural monopoly. On the other hand, however, the value of network externalities is not infinite, and is likely to taper off after a thick and sufficiently large network is reached, where the value of adding extra users and reducing waiting times becomes marginally insignificant. A similar conclusion applies to the role of data for matching purposes, which is likely to be much smaller when compared to their role in horizontal search, although they may retain value for the more predictive purpose of algorithmic route planning and routing. With regard to supply-side scale economies, the cost of developing the matching technology are also arguably smaller than search, making entry more feasible. The possibility of natural monopoly is therefore not remote but significantly lower than in horizontal search, and it is largely dependent on the local conditions of demand – the extent and density of the population, the availability of alternative methods of transportation, and so on.

As the three case studies illuminate, the relative importance of scale on the supply side, on the demand side in the form of network externalities, and with regard to data is an empirical matter, but these factors are likely to play a rather different role in each platform market. Hence, while many of the factors enabled by technological change make the likelihood of natural monopoly higher in the current generation of platforms compared to their older predecessors, the identified drivers of concentration remain highly heterogeneous and specific to the features of each market. As a result, some digital platforms are prone to be natural monopolies, while other can feasibly sustain coexisting, competing platforms and competition.

In addition, the book has also shown that the source of natural monopolies in digital platform industries may often differ from standard natural monopolies and network utilities-based subadditivity on the supply side, and that as a result there may be different degrees of contestability across platform markets depending on the relative importance of various drivers of concentration. In particular, in contrast to standard network utilities based on supply-side economies of scale where entry barriers are generally high and entry and contestability unlikely, platform markets that derive natural monopoly features from the strength of network externalities can potentially be made more contestable than standard public utility industries through policies that reduce the costs of switching and promote potential competition by facilitating entry that depends on demand-side network externalities and the development of a sufficiently large network of users. Adding to this feature the extremely rapid pace of technological change and the prospect of global platform competition as additional threats to entrenched market positions and potential sources of displacement, there appears to be more room than in standard network utilities for

policy intervention that focuses on making the position of some large digital platforms contestable, even when they possess naturally monopolistic features.

7.1.2 *Break-Up Policies*

The various forms of scale associated with digital industries and the resulting
tendencies toward natural concentration suggest that policies that focus on artificial
fragmentation such as breaking up some of the large tech platforms are generally
undesirable. In this regard, it is useful to distinguish between forms of horizontal and
vertical break-up. Horizontal break-ups create artificial fragmentation by breaking
up a large platform into smaller, competing firms – for example, breaking Facebook
in order to create competing social networks. The logic of this policy approach is for
the most part antithetical to the economic features at play in digital platform
markets.

Vertical break-ups are in contrast potentially more pertinent. Vertical separation, as a way to address discriminatory behavior by a vertically integrated monopolist, has more pertinence in this context in that it cuts at the root incentives to
discriminate – for example, separating Google search from some of its specialized
services to eliminate various forms of search bias. However, as was argued in this
book, it remains a last resort remedy for issues that may be better addressed
through access remedies. Another area where vertical separation may be potentially pertinent is also deintegration of acquisitions that post-mergers are revealed
to be problematic, such as the acquisition of Instagram by Facebook. The
problem of this policy is that the goal of blocking this kind of mergers is generally
to preserve nascent potential competitors, despite the presence of efficiencies that
the acquisition may create. Setting aside the costs of break-ups, it is unclear how
effectively post-merger separation can foster potential competition once the two
firms have already been integrated; meanwhile, some efficiencies may have
materialized as a result of the merger, and separation must deal with undoing
some of these synergies.

7.1.3 *The Economics of Platforms and the Boundaries of Desirable Legal Changes*

While break-ups and policies that promote artificial fragmentation appear generally
incompatible with the economic and technological features of digital platforms, the
search for desirable policy approaches to market power in these industries entails
a complex determination, which is connected to larger important questions raised
by the economics of platform markets at large: are the economic features of markets
with multiple sides intrinsically different from standard markets? And, if so, do they
represent a challenge to the fundamental principles, assumptions, and legal tools
applied in competition policy enforcement?

Some views suggest that everything needs to be rethought in platform markets, that new tools need to be developed to address the specific features of platforms in antitrust cases, or that established goals need to be abandoned. Different views instead argue that everything is the same in platform markets, and, therefore, that normal antitrust policy and industrial organization models continue to apply. Other views propose various refinements to standard tools and policy approaches, without, however, altering the fundamental principles at the basis of competition law enforcement. This book has supported this latter position.

First, the book has argued that while platform markets have specific economic features that may distinguish them from single-sided ones, the importance of multisidedness is a matter of degree rather than a black-and-white distinction. Hence, what matters is not whether a market is labeled as multisided, but rather whether the economic consequences of multisidedness are relevant enough in a given context, and whether these differences can be accommodated within the established legal framework. On this basis, the book has concluded that there is no need to rethink the fundamental principles of competition law in platform industries, but that there is room for tailored adjustment and refinements to fill some of the gaps in the current tools, whether it is refining tests for predation, the legal framework for balancing competitive effects, or policy approaches in highly concentrated platform markets.

Analogous conclusions apply to digital platforms. On the one hand, the book has stressed the heterogeneous features that distinguish different digital platform markets from one another, both from an economic perspective and in terms of regulatory issues that may be specific to each sector. Looking for example at the digital platforms evaluated in the three case studies, none represents a pure platform but rather different hybrid forms of platform intermediation – for example, Amazon is not a pure market maker, but a hybrid marketplace where it also directly supplies products in competition with third-party sellers; Uber sets prices centrally instead of allowing independent drivers to set their own fares, and so on. Likewise, the importance of multisidedness for natural concentration varies substantially, as indirect network externalities have different strength and play different roles in e-commerce, ride hailing, and horizontal search.

On the other hand, the book has at the same time identified a mix of recurring technological and economic forces that may demand tailored policy adjustments in digital platform industries. Among other things, the importance of data and digitalization expands prediction and matching capabilities, which generally enhance concentration tendencies, and technological change affects the application of standard policy approaches, limiting the feasibility of standard ex ante regulation but at the same time revealing the institutional limitations of an ex post approach based on Schumpeterian competition and contestability. As a result, the book has identified some gaps in current policy instruments that affect intervention in the context of digital platforms. These identified gaps are often more institutional than substantive, and do not entail the creation of radically novel approaches. Rather, they demand an attempt to build on established principles to increase the strength of current tools.

7.1.4 *Institutional Refinements for a Schumpeterian Framework*

This book has argued that substantive changes to competition laws cannot represent, by themselves, a panacea for the market power issues at play in digital industries, being either not necessarily desirable or not sufficiently effective. First, substantive changes will inevitably gravitate toward emphasis on the protection of small competitors and will carve in the legislative text special exceptions for the digital sector, militating against the generalist aspiration of competition laws. Second, even when desirable substantive changes are introduced, enforcement remains excessively slow and unsuited for remedies that require ongoing monitoring. As a result, rather than focusing solely on changes to various substantive areas of competition laws (for example, reforming merger regulations, or changing doctrinal or procedural aspects of refusal to deal provisions), this book has instead argued that a more promising approach is empowering competition authorities with the necessary power to oversee some digital markets in which identified structural features make competition and exercises of market power particularly problematic. These powers may include tools to: address distortions of potential competition through faster and simplified procedures to foster contestability; implement ad hoc review of preemptive mergers outside the standard merger review process in industries where such acquisitions can be particularly pernicious; implement and monitor remedies that may require ongoing oversight such as access remedies and possibly selected forms of exploitative exercises of market power, especially in markets with low contestability.

This particular emphasis on the institutional dimension of intervention is justified by the fact that a competition policy approach based on contestability is limited by important institutional constraints, and that supporters of a contestability framework[373] tend to assume away the institutional limitations of ex enforcement as a meaningful instrument against market power in digital industries. In particular, a Schumpeterian form of competition policy intervention assumes the possibility that markets can be made contestable and entry encouraged through antitrust enforcement alone. These are strong assumptions. While in some contexts, dominant positions may be made contestable, in other markets, the force of potential competition may remain critically weak. Likewise, competition policy can be oriented toward a contestability framework, yet enforcement needs to move more quickly and, in some markets, may require the complementary role of ex ante rules and remedies that are more regulatory in nature.

---

[373] For a discussion on contestability, see, for instance, Tirole (2017), *supra*, note 11.

Hence, as it was argued throughout this book, while a contestability-based competition policy is likely to represent the most promising form of intervention against market power in digital platform markets at a general level, making this approach effective requires a strengthening of institutional capabilities attuned to the economic and technological characteristics of digital industries. As a result, the boundaries between ex post forms and ex ante forms of intervention tend to overlap and gravitate toward more complementarity between regulatory and competition law instruments.[374]

7.1.5 *Political Economy Considerations*

Future policy approaches in digital platform markets are likely to follow the lead of major jurisdictions, where the balance between a race to the top and a race to the bottom with regard to intervention is likely to be affected by a number of factors. As a starting point, it is likely that jurisdictions where most of the large digital platforms are based and originate (for example, the United States) will favor lower standards, driving an overall race to the bottom. At the same time, countries that hope to foster their digital industries and where domestic firms may rely on access to large and established foreign platforms may instead favor stricter approaches (for example, the European Union and countries following the European lead). It is thus plausible that large jurisdictions that favor stricter standards and have the ability to exercise indirect regulatory influence may ignite a contrasting global race to the top, especially if the benefits for global platforms of complying with a uniform global standard exceed the benefits of adhering to multiple, different regulatory requirements. Adding to this effect, domestic concerns over privacy, excessive concentration, and other policy issues related to digital platforms may tilt preferences even in less interventionist jurisdictions, eventually leading toward stricter regulatory standards. Moreover, international competition may also alter the balance of domestic considerations, with less interventionist countries plausibly becoming stricter if foreign platforms become dominant by displacing domestic firms in some sectors.

The presence of multiple, diverging standards is likely to increase compliance costs for global platforms across jurisdictions, and political economy considerations may create frictions against cross-border cooperation. Nonetheless, variations across regulatory initiatives are not necessarily problematic in the long term, insofar as they may eventually promote a de facto globalization of standards that is closer to the optimal.

7.2 CONCLUSION

The conclusions reached in this book show the failures of broad generalizations in favor or against intervention in digital platform markets. First, the book has criticized

---

[374] For recent policy approaches and proposals for the digital economy, see various reports cited *supra*, note 12.

approaches that use the term platform as a label to describe a homogeneous and unitary category, showing instead that the platform model can display a substantial degree of heterogeneity, and that multisided externalities can often be only tangential and not necessary determinant of natural concentration. Second, the position taken in this book differs from the prevailing positions in favor and against intervention in digital markets. For instance, some commentators, such as Jonathan Taplin in *Move Fast and Break Things*,[375] have advocated for breaking up tech giants; others, Jonathan Tepper in *The Myth of Capitalism*,[376] for instance, have proposed blocking any merger that materially reduces the number of firms in a market, breaking up and reversing problematic mergers, and introducing new laws for predatory pricing; in a similar vein, proponents of "Hipster" or "Brandeis." Antitrust have suggested abandoning the consumer welfare standard in favor of multiple objectives that include protection of small businesses, preserving deconcentrated market structures, and tackling excessive concentration of economic and political power.[377] All these proposals, in one form or another, attempt to address market power and platform competition by deconcentrating markets and inducing fragmentation. Hence, they fail to appreciate that the enhanced likelihood of natural monopolies in platform markets will generate efficient concentration that is better dealt with through policies that accept various degrees of natural concentration.

At the opposite end of the spectrum, proponents of laissez-faire instead generally claim that no intervention is required in tech markets because market forces will discipline incumbents and innovative entrants will eventually erode and displace current monopolist.[378] However, these positions also fail to appreciate or underplay the tools that dominant firms, especially if naturally monopolistic and safeguarded by high entry barriers, have at their disposal to delay or prevent displacement, and dismiss the intra-platform distortions that can occur while a platform enjoys an uncontested dominant position.

More intermediate and nuanced positions that build on refinements to the Schumpeterian thesis, such as that espoused by, among others, Jean Tirole in *Economics for the Common Good*,[379] acknowledge the need to intervene by adopting a competition policy focused on contestability and facilitating entry that aims at competing for the market, rather than within the market. Yet even these more refined positions, in their embrace of competition policy as the most desirable approach to digital platforms, fall short of taking seriously some institutional limitations of antitrust enforcement based on a Schumpeterian and contestability

[375]   Jonathan Taplin, *Move Fast and Break Things: How Facebook, Google, and Amazon Cornered Culture and Undermined Democracy* (New York: Little, Brown, 2017).
[376]   Tepper, *supra*, note 39.
[377]   Medvedovsky, *supra*, note 5.
[378]   Evans (2017), *supra*, note 371.
[379]   Tirole (2017), *supra*, note 11.

framework. As this book has attempted to emphasize, many of the market power concerns at play in digital platform markets challenge the institutional reach of ex post enforcement, entailing forms of intervention and remedies that competition authorities or courts are generally not well-placed to perform and implement. Thus, the prospect of competition policy based on a contestability framework that promotes Schumpeterian and dynamic competition in digital platform markets inevitably entails the need to complement standard competition policy with more regulatory forms of intervention, where the respective institutional limitations of ex post and ex ante approaches are likely to shape policy approaches to market power more than is generally appreciated.

Bibliography

BOOKS

Baumol, William J., John C. Panzar, and Robert D. Willig. *Contestable Markets and the Theory of Industry Structure* (New York: Harcourt Brace Jovanovich, 1982).

Berg, Sanford V. and John Tschirhart. *Natural Monopoly Regulation: Principles and Practice*, Cambridge Surveys of Economic Literature (Cambridge: Cambridge University Press, 1988).

Blair, Roger D. and D. Daniel Sokol, eds. *The Cambridge Handbook of Antitrust, Intellectual Property, and High Tech* (Cambridge: Cambridge University Press, 2017).

Bork, Robert H. *The Antitrust Paradox*, 2nd ed. (New York: Free Press, 1993).

Botsman, Rachel and Roo Rogers. *What's Mine Is Yours: The Rise of Collaborative Consumption* (New York: HarperCollins, 2010).

Chandler Jr, Alfred D. *The Visible Hand* (Cambridge, MA: Harvard University Press, 1977).

Chopra, Sunil and Peter Meindl. *Supply Chain Management: Strategy, Planning, and Operation* (Pearson: London, 2014).

Christensen, Clayton M. *The Innovator's Dilemma: When New Technologies Cause Great Firms to Fail* (Cambridge, MA: Harvard Business School Press, 1997).

Croley, Steven P. *Regulation and Public Interests: The Possibility of Good Regulatory Government* (Cambridge, MA: Princeton University Press, 2009).

Elhauge, Einer and Damien Geradin. *Global Antitrust Law and Economics*, 2nd ed., University Casebook Series (New York: Foundation Press Thomson/West 2011).

Evans, David and Richard Schmalensee. *Matchmakers: The New Economics of Multisided Platforms* (Cambridge, MA: Harvard Business Review Press, 2016).

Ezrachi, Ariel and Maurice E. Stucke. *Virtual Competition: The Promise and Perils of the Algorithm-Driven Economy* (Cambridge, MA: Harvard University Press, 2016).

Fox, Eleanor M. and Michael J. Trebilcock. *The Design of Competition Law Institutions, Global Norms, Local Choices* (Oxford: Oxford University Press, 2013).

Galloway, Scott. *The Four: The Hidden DNA of Amazon, Apple, Facebook, and Google* (London: Penguin, 2017).

Goldin, Claudia and Lawrence F. Katz. *The Race Between Education and Technology* (Cambridge, MA: Harvard University Press, 2009).

Kahn, Alfred. *The Economics of Regulation: Principles and Institutions* (Cambridge, MA: MIT Press, 1988).

Laffont, Jean-Jacques and Jean Tirole. *A Theory of Incentives in Procurement and Regulation* (Cambridge, MA: MIT Press, 1993).

Lanier, Jaron. *Who Owns The Future?* (London: Penguin, 2013).

Letwin, William. *Law and Economic Policy in America* (Chicago: University of Chicago Press, 1981).

Marx, Karl. *A Contribution to the Critique of Political Economy* (Moscow: Progress Publishers, 1859).

McKee, Derek and Teresa Scassa, eds. *Law and the "Sharing Economy": Regulating Online Market Platforms* (Ottawa: University of Ottawa Press, 2018).

Motta, Massimo. *Competition Policy: Theory and Practice* (Cambridge: Cambridge University Press, 2004).

Parker, Geoffrey G., Marshall W. Van Alstyne, and Sangeet Paul Choudary. *Platform Revolution: How Networked Markets Are Transforming the Economy and How to Make Them Work for You* (New York: W.W. Norton & Company, 2016).

Peltzman, Sam and Clifford Winston. *Deregulation of Network Industries: What's Next?* (Washington, DC: AEI-Brookings Joint Center for Regulatory Studies, 2000).

Posner, Richard. *Antitrust Law*, 2nd ed. (Chicago: University of Chicago Press, 2001).

Ramanadham, V. V. *The Economics of Public Enterprise* (London: Routledge, 1991).

Rifkin, Jeremy. *The Zero Marginal Cost Society: The Internet of Things, the Collaborative Commons, and the Eclipse of Capitalism* (New York: Macmillan, 2014).

Roth, Alvin E. *Who Gets What and Why: The New Economics of Matchmaking and Market Design* (Boston, MA: Houghton Mifflin Harcourt, 2015).

Scherer, F. M. and David Ross. *Industrial Market structure and Economic Performance*, 3rd ed. (Boston, MA: Houghton Mifflin, 1990).

Schmalensee, Richard. *The Control of Natural Monopolies* (Lexington, MA: Lexington Books, 1979).

Schumpeter, Joseph A. *Capitalism, Socialism, and Democracy* (London: Harper & Brothers, 1942).

Seager, Henry Rogers and Charles Adams Gulick. *Trust and Corporation Problems* (New York: Harper, 1929).

Sharkey, William W. *The Theory of Natural Monopoly* (Cambridge: Cambridge University Press, 1982).

Shy, Oz. *The Economics of Network Industries* (Cambridge: Cambridge University Press, 2001).

Slee, Tom. *What's Yours Is Mine: Against the Sharing Economy* (New York: Penguin, 2016).

Srinivasan, Bhu. *Americana: A 400-Year History of American Capitalism* (New York: Penguin, 2017).

Stone, Brad. *The Everything Store: Jeff Bezos and the Age of Amazon* (New York: Little, Brown, 2013).

Sundararajan, Arun. *The Sharing Economy: The End of Employment and the Rise of Crowd-Based Capitalism* (Cambridge, MA: MIT Press, 2016).

Susskind, Richard. *The Future of Law: Facing the Challenges of Information Technology* (Oxford: Clarendon Press, 1998).

Susskind, Richard and Daniel Susskind. *The Future of the Professions: How Technology Will Transform the Work of Human Experts* (Oxford: Oxford University Press, 2016).

Taplin, Jonathan. *Move Fast and Break Things: How Facebook, Google, and Amazon Cornered Culture and Undermined Democracy* (New York: Little, Brown, 2017).

Tepper, Jonathan. *The Myth of Capitalism: Monopolies and the Death of Competition* (Hoboken, NJ: John Wiley & Sons, 2018).

Tirole, Jean. *Economics for the Common Good* (Cambridge, MA: Princeton University Press, 2017).

Trebilcock, Michael J., Ralph A. Winter, and Edward M. Iacobucci. *The Law and Economics of Canadian Competition Policy* (Toronto: University of Toronto Press, 2002).

Van Parijs, Philippe and Yannick Vanderborght. *Basic Income, A Radical Proposal for a Free Society and a Sane Economy* (Cambridge, MA: Harvard University Press, 2017).

Vickers, John and George K. Yarrow. *Privatization: An Economic Analysis*, MIT Press Series on the Regulation of Economic Activity 18 (Cambridge, MA: MIT Press, 1988).

Williamson, Oliver E. *Markets and Hierarchies, Analysis and Antitrust Implications: A Study in the Economics of Internal Organization* (New York: Free Press, 1975).

Wu, Tim. *The Master Switch: The Rise and Fall of Information Empires*, 1st ed. (New York: Alfred A. Knopf, 2010).

   The Curse of Bigness: Antitrust in the New Gilded Age (New York: Columbia Global Reports, 2018).

ARTICLES

Abrahamson, Zachary. "Essential Data" (2014) 124, no. 3, *Yale Law Journal*, available at https://digitalcommons.law.yale.edu/ylj/vol124/iss3/7.

Aghion, Philippe, Nick Bloom, Richard Bundell, Rachel Griffith, and Peter Howitt. "Competition and Innovation: An Inverted-U Relationship" (2005) 120, no. 2, *Quarterly Journal of Economics*, 701.

Akman, Pinar. "The Theory of Abuse in Google Search: A Positive and Normative Assessment Under EU Competition Law," SSRN Scholarly Paper ID 2811789 (Rochester, NY: Social Science Research Network, 2016).

Alarie, Benjamin, Anthony Niblett, and Albert H. Yoon. "Law in the Future" (2016) 66, no. 4, UTLJ, 423.

Alchian, Armen and Harold Demsetz. "Production, Information Costs, and Economic Organization" (1972) 62, no. 5, *American Economic Review*, 777.

Amelio, Andrea and Bruno Jullien. "Tying and Freebies in Two-Sided Markets" (2012) 30, no. 5, *International Journal of Industrial Organization*, 436.

Amelio, Andrea, Liliane Karlinger, and Tommaso Valletti. "Exclusionary Practices and Two-sided Platforms." Note by Andrea Amelio, Liliane Karlinger, and Tommaso Valletti, "Hearing on Re-Thinking the Use of Traditional Antitrust Enforcement Tools in Multi-Sided Markets," DAF/COMP/WD(2017)34/FINAL (OECD, 2017).

Anchustegui, Ignacio Herrera and Julian Nowag. "Buyer Power in the Big Data and Algorithm Driven World: the Uber and Lyft Example" (2017) CPI Antitrust Chronicle, available at www.competitionpolicyinternational.com/wp-content/uploads/2017/09/CPI-Anchustegui-Nowag.pdf.

Andreu, Enrique and Jorge Padilla. "Quantifying Horizontal Merger Efficiencies in Multi-Sided Markets: An Application to Stock Exchange Mergers" – Note by Enrique Andreu and Jorge Padilla, "Hearing on Re-Thinking the Use of Traditional Antitrust Enforcement Tools in Multi-Sided Markets," DAF/COMP/WD(2017)37/FINAL (2017).

Areeda, Phillip. "Essential Facilities: An Epithet in Need of Limiting Principles" (1989) 58 no. 3, *Antitrust Law Journal*, 841.

Argentesi, Elena and Lapo Filistrucchi. "Estimating Market Power in a Two-Sided Market: The Case of Newspapers" (2007) 22, no. 7, *Journal of Applied Econometrics*, 1247.

Argentesi, Elena and Marc Ivaldi. "Market Definition in the Printed Media Industry: Theory and Practice," SSRN Scholarly Paper ID 779107 (Rochester, NY: Social Science Research Network, 2005).

Argenton, Cédric and Jens Prüfer. "Search Engine Competition with Network Externalities" (2012) 8, no. 1 Jnl of Competition Law & Economics, 73.

Armstrong, Mark. "Competition in Two-Sided Markets" (2006) 37, no. 3, *RAND Journal of Economics*, 668.

Armstrong, Mark and David E. M. Sappington. "Regulation, Competition and Liberalization" (2006) 44, no. 2, *Journal of Economic Literature*, 325.

Armstrong, Mark and Julian Wright. "Two-sided Markets, Competitive Bottlenecks and Exclusive Contracts" (2007) 32, no. 2, *Economic Theory*, 353.

Arrow, Kenneth. "Economic Welfare and the Allocation of Resources for Invention" in *The Rate and Direction of Economic Activities: Economic and Social Factors* (Cambridge, MA: Princeton University Press, 1962).

Autor, David, David Dorn, Lawrence F. Katz, Christina Patterson, and John Van Reenen. "Concentrating on the Fall of the Labor Share" (2017) 107, no. 5, *American Economic Review*, 180.

"The Fall of the Labor Share and the Rise of Superstar Firms" (2017) Working Paper, available at https://scholar.harvard.edu/lkatz/publications/fall-labor-share-and-rise-superstar-firms.

Azar, José, Sahil Raina, and Martin C Schmalz. "Ultimate Ownership and Bank Competition," SSRN Scholarly Paper ID 2710252 (Rochester, NY: Social Science Research Network, 2016).

Azar, José, Martin C. Schmalz, and Isabel Tecu. "Anticompetitive Effects of Common Ownership," SSRN Scholarly Paper ID 2427345 (Rochester, NY: Social Science Research Network, 2018).

Baker, Jonathan B. "Market Power in the U.S. Economy Today" (March 20, 2017), available at https://equitablegrowth.org/market-power-in-the-u-s-economy-today/.

Baker, Jonathan B. and Judith A. Chevalier. "The Competitive Consequences of Most-Favored-Nation Provisions" (2012) 27, *Antitrust*, 20.

Baker, Jonathan B. and Fiona Scott Morton. "Antitrust Enforcement Against Platform MFNs" (2018) 127, no. 7, Yale LJ, 2176.

Baker, Jonathan, Nancy Rose, Steven Salop, and Fiona Scott Morton. "Five Principles for Vertical Merger Enforcement Policy," Georgetown Law Faculty Publications and Other Works 2148–2019 (2019), available at https://ssrn.com/abstract=3351391.

Barkai, Simcha. "Declining Labor and Capital Shares" (2017) Working Paper, available at www.london.edu/faculty-and-research/academic-research/d/declining-labor-and-capital-shares.

Baxter, William F. "Bank Interchange of Transactional Paper: Legal and Economic Perspectives" (1983) 26, no. 3, *Journal of Law and Economics*, 541.

Behringer, Stefan and Lapo Filistrucchi. "Areeda–Turner in Two-Sided Markets" (2015) 46, no. 3, Rev Ind Organ, 287.

Belleflamme, Paul and Martin Peitz. "Platforms and Network Effects," Working Papers 16–14 (University of Mannheim, Department of Economics, 2016).

Benkler, Yochai. "Sharing Nicely: On Shareable Goods and the Emergence of Sharing as a Modality of Economic Production" (2004) 114 Yale LJ, 273.

Bessen, James E. "Information Technology and Industry Concentration," SSRN Scholarly Paper ID 3044730 (Rochester, NY: Social Science Research Network, 2017).

Blonigen, Bruce A. and Justin R. Pierce. "Evidence for the Effects of Mergers on Market Power and Efficiency" Finance and Economics Discussion Series 2016–082 (Board of Governors of the Federal Reserve System (US), 2016).

Boffa, Federico and Lapo Filistrucchi. "Optimal Cartel Prices in Two-Sided Markets" SSRN Scholarly Paper ID 2506510 (Rochester, NY: Social Science Research Network, 2014).

Boik, Andre and Kenneth S. Corts. "The Effects of Platform Most-Favored-Nation Clauses on Competition and Entry" (2016) 59, no. 1, *Journal of Law and Economics*, 105.

Bortolotti, B., M. Fantini, and D. Siniscalco. "Privatisation Around the World: Evidence from Panel Data" (2004) 88, no. 1–2, *Journal of Public Economics*, 305.

Bower, Joseph and Clayton Christensen. "Disruptive Technologies: Catching the Wave" (1995) 73 *Harvard Business Review*, 43.

Brekke, Kurt. "Measuring Market Power in Multi-Sided Markets" – Note by Kurt Brekke, "Hearing on Re-Thinking the Use of Traditional Antitrust Enforcement Tools in Multi-Sided Markets," DAF/COMP/WD(2017)31/FINAL (OECD, 2017).

Brill, Julie. "Statement of the Commission Regarding Google's Search Practices" Statement 111-0163 (Washington, DC: Federal Trade Commission, 2013).

Brin, S. and L. Page. "The Anatomy of a Large-Scale Hypertextual Web Search Engine" (1998) 30 *Computer Networks and ISDN Systems*, 107–117.

Budzinski, Oliver and Karoline Henrike Köhler. "Is Amazon the Next Google?" Working Paper 97 (Ilmenau Economics Discussion Papers, 2015).

Caillaud, Bernard and Bruno Jullien. "Chicken & Egg: Competition Among Intermediation Service Providers" (2003) 34, no. 2 *RAND Journal of Economics*, 309.

Cairns, Robert and Liston-Heyes Catherine. "Competition and Regulation in the Taxi Industry" (1996) 59, no. 1, *Journal of Public Economics*, 1.

Carlton, Dennis W. and Michael Waldman. "The Strategic Use of Tying to Preserve and Create Market Power in Evolving Industries" (2002) 33, no. 2 *RAND Journal of Economics*, 194.

Carlton, Dennis W. and Ralph A. Winter. "Vertical MFN's and the Credit Card No-Surcharge Rule," SSRN Scholarly Paper ID 2982115 (Rochester, NY: Social Science Research Network, 2018).

Casey, Anthony J. and Anthony Niblett. "Self-Driving Laws" (2016) 66, no. 4, UTLJ, 429.

Cetin, Tamer and Elizabeth Deakin. "Regulation of Taxis and the Rise of Ridesharing" (2017) Transport Policy, available at www.sciencedirect.com/science/article/pii/S0967070X17300409.

Chandra, Ambarish and Allan Collard-Wexler. "Mergers in Two-Sided Markets: An Application to the Canadian Newspaper Industry" (2009) 18, no. 4, *Journal of Economics & Management Strategy*, 1045.

Choi, Jay Pil and oh-Shin Jeon. "A Leverage Theory of Tying in Two-Sided Markets," SSRN Scholarly Paper ID 2834821 (Rochester, NY: Social Science Research Network, 2016).

Coase, R. H. "The Nature of the Firm" (1937) 4, no. 16 *Economica*, 386.

Codagnone, Cristiano and Bertin Martens. "Scoping the Sharing Economy: Origins, Definitions, Impact and Regulatory Issues," JRC Technical Reports Institute for Prospective Technological Studies Digital Economy Working Paper JRC100369 (2016).

Collyer, Kate, Hugh Mullan, and Natalie Timan. "Measuring Market Power in Multi-Sided Markets" – Note by Kate Collyer, Hugh Mullan and Natalie Timan, DAF/COMP/WD (2017)35/FINAL (2017).

Cohen, Molly and Arun Sundararajan. "Self-Regulation and Innovation in the Peer-to-Peer Sharing Economy" (2015) 82 U Chi L Rev Dialogue, 116.

Cohen, Peter, et al. "Using Big Data to Estimate Consumer Surplus: The Case of Uber" (2016), available at awww.datascienceassn.org/sites/default/files/Using%20Big%20Data%20to%20Estimate%20Consumer%20Surplus%20at%20Uber.pdf.

Cornière, Alexandre de and Greg Taylor. "Integration and Search Engine Bias" (2014) 45, no. 3, *RAND Journal of Economics*, 576.

Crane, Daniel A. "Balancing Effects Across Markets" (2015) 80, no. 2, *Antitrust Law Journal*, 397.

De Loecker, Jan, Jan Eeckhout, and Gabriel Unger. "The Rise of Market Power and the Macroeconomic Implications," Draft, November 22, 2018.

Decker, Ryan, John Haltiwanger, Ron Jarmin, and Javier Miranda. "The Role of Entrepreneurship in US Job Creation and Economic Dynamism" (2014) 28, no. 3, *Journal of Economic Perspectives*, 3.

"The Secular Decline in Business Dynamism in the U.S.," Working Paper (Ann Arbor: University of Maryland, 2014).

Delbono, Flavio and Luca Lambertini. "Innovation and Product Market Concentration: Schumpeter, Arrow and the Inverted-U Shape Curve," SSRN Scholarly Paper ID 2981677 (Rochester, NY: Social Science Research Network, 2017).

Demsetz, Harold. "The Cost of Transacting" (1968) 82, no. 1, *Quarterly Journal of Economics*, 33.

"Why Regulate Utilities?" (1968) 11, no. 1, *Journal of Law and Economics*, 55.

"Information and Efficiency: Another Viewpoint" (1969) 12 J Law Econ, 1.

Dempsey, Paul Stephen. "Taxi Industry Regulation, Deregulation, and Reregulation: The Paradox of Market Failure," SSRN Scholarly Paper ID 2241306 (Rochester, NY: Social Science Research Network, 1996).

Dewenter, Ralf, Justus Haucap, and Tobias Wenzel. "Semi-Collusion in Media Markets" (2011) 31, no. 2, *International Review of Law and Economics*, 92.

Dolmans, Maurits and Thomas Graf. "Analysis of Tying Under Article 82 EC: The European Commission's Microsoft Decision in Perspective" (2004) 27, no. 2, *World Competition*, 225.

Dou, Zhicheng, Ruihua Song, and Ji-Rong Wen. "A Large-scale Evaluation and Analysis of Personalized Search Strategies" (2007) New York: ACM, available at https://dl.acm.org/citation.cfm?id=1242651

Dube, Aindrajit, et al. "Monopsony in On-line Labor Markets" (2018) Draft (Paper under Preparation).

Ducci, Francesco. "Procedural Implications of Market Definition in Platform Cases" (jnz017, 2019) *Journal of Antitrust Enforcement*.

Ducci, Francesco and Michael Trebilcock. "The Revival of Fairness Discourse in Competition Policy" (2019) 64 *The Antitrust Bulletin*, 79–104.

Economides, Nicholas and Ioannis Lianos. "The Elusive Antitrust Standard on Bundling in Europe and in the United States at the Aftermath of the Microsoft Cases" (2009) 76 *Antitrust Law Journal*, 483–567.

Edelman, Benjamin G. "Does Google Leverage Market Power Through Tying and Bundling?" (2015) 11, no. 2, *Journal of Competition Law and Economics*.

Edelman, Benjamin G. and Damien Geradin. "Efficiencies and Regulatory Shortcuts: How Should We Regulate Companies Like Airbnb and Uber" (2015) 19 Stan Tech L Rev, 293.

Edelman, Benjamin G. and Julian Wright. "Price Coherence and Excessive Intermediation," SSRN Scholarly Paper ID 2513513 (Rochester, NY: Social Science Research Network, 2015).

Einav, Liran, Chiara Farronato, and Jonathan Levin. "Peer-to-Peer Markets" (2016) 8, no. 1, *Annual Review of Economics*, 615.

Elhauge, Einer. "Horizontal Shareholding" (2015) 129 Harv L Rev, 1267.

Evans, David S. "The Antitrust Economics of Multi-Sided Platform Markets" (2003) 20 Yale J on Reg, 325.

"Multisided Platforms, Dynamic Competition, and the Assessment of Market Power for Internet-Based Firms," SSRN Scholarly Paper ID 2746095 (Rochester, NY: Social Science Research Network, 2016).

"Why the Dynamics of Competition for Online Platforms Leads to Sleepless Nights But Not Sleepy Monopolies," SSRN Scholarly Paper ID 3009438 (Rochester, NY: Social Science Research Network, 2017).

Evans, David S. and Michael Noel. "Defining Antitrust Markets When Firms Operate Two-Sided Platforms" (2005) 2005 Colum Bus L Rev, 667.

Evans, David S. and Richard Schmalensee. "The Industrial Organization of Markets with Two-Sided Platforms," NBER Working Paper No. 11603 (Cambridge, MA: National Bureau of Economic Research, 2005).

"The Antitrust Analysis of Multi-sided Platform Businesses" in *Oxford Handbook on International Antitrust Economics* (Oxford: Oxford University Press, 2015).

"Debunking the 'Network Effects' Bogeyman," SSRN Scholarly Paper ID 3148121 (Rochester, NY: Social Science Research Network, 2017).

"Network Effects: March to the Evidence Not to the Slogans," SSRN Scholarly Paper ID 3027691 (Rochester, NY: Social Science Research Network, 2017).

"Ignoring Two-Sided Business Reality Can Also Hurt Plaintiffs" (2018) *Competition Policy International*.

Ezrachi, Ariel and Maurice E Stucke. "Artificial Intelligence & Collusion: When Computers Inhibit Competition" (2017) 2017 U Ill L Rev, 1775.

Farrell, Joseph and Michael L Katz. "Competition or Predation? Consumer Coordination, Strategic Pricing and Price Floors in Network Markets" (2005) 53, no. 2, *Journal of Industrial Economics*, 203.

Farrell, Joseph and Garth Saloner. "Standardization, Compatibility, and Innovation" (1985) 16, no. 1, *RAND Journal of Economics*, 70.

Farronato, Chiara and Audrey Fradkin. "Market Structure with the Entry of Peer-to-Peer Platforms: The Case of Hotels and Airbnb" (2016) Unpublished Draft, available at https://editorialexpress.com/cgi-bin/conference/download.cgi?db_name=IIOC2016&paper_id=285.

Filistrucchi, Lapo. "How Many Markets Are Two-Sided?" (2011) 1 *Antitrust Chronicle*, available at https://econpapers.repec.org/article/cpiatchrn/1.1.2011_3ai=5804.htm.

"Market Definition in Multi-Sided Markets" – Note by Dr Lapo Filistrucchi, "Hearing on Re-Thinking the Use of Traditional Antitrust Enforcement Tools in Multi-Sided Markets," DAF/COMP/WD(2017)27/FINAL (OECD, 2017).

Filistrucchi, Lapo, Damien Geradin, and Eric Van Damme. "Identifying Two-Sided Markets" (2013) 36 *World Competition*, 33.

Filistrucchi, Lapo, Damien Geradin, Eric Van Damme, and Pauline Affeldt. "Market Definition in Two-Sided Markets: Theory And Practice" (2014) 10, no. 2, Jnl of Competition Law & Economics, 293.

Filistrucchi, Lapo, Tobias J. Klein, and Thomas O. Michielsen. "Assessing Unilateral Merger Effects In a Two-Sided Market: An Application to the Dutch Daily Newspaper Market" (2012) 8, no. 2, Jnl of Competition Law & Economics, 297.

Fletcher, Amelia. "Predatory Pricing in Two-Sided Markets: A Brief Comment," SSRN Scholarly Paper ID 987875 (Rochester, NY: Social Science Research Network, 2007).

Gal, Michal and Daniel L. Rubinfeld. "The Hidden Costs of Free Goods: Implications for Antitrust Enforcement" (2016) 80, no. 401, *Antitrust Law Journal*, available at https://papers.ssrn.com/abstract=2529425.

Gallick, Edward C. and David E. Sisk. "A Reconsideration of Taxi Regulation" (1987) 3, no. 1, *Journal of Law, Economics, and Organization*, 117.

"Specialized Assets and Taxi Regulation: An Inquiry into the Possible Efficiency Motivation of Regulation," Working Paper No. 119 (Washington, DC: Bureau of Economics, Federal Trade Commission, 1984).

Gegax, Douglas and Kenneth Nowotny. "Competition and the Electric Utility Industry: An Evaluation" (1993) 10, no. 1, *Yale Journal on Regulation*, available at https://digitalcommons.law.yale.edu/yjreg/vol10/iss1/4.

Gibbons, Robert. "Four Formal(izable) Theories of the Firm?" (2005) 58, no. 2, *Journal of Economic Behavior & Organization*, 200.

Goldberg, Victor P. "Regulation and Administered Contracts" (1976) 7, no. 2, *Bell Journal of Economics*, 426.

Goolsbee, Austan and Judith Chevalier. "Measuring Prices and Price Competition Online: Amazon and Barnes and Noble," NBER Working Papers 9085 (National Bureau of Economic Research, Inc., 2002).

Greenfield, Rebecca. "Why Google Pays Apple $1 Billion a Year", *The Atlantic* (February 12, 2013), available at www.theatlantic.com/technology/archive/2013/02/why-google-pays-apple-1-billion-year/318451/.

Grossman, Sanford J. and Oliver D. Hart. "The Costs and Benefits of Ownership: A Theory of Vertical and Lateral Integration" (1986) 94, no. 4. *Journal of Political Economy*, 691.

Grullon, Gustavo, Yelena Larkin, and Roni Michaely. "Are U.S. Industries Becoming More Concentrated?," SSRN Scholarly Paper ID 2612047 (Rochester, NY: Social Science Research Network, 2018).

Hagiu, Andrei and Julian Wright. "Marketplace or Reseller?" (2014) 61, no. 1, *Management Science*, 184.

"Multi-Sided Platforms," Working Paper No. 15–037 (Harvard Business School, 2014).

Hart, Oliver and John Moore. "Property Rights and the Nature of the Firm" (1990) 98, no. 6, *Journal of Political Economy*, 1119.

"Contracts as Reference Points" (2008) 123, no. 1, Q J Econ, 1.

Holmstrom, Bengt and Paul Milgrom. "The Firm as an Incentive System" (1994) 84, no. 4, *American Economic Review*, 972.

Hoofnagle, Chris Jay and Jan Whittington. "Free: Accounting for the Costs of the Internet's Most Popular Price" (2013) 61 UCLA L Rev, 606.

Hu, H., et al. "Toward Scalable Systems for Big Data Analytics: A Technology Tutorial" (2014) 2 *IEEE Access*, 652.

Hunt, Robert M. "An Introduction to the Economics of Payment Card Networks" (2003) 2, no. 2, *Review of Network Economics*, available at www.degruyter.com/view/j/rne.2003.2.issue-2/rne.2003.2.2.1020/rne.2003.2.2.1020.xml.

Iacobucci, Edward. "Tying as Quality Control: A Legal and Economic Analysis," SSRN Scholarly Paper ID 293602 (Rochester, NY: Social Science Research Network, 2001).

"The Superior Propane Saga: The Efficiencies Defence in Canada" in *Competition Law Around the World in Fourteen Stories* (Alphen aan den Rijn, The Netherlands: Kluwer Law International, 2013).

Iacobucci, Edward and Francesco Ducci. "The Google Search Case in Europe: Tying and the Single Monopoly Profit Theorem in Two-Sided Markets" (2019) 47, no. 1, *European Journal of Law and Economics*, 15.

Iacobucci, Edward M. and Michael J. Trebilcock. "The Design of Regulatory Institutions for the Canadian Telecommunications Sector" (2007) Canadian Public Policy, available at www.utpjournals.press/doi/abs/10.3138/cpp.33.2.127.

"The Role of Crown Corporations in the Canadian Economy: An Analytical Framework" (2012), available at https://tspace.library.utoronto.ca/handle/1807/89449.

Jiang, Yabing. "E-Book Platform Competition in the Presence of Two-Sided Network Externalities," SSRN Scholarly Paper ID 2164395 (Rochester, NY: Social Science Research Network, 2012).

Joskow, Paul. "Regulation of Natural Monopoly" in *Handbook of Law and Economics* (Amsterdam: Elsevier, 2007), p. 1227.

"Incentive Regulation in Theory and Practice: Electricity Distribution and Transmission Networks" in *Economic Regulation and Its Reform: What Have We Learned?* (Chicago: University of Chicago Press, 2014), p. 291.

Jullien, Bruno. "Competition in Multi-sided Markets: Divide and Conquer" (2011) 3, no. 4, *American Economic Journal: Microeconomics*, 186.

Karabarbounis, Loukas and Brent Neiman. "The Global Decline of the Labor Share" (2014) 129, no. 1, Q J Econ, 61.

Katz, Michael. "Exclusionary Conduct in Multi-Sided Markets" – Note by Michael Katz (OECD, 2017).

Katz, Michael and Jonathan Sallet, "Multisided Platforms and Antitrust Enforcement (2017) 127 *Yale Law Journal*, 2142.

Katz, Michael L. and Carl Shapiro. "Network Externalities, Competition, and Compatibility" (1985) 75, no. 3, *American Economic Review*, 424.

Khan, Lina M. "Amazon's Antitrust Paradox" (2016) 126 Yale L J, 710.

Kirkwood, John B. "Collusion to Control a Powerful Customer: Amazon, E-Books, and Antitrust Policy" (2014) 69 U Miami L Rev, 1.

Klein, Benjamin, Robert G. Crawford and Armen A. Alchian. "Vertical Integration, Appropriable Rents, and the Competitive Contracting Process" (1978) 21, no. 2, *Journal of Law and Economics*, 297.

Lao, Marina. "Networks, Access, and Essential Facilities: From Terminal Railroad to Microsoft" (2009) 62 SMU L Rev, 557.

"Search, Essential Facilities, and the Antitrust Duty to Deal" (2012) 11 *Northwestern Journal of Technology and Intellectual Property*, 275.

"'Neutral' Search as a Basis for Antitrust Action?," SSRN Scholarly Paper ID 2245295 (Rochester, NY: Social Science Research Network, 2013).

Lee, Robin S. "Vertical Integration and Exclusivity in Platform and Two-Sided Markets" (2013) 103, no. 7, *American Economic Review*, 2960.

Lefouili, Yassine and Joana Pinho. "Collusion in Two-Sided Markets," SSRN Scholarly Paper ID 3049356 (Rochester, NY: Social Science Research Network, 2017).

Lerner, Andres V. "The Role of 'Big Data' in Online Platform Competition," SSRN Scholarly Paper ID 2482780 (Rochester, NY: Social Science Research Network, 2014).

Lipsky, Abbott B. Jr and J. Gregory Sidak. "Essential Facilities" (1998) 51 Stan L Rev, 1187.

Luca, Michael, et al. "Does Google Content Degrade Google Search? Experimental Evidence," Harvard Business School Working Paper 16–035 (Harvard Business School, 2016).

Luchetta, Giacomo. "Is the Google Platform a Two-Sided Market?" (2014) 10, no. 1, *Journal of Competition Law and Economics*, 185.

Maurer, Stephen M. and Suzanne Scotchmer. "The Essential Facilities Doctrine: The Lost Message of Terminal Railroad," SSRN Scholarly Paper ID 2407071 (Rochester, NY: Social Science Research Network, 2014).

Medvedovsky, Konstantin. "Antitrust Chronicle – Hipster Antitrust" (April 18, 2018), available at Competition Policy International www.competitionpolicyinternational.com/anti trust-chronicle-hipster-antitrust/.

Moore, Adrian T. and Ted Balaker. "Do Economists Reach a Conclusion on Taxi Deregulation?" (2006) 3, no. 2, Econ J Watch, 109.

Munoz, Cecilia, Megan Smith, and D. J. Patil. "Big Data: A Report on Algorithmic Systems," Opportunity, and Civil Rights, Obama Administration's Big Data Working Group (Washington, DC: Executive Office of the President, 2016).

Naidu, Suresh, Eric A. Posner, and E. Glen Weyl. "Antitrust Remedies for Labor Market Power," SSRN Scholarly Paper ID 3129221 (Rochester, NY: Social Science Research Network, 2018).

Netter, Jeffry M. and William L. Megginson. "From State to Market: A Survey of Empirical Studies on Privatization" (2001) 39, no. 2, *Journal of Economic Literature*, 321.

Ohlhausen, Maureen K. "Antitrust Enforcement in the Digital Age" (2017) Remarks Before the Global Antitrust Enforcement Symposium Georgetown University.

Pagano, Anthony M. and Claire E. McKnight. "Economies of Scale in the Taxicab Industry: Some Empirical Evidence from the United States" (1983) 17, no. 3, *Journal of Transport Economics and Policy*, 299.

Parker, Geoffrey G. and Marshall W. Van Alstyne. "Two-Sided Network Effects: A Theory of Information Product Design" (2005) 51, no. 10, *Management Science*, 1494.

Pasquale, Frank and Oren Bracha. "Federal Search Commission? Access, Fairness and Accountability in the Law of Search" (2008) 93 *Cornell Law Review*, 1149.

Peltzman, Sam. "Toward a More General Theory of Regulation" (1976) 19, no. 2, *Journal of Law and Economics*, 211.

Pitofsky, Robert, Donna Patterson, and Jonathan Hooks. "The Essential Facilities Doctrine Under United States Antitrust Law" (2002) 70 *Georgetown Law Faculty Publications and Other Works*, 443.

Pollock, Rufus. "Is Google the Next Microsoft: Competition, Welfare and Regulation in Online Search" (2010) 9, no. 4, *Review of Network Economics*, available at www .degruyter.com/view/j/rne.2010.9.issue-4/rne.2010.9.4.1240/rne.2010.9.4.1240.xml.

Posner, Eric A. "Why Uber Will – And Should – Be Regulated" *Slate* (January 5, 2015), available at: www.law.uchicago.edu/news/eric-posner-why-uber-will-and-should-be-regulated.

Posner, Eric A., Fiona M. Scott Morton, and E. Glen Weyl. "A Proposal to Limit the Anti-Competitive Power of Institutional Investors," SSRN Scholarly Paper ID 2872754 (Rochester, NY: Social Science Research Network, 2017).

Posner, Richard. "Natural Monopoly and Its Regulation" (1973) *Journal of Reprints for Antitrust Law and Economics*, 335.

Rauch, Daniel and David Schleicher. "Like Uber, But for Local Governmental Policy: The Future of Local Regulation of the "Sharing Economy," SSRN Scholarly Paper ID 2549919 (Rochester, NY: Social Science Research Network, 2015).

Rochet, Jean-Charles and Jean Tirole. "An Economic Analysis of the Determination of Interchange Fees in Payment Card Systems" (2003) 2, no. 2, *Review of Network Economics*, 69.

"Platform Competition in Two-Sided Markets" (2003) 1, no. 4, *Journal of the European Economic Association*, 990.

"Two-Sided Markets: A Progress Report" (2006) 37, no. 3, *RAND Journal of Economics*, 645.

"Tying-in Two-Sided Markets and the Honour All Cards Rule," CEPR Discussion Papers 6132 (2007) C.E.P.R. Discussion Papers.

Rohlfs, Jeffrey. "A Theory of Interdependent Demand for a Communications Service" (1974) 5, no. 1, *Bell Journal of Economics*, 16.

Romanyuk, Gleb and Alex Smolin. "Cream Skimming and Information Design in Matching Markets," *American Economic Journal: Microeconomics*, available at www.aeaweb.org /articles?id=10.1257/mic.20170154.

Rosse, James N. "Daily Newspapers, Monopolistic Competition, and Economies of Scale" (1967) 57, no. 2, *American Economic Review*, 522.

Ruhmer, Isabel. "Platform Collusion in Two-Sided Markets" (Frankfurt a. M.: Verein für Socialpolitik, 2010).

Rysman, Marc. "Competition Between Networks: A Study of the Market for Yellow Pages" (2004) 71, no. 2, Rev Econ Stud, 483.

"The Economics of Two-Sided Markets" (2009) 23, no. 3, *Journal of Economic Perspectives*, 125.

Salop, Steven C. "Invigorating Vertical Merger Enforcement," SSRN Scholarly Paper ID 3052332 (Rochester, NY: Social Science Research Network, 2018).

Shapiro, Carl. "Antitrust in a Time of Populism," SSRN Scholarly Paper ID 3058345 (Rochester, NY: Social Science Research Network, 2017).

"Protecting Competition in the American Economy: Merger, Control, Tech Titans, Labour Markets" (2019) 33 *Journal of Economic Perspectives*, 69.

Shelanski, Howard A. and J. Gregory Sidak. "Antitrust Divestiture in Network Industries" (2001) 68 U Chi L Rev, 1.

Shleifer, Andrei. "State versus Private Ownership" (1998) 12, no. 4, *Journal of Economic Perspectives*, 133.

Smith, D., C. Andrew, and Michael J Trebilcock. "State-Owned Enterprises in Less Developed Countries: Privatization and Alternative Reform Strategies" (2001) 12, no. 3, *European Journal of Law and Economics*, 217.

Stigler, George. "The Theory of Economic Regulation" (1971) 2, no. 1, *Bell Journal of Economics*, 3.

Stiglitz, Joseph. "Toward a Broader View of Competition Policy" in *Competition Policy for the New Era: Insights from the BRICS Countries* (Oxford: Oxford University Press, 2017), p. 4.

Stucke, Maurice E. and Ariel Ezrachi. "When Competition Fails to Optimize Quality: A Look at Search Engines" (2016) 18 Yale JL & Tech, 70.

Stucke, Maurice E. and Allen P. Grunes. "Debunking the Myths Over Big Data and Antitrust" (2015) Legal Studies Research Paper Series Research Paper, 276 University of Tennessee.

Taplin, Jonathan. "Opinion: Is It Time to Break Up Google?", *New York Times* (January 20, 2018), available at www.nytimes.com/2017/04/22/opinion/sunday/is-it-time-to-break-up-google.html.

Thepot, Florence. "Market Power in Online Search and Social Networking: A Matter of Two-Sided Markets" (2013) 36, no. 2, *World Competition*, 195.

Trebilcock, Michael J. "The Fracturing of the Post-War Free Trade Consensus: The Challenges of Reconstructing a New Consensus," Paper Delivered at the University of Toronto Faculty of Law (2017).

Tucker, Darren S. and Hill Wellford. "Big Mistakes Regarding Big Data," SSRN Scholarly Paper ID 2549044 (Rochester, NY: Social Science Research Network, 2014).

Varian, Hal R. "Economics of Information Technology" (2003) University of California, Berkeley, available at http://people.ischool.berkeley.edu/~hal/Papers/mattioli/mattioli.pdf.

Waller, Spencer and Brett Frischmann. "Revitalizing Essential Facilities" (2008) 74, no. 1, *Faculty Publications & Other Works*, available at https://lawecommons.luc.edu/facpubs/72.

Ward, Patrick "Testing for Multisided Platform Effects in Antitrust Market Definition" (2017) 84 *University of Chicago Law Review*, 2059.

Werden, Gregory J. "The Law and Economics of the Essential Facility Doctrine" (1987) 32 St Louis U LJ, 433.

"Cross-Market Balancing of Competitive Effects: What Is the Law, and What Should It Be" (2017) 43 J Corp L, 119.

Weyl, E. Glen. "A Price Theory of Multi-sided Platforms" (2010) 100, no. 4, *American Economic Review*, 1642.

Weyl, E. Glen and Alexander White. "Let the Right 'One' Win: Policy Lessons from the New Economics of Platforms" (2014) Coase-Sandor Working Paper Series in Law and Economics No. 709–2014.

Wismer, Sebastian and Arno Rasek. "Market Definition in Multi-sided Markets" – Note by Sebastian Wismer and Arno Rasek, "Hearing on Re-Thinking the Use of Traditional Antitrust Enforcement Tools in Multi-Sided Markets," DAF/COMP/WD(2017)33/FINAL (2017).

Whinston, Michael. "Tying, Foreclosure, and Exclusion" (1990) 80, no. 4, *American Economic Review*, 837.

Williamson, Oliver. "Economies as an Antitrust Defense: The Welfare Tradeoffs" (1968) 58, no. 1, *American Economic Review*, 18.

"The Vertical Integration of Production: Market Failure Considerations" (1971) 61, no. 2, *American Economic Review*, 112.

"Franchise Bidding for Natural Monopolies-in General and with Respect to CATV" (1976) 7, no. 1, *Bell Journal of Economics*, 73.

"Assessing Vertical Market Restrictions: Antitrust Ramifications of the Transaction Cost Approach" (1979) 127, no. 4, *University of Pennsylvania Law Review*, 953.

"Transaction-Cost Economics: The Governance of Contractual Relations" (1979) 22, no. 2, *Journal of Law and Economics*, 233.

Winston, Clifford. "Economic Deregulation: Days of Reckoning for Microeconomists" (1993) 31, no. 3, *Journal of Economic Literature*, 1263.

Wright, Joshua and John Yun, "Burdens and Balancing in Multisided Markets: The First Principles Approach of Ohio v. American Express" (forthcoming, 2019) *Review of Industrial Organization*.

Wu, Tim. "Antitrust via Rulemaking: Competition Catalysts," SSRN Scholarly Paper ID 3058114 (Rochester, NY: Social Science Research Network, 2017).

"After Consumer Welfare, Now What? The 'Protection of Competition' Standard in Practice" (2018) CPI Antitrust Chronicle, available at www.competitionpolicyinternational.com/wp-content/uploads/2018/04/CPI-Wu.pdf.

"The American Express Opinion, Tech Platforms & the Rule of Reason" (forthcoming, 2018) *Journal of Antitrust Enforcement*, available at https://ssrn.com/abstract=3326667.

Zervas, Georgios, Davide Proserpio, and John W. Byers. "The Rise of the Sharing Economy: Estimating the Impact of Airbnb on the Hotel Industry" (2017) 54, no. 5, *Journal of Marketing Research*, 687.

Zhu, Feng and Liu Quihong. "Competing with Complementors: An Empirical Look at Amazon.com" (2015), available at https://mackinstitute.wharton.upenn.edu/wp-content /uploads/2015/04/Zhu-Feng-Liu-Qihong_Competing-with-Complementors.-An-Empirical-Look-at-Amazon.com_.pdf.

Zingales, Luigi. "Towards a Political Theory of the Firm" (2017) 31, no. 3, *Journal of Economic Perspectives*, 113.

REPORTS, LEGISLATION, REGULATIONS, AND GUIDELINES

Australian Competition and Consumer Commission, *Digital Platforms Inquiry: Final Report* (2019).

Autorité de la Concurrence & the Bundeskartellamt. *Competition Law and Data* (2016).

Bundeskartellamt. *Amazon Removes Price Parity Obligation for Retailers on Its Marketplace Platform*, Case Report B6-46/12 (2013).

Competition Act, RSC, 1985, c. C. 34.

Competition Bureau of Canada. *Big Data and Innovation: Implications for Competition Policy in Canada*, Draft for Public Consultation (Gatineau: QC, 2017).

European Commission. *Communication from the Commission – Notice – Guidelines on the Application of Article 81(3) of the Treaty (Text with EEA relevance)*, Guidelines Document 52004XC0427(07) (European Commission, 2004).

Communication from the Commission – Guidance on the Commission's Enforcement Priorities in Applying Article 82 of the EC Treaty to Abusive Exclusionary Conduct by Dominant Undertakings, Guidance Document OJ C 45, 24.2.2009 (Brussels: European Commission, 2009).

Antitrust: Commission Probes Allegations of Antitrust Violations by Google, Press Release IP/10/1624 (Brussels: European Commission, 2010).

Antitrust: Commission Seeks Feedback on Commitments Offered by Google to Address Competition Concerns, Press Release (Brussels: European Commission, 2013).

Antitrust: Commission Opens Formal Investigation Against Google in Relation to Android Mobile Operating System, Fact Sheet Memo/15/4782 (Brussels: European Commission, 2015).

Antitrust: Commission Sends Statement of Objections to Google on Comparison Shopping Service, Fact Sheet Memo/15/4781 (Brussels: European Commission, 2015).

Antitrust: Commission Sends Statement of Objections to Google on Comparison Shopping Service; Opens Separate Formal Investigation on Android, Press Release (Brussels: European Commission, 2015).

Antitrust: Commission Takes Further Steps in Investigations Alleging Google's Comparison Shopping and Advertising-Related Practices Breach EU Rules, Press Release (Brussels: European Commission, 2016).

Mergers: Commission Alleges Facebook Provided Misleading Information About WhatsApp Takeover, Press Release (Brussels: European Commission, 2016).

Antitrust: Commission Accepts Commitments from Amazon on E-books, Press Release IP/17/ 1223 (2017).

Mergers: Commission Fines Facebook €110 Million for Providing Misleading Information About WhatsApp Takeover, Press Release (Brussels: European Commission, 2017).

Staff Working Document on the Free Flow of Data and Emerging Issues of the European Data Economy, Working Document (Brussels: European Commission, 2017).

Competition Policy for the Digital Era, Final Report (April 4, 2019).

European Union. Consolidated Versions of the Treaty on the Functioning of the European Union (TFEU) [2016] OJ C202/1.

Federal Trade Commission. *FTC Consumer Protection Staff Updates Agency's Guidance to Search Engine Industry on the Need to Distinguish Between Advertisements and Search Results*, Press Release (Washington, D.C., 2013).

  Big Data: A Tool for Inclusion or Exclusion? Understanding the Issues, FTC Report (2016).

Ramirez, Edith, Maureen K. Ohlhausen, and Terrell P. McSweeny. The "Sharing" Economy: Issues Facing Platforms, Participants & Regulators, Federal Trade Commission Staff Report (Federal Trade Commission, 2016).

ILSR Report. Mitchell, Stacy and Olivia LaVecchia. Report: How Amazon's Tightening Grip on the Economy Is Stifling Competition, Eroding Jobs, and Threatening Communities (November 29, 2016) Institute for Local Self-Reliance.

OECD. *Two Sided Markets*. Report and supporting documents (2009).

  Exploring the Economics of Personal Data: A Survey of Methodologies for Measuring Monetary Value. OECD Digital Economy Papers No. 22 (2013).

  Data-Driven Innovation (2015).

  Disruptive Innovations and Their Effect on Competition (2015).

  Big Data: Bringing Competition Policy to the Digital Era (2016).

  Working Party on Measurement and Analysis of the Digital Economy. New Forms of Work in the Digital Economy, Background Report JT03398022 (Committee on Digital Economy Policies CDEP, 2016).

  Rethinking Antitrust Tools for Multi-Sided Platforms (2018).

Price Waterhouse Coopers. *The Sharing Economy*, Consumer Intelligence Series (2015).

Sherman Act, 1890, USC.

University of Chicago Booth School of Business – George Stigler Center for the Study of the Economy and the State, Report by the Committee for the Study of Digital Platforms Market Structure and Antitrust Subcommittee (2019).

UK Report of the Digital Competition Expert Panel, *Unlocking Digital Competition* (2019).

US Council of Economic Advisers. *Benefits of Competition and Indicators of Market Power*, Issues Brief (Washington, DC: Obama White House, 2016).

CASES CITED

Aspen Highlands Skiing Corp. v. Aspen Skiing Co. [1984] 738 F 2d 1509 (Court of Appeals, 10th Circuit).

Aspen Skiing Co. v. Aspen Highlands Skiing Corp. [1985] 472 US 585 (Supreme Court).

Canada (Commissioner of Competition) v. Superior Propane Inc. [2003] 53 FC 529 (Federal Court of Appeal).

Case AT.40099 – *Google Android*, 2018 European Commission.

Case ATC.39740 – *Google Search (Shopping)*, 2018 European Commission.

Case COMP/AT39847 – *E-Books*, 2012 European Commission.

Case COMP/M4731 – *Google/DoubleClick*, 2008 European Commission.

Case COMP/M5727 – *Microsoft/Yahoo! Search Business*, 2010 European Commission.

Case COMP/M7217 *Facebook/WhatsApp*, 2014 European Commission.

Case M8124 – *Microsoft/LinkedIn*, 2016 European Commission.

Continental TV Inc. v. GTE Sylvania, Inc. [1977] 433 US 36 (US Supreme Court).

Desoto Cab Company, Inc. d.b.a Flywheel Taxi v. Uber Technologies, Inc. 2016 District Court Northern District of California San Francisco Division.

Federal Trade Commission, *In the Matter of Google Inc.*, FTC File Number 111–0163 (2013).

Groupement des cartes bancaires (CB) v. European Commission, EU:C:2014:2204, 2014, European Court of Justice (Third Chamber).

IMS Health GmbH & Co. OHG v. NDC Health GmbH & Co. KG [2004] 2004 I-05039 (European Court of Justice (Fifth Chamber).

Istituto Chemioterapico Italiano S.p.A and Commercial Solvents Corporation v. Commission of the European Communities, 1974 European Court of Justice.

Lorain Journal Co. v. United States [1951] 342 US 143 (US Supreme Court).

Maryland v. United States [1983] 460 US 1001 (Supreme Court).

MasterCard Inc. v. Comm'n, 2014 EU:C:2014:2201, 2014, European Court of Justice (Third Chamber).

MCI Communications v. American Tel & Tel Co. [1983] 708 F 2d 1081 (Court of Appeals, 7th Circuit).

Meyer v. Kalanick, 2016 United States District Court, SDNY.

Michael Gonzales v. Uber Technologies, Inc. et al., 2018 California Northern District Court.

Microsoft v. Commission [2007] 3619 ECR II (Court of Justice of the European Union First Instance).

National Bancard Corp(NaBanco) v. Visa USA, Inc. [1986] 779 F 2d 592 (Court of Appeals, 11th Circuit).

Ohio v. American Express Co. (AmEx), 138 S.Ct. 2274 (2018).

Oscar Bronner GmbH & Co. KG v. Mediaprint Zeitungs- und Zeitschriftenverlag GmbH & Co. KG, Mediaprint Zeitungsvertriebsgesellschaft mbH & Co. KG and Mediaprint Anzeigengesellschaft mbH & Co. KG [1998] European Court Reports (European Court of Justice Sixth Chamber).

Otter Tail Power Co. v. United States [1972] 410 US 366 (Supreme Court).

Radio Telefis Eireann (RTE) and Independent Television Publications Ltd (ITP) v. Commission of the European Communities [1995] 1995 I-00743 (European Court of Justice).

Sea Containers v. Stena Sealink – Interim Measures [1994] OJ No L.

Standard Oil Co. of NJ v. United States [1911] 221 US 1 (Supreme Court).

Times-Picayune Pub Co. v. United States [1953] 345 US 594 (US Supreme Court).

United States of America v. Visa USA, Inc., Visa International Corp, and MasterCard International, Incorporated, 2003 United States Court of Appeals, Second Circuit.

United States v. American Express Company, 2016 Court of Appeals, Second Circuit.

United States v. American Tel and Tel Co. [1983] 552 F Supp 131 (Dist Court).

United States v. Apple Inc. [2013] 952 F Supp 2d 638 (Dist Court, SDNY).

United States v. Apple, Inc., 2015 2d Cir 28–29.

United States v. Microsoft Corp. [1995] 56 F 3d 1448 (Court of Appeals, Dist of Columbia Circuit).

United States v. Microsoft Corp. [1998] 147 F 3d 935 (Court of Appeals, Dist of Columbia Circuit).

United States v. Microsoft Corp. [2001] 253 F 3d 34 (Court of Appeals, Dist of Columbia Circuit).

United States v. Otter Tail Power Company [1971] 331 F Supp 54 (Dist Court).

United States v. Philadelphia Nat'l Bank [1963] 374 US 321 (US Supreme Court).
United States v. Terminal Railroad Assn of St Louis [386AD] 224 US 383 (US Supreme Court).
United States v. Topco Associates, Inc. [1971] 405 US 596 (Supreme Court).
Verizon Communications Inc. v. Law Offices of Curtis V. Trinko, LLP [2003] 540 US 398 (Supreme Court).

Index

Index

CPSIA information can be obtained
at www.ICGtesting.com
Printed in the USA
LVHW022305230720
661406LV00013B/337